T0244395

Twentieth-Century Man

Twentieth-Century Man

The Wild Life of Peter Beard

Christopher Wallace

An Imprint of HarperCollins*Publishers*

HarperCollins books may be purchased for educational, business, or sales promotional use. For information, please email the Special Markets Department at SPsales@harpercollins.com.

Ecco® and HarperCollins® are trademarks of HarperCollins Publishers.

FIRST EDITION

Designed by Jennifer Chung
Frontispiece by Mark Green Photography

Library of Congress Cataloging-in-Publication Data has been applied for.

ISBN 978-0-06-306641-0

23 24 25 26 27 LBC 5 4 3 2 1

Contents

Preface

I think I first *really* got into Peter Beard when I was in college, around the time I fell in thrall to the Beats and all the other mad-bad artists living out loud whom I hoped right then to emulate. I was a jock at the time, the quarterback of my college football team, and I was desperate for something else, for adventure, for real stakes, for modes of expression and just a comfortable grasp on selfhood and identity that PB—with his derring-do and real-life grand adventuring, his live-first-ask-questions-never attitude—seemed so perfectly to embody.

For a young guy (I was in my late teens, or maybe just twenty at the time), Beard was all of that adolescent lust, vigor, angst, and ambition I dreamed of, writ large. He was, for me, the perfect representation of the American id: if you had all the money in the world, what would you do, if not use it to traipse around the world collecting the wildest, most outrageous experiences, as he did? If you had movie-star good looks and charm to burn, how better to spend that than at the best parties with the greatest artists, supermodels, and rock stars of the jet set? And he also had passion—probably more like obsession—about the faults of the entire human experiment, the ways in which our consumption of the world's resources would come to consume us all. And that appealed to me too—that purpose, a calling greater than oneself, to vibrate with creativity, with a message, at such high frequency that if you didn't turn it into art, you would just explode.

Later, when I first met PB, in April 2016, in putting together the last big profile on him, for *Interview* magazine, we talked for a long time about the grand old gentlemen explorers, links in this long chain of adventurers from which he was sympathetically descended. And we talked about East Africa, where he had set his sights as an ambitious young artist, while still in college, when he first visited there with Darwin's grandson, Quentin Keynes. But PB was shy to accept the symbolism I found in all of this—of his finding the starkest expression of our destruction in the very birthplace of man, in the cradle itself. He wasn't trapped in his subconscious as I was, looking for symbols and symmetry. "Just keep moving forward," he told me, more than once. In a way, he trusted his subconscious to sort it all out, to just keep living and producing the work, letting the chips fall where they may. "There are two sure things in life: birth and death," he said. "And in between there, this basically meaningless time that is as good as *what you make out of it*." Which might be something out of Sartre or Camus, my great heroes at the time I first fell in love with PB's work. And if we are to think of existentialism as the idea that you are what you do, Peter was a great example of it: a man of action, maybe the last great romantic adventurer, and his work changed the world.

"He led the way," said Paul Theroux. "He was really the first person to chronicle the decline of wildlife—the majestic megafauna of East Africa, elephants, lions, cheetahs—and he did it in a characteristic way, by depicting the deaths in iconic images, and writing about his own experiences, using texts from classic books related to Africa."

But it wasn't just the content of his work that was avant-garde; his perfectly recognizable style, too, anticipated so much of the way we see now. His collages of sex, gore, and the sublime, borrowing an image here, a found item there, and even his own blood, were "remixing" before that became the primary creative mode of the digital age. More than that: in a perfectly twentieth-century way, before personal branding and the cult of identity washed over us, *PB was his art.* Those experiences he'd gone so far and suffered so dearly for (getting trampled by an elephant in the process) were the material. PB's whirring life and mind were the main event—his canvases, just artifacts of his process, of his being.

And who he was is incredibly significant. Via his friends, Keynes and Karen Blixen, whom he would eventually become a neighbor of in Kenya, he could touch that old Africa, the big-game trophy-hunting colonialist Africa. At home, he was descended from two industrial-age fortunes—tobacco and railroad: American icons and American sins, both. He overlapped or interacted with many of the great artistic traditions of the 1900s, from his collaborations with the painter Francis Bacon to his dialogues with Warhol, from Picasso to experimental film (with the Mekas brothers). He was high society within the last American generation to recognize the claim through family name. He was famous when fame was still something you went out and did in person, working a room, wowing a crowd, earning it over and over, at every appearance, every night. And still he kept just going forward.

By the time I met him, of course, that fame—as an artist, playboy, activist, and adventurer—had dimmed somewhat, even if his feverish energy certainly had not. Gone were the days of playing around with the Rolling Stones and Lee Radziwill out east, of blitzing Studio 54 with the Factory crowd and photographing supermodels in the bush (and in the buff); gone the days of his collaborations with Bacon, of traipsing hither and thither across Africa from his forty-five-acre bolt-hole in Nairobi. He was seventy-eight at the time and no longer really producing books or shows of his art, though he was still making it—he was incapable of not pressing the world through the thresher of his vision and process (and during my stay he was never not snapping pictures or scribbling or rubbing pastels over photographs). When there was news of him, Page 6–type stuff of his running off on a debauch, bringing hookers home, or saying something crude, it was not altogether flattering. But if his reputation was a bit messy (in large part because he was a mess), and his faculties downgraded by a series of strokes, he was, for me, still the author of the greatest images of my childhood, images that made me crave life and adventure and the scars that came along with them. So when I went out to his famous home in Montauk for a series of interviews, I went looking for a legend, and maybe even a childish idea of returning my hero to his former glory. But I needn't have bothered. Peter Beard did not need my help or that of any other mortal to be something out of myth. He was, and would always be, "Half Tarzan, half Byron," as Bob Colacello once described him.

"This is it. This is existentialism," Beard said while we were sitting outside on his Montauk property—the easternmost residence on Long Island, looking out on infinity—talking about art and life and death. Spring was then rushing into full bloom, and with it, dozens of birds and the families of local deer were celebrating the warming sun with song and wobbly-limbed dance. Over the course of his career, whether he was photographing the wildest creatures of East Africa or the finer-boned figures of the East End, in his writing, his diaries, or the monumental collages that bring them all together, Beard had made a living, and his legend, wrapping his work around such elemental, earthen subjects (the mass die-off of the elephants; the erotic life force of a nude; the native beauty of the natural world), often blurring the distinctions between them in the process.

His totemic book *The End of the Game*, made when he was only twenty-five, some of which he'd written and photographed while working for a warden in Tsavo game reserve, is a grand meditation on the balance between life and death, set in Kenya, where Beard had spent as much of his time as possible. The book is still the most provocative and impressive statement on man's relationship to the natural world I've ever read, and—spoiler—it does not have a happy ending (everyone dies). But even in his relative dotage,

Beard was, by contrast, the most vividly alive person I'd ever met, buzzing with the ebullience and energy of a child and converting all of his wide-eyed wonder into his work and his adventures.

PB and I walked around the property at dusk on the night that I arrived. He loved taking pictures at sunset as much as I did, and with very little cajoling he convinced me to stay the night, the weekend, forever. The grounds around his little cabin were an endless maze of thicket-like trees, with little warrens for deer and whatever else sorts of creatures make their home out there. PB of course knew every inch of the terrain. He'd been coming out to fish in Montauk with his dad since he was a child. And he'd had this land for his entire adult life.

In the lulls of our conversation, I would just leap forward and start yammering on about something inane, some supermodel he'd photographed, a picture that had meant the world to me as a boy. *The End of the Game* is subtitled *The Last Word from Paradise*, and the painful irony is that conclusive statements seemed to be primarily what now eluded him. He would wade through memories and ideas dimmed by the strokes, looking for last words in vain. But somehow he was remarkably unflustered by it. Stammering after some reference, some word or thought or hoary old name, he would, at times in our days-long chat, give up, cross his arms, and smirk at me as if to say, "Well, what are ya gonna do?"

At my insistence—though he would've liked to continue—we took several breaks during our conversations, to get sushi, to watch TV, to gossip. In the purple Montauk evening, we clambered down the sea stairs to watch the sea turn golden green, then lilac. The wet stone beach where the cliffside had fallen in looked like a slippery stack of potatoes in coral, mustard, mauve. I felt terribly protective of him, a man a few years younger than my father. But, as if! As if I could lend any sort of support to a man who had stared down lions.

He'd written about the scrapes and the scares, about his ideas and experiences and adventures, of course, in bits and pieces. But throughout our time together, I sort of teasingly, but entirely earnestly, wondered if he might not write a proper full-length story of his life. He shrugged me off, of course, saying something along the lines of it being too late. Maybe he didn't want to bother, didn't have the patience, or simply no longer wanted to reckon with the past. Maybe he suspected that I secretly hoped to help him with that project or was merely asking permission.

Well, be very careful what you wish for. The following is not the story as Peter would have told it. Not that I wasn't at times trying to sort of put him in the witness box. But this is very much my reading of the man, of his life, and his work. Granted, I felt privileged to have insight into the subject, having studied him quite closely and then been able to compare notes with him while he was alive. I felt fortunate that I remained in touch with him, and with Nejma and Zara throughout the rest of his life. From the time he passed, though, and since I agreed to do this book about a month later, both Nejma and Zara have been incommunicado. Similarly, some of his friends and intimates chose not to participate. At the risk of sounding insecure or jaded, I actually found this to be quite understandable, a sign of our times and the attention economy. Having a Peter story, a memory, or a souvenir of an experience with him is, in many cases, a treasured thing, and those in possession of one or several would like to share it themselves, on their own feed, to profit from it directly, whether in the form of likes or attention or otherwise.

Happily, I did have incredible conversations with many of Peter's nearest and dearest, and this book is all the richer for it. And from his own writings, the contemporaneous record, and the recollections of those closest to him I think I came fairly close to getting a picture of one of the most complicated people I've ever known. Was he, for example, as profligately generous as he seemed, giving away pieces he had worked on tirelessly, or did he simply no longer care for the pieces when he was done with them? Was he bigoted, racist, cruel, stubborn, closed-minded, but also wildly intuitive, wise beyond measure, vain and yet unaffected, trapped and free, dying to live and vice versa? Well, yes. In my experience he was all of those things and more. He was not just the sum of his works but also, as a self-proclaimed existentialist, one who must be defined by them. He was, in one very specific personality, all of the best and worst of the twentieth century, of the American century. Privileged by empire and by the lottery of good looks, he was ambitious, adventurous, insolent, insecure, grandiloquent, debauched, petty, narcissistic, crass, cruel, and absolutely awful by turns. And then simply brilliant beyond description, charming, intelligent, urbane, witty, profound in his work, pathfinding in his use of media (indeed, by his use of "the media" as material to be woven into his work), and maybe something nigh on prophetic.

I keep sort of jokingly referring to him in my notes as the Tinker Bell of Tsavo—tragic, brilliant, necessary, and enduring, who depended so dearly on the attention and affections of others—or else as a kind of Cocaine Cassandra. Partying with the jet-set crowd and celebrating his fortieth birthday at Studio 54 made him a man of his times, for sure. But I wonder if his particular message about life on this planet, his visionary journals, which he maintained for decades, and indeed his lifelong project to uncivilize himself, to re-wild himself, as we might say today, will continue to inform our lives for years to come.

I have attempted to put all of that on the pages before you, to consider Peter Beard's life and times, his work and his philosophy, if we can call it that, in my own way. Though there are, inevitably, failings in the following, they are surely not because of a want of information. They are just my failings as a writer to adequately contend with, express, analyze, and contextualize a life—a fascinating and maybe important life but without doubt a singular life with all of its specificity and contradiction, its mysteries and eccentricities.

Twentieth-Century Man

CHAPTER 1

Longing for Darkness

The need to escape, to run and hide, to be on his own, alone, on his own terms—he'd felt this call to flight all of his life, in varying degrees, and he felt it now.

No longer wanting to be a burden to his loved ones who had been tending to him, perhaps, or finally fed up with being fussed over, sick of his confinement to the downstairs couch, or just sick and tired of being sick and tired, subject to that characteristic restlessness, Peter Beard had to get up, had to move, had to get gone.

In the late winter afternoon gloaming out east, at his home in Montauk, the easternmost residence on all of Long Island, Peter turned his body to set his feet on the worn oak-board floors. The brass student lamp, roughly bandaged with blue gaffer's tape, by which he read and worked here at his command center on the couch, shone on his pile of pastels and charcoal on the coffee table, casting shadows on the scattered assemblage of remotes, jars of paints, corks, shells, a lighter or two, pencils, glue sticks, rolls of masking tape, and stacks of reading materials. No warmth came from the freestanding cast-iron fireplace in the corner as it sat and glared at him, dark and cold. The thin, naked board-and-beam walls here, as in the rest of his house—like every surface in the rest of his world—were covered in layers of posted and pinned pictures, ephemera, doodles, news clippings, magazine tear sheets, and posters for his previous exhibitions.

As he had done countless times over the years, Peter rocked himself to stand, his bodyweight pulling taut the Kenyan *kikoi* that lay across the couch. Navigating on instinct as much as anything, he passed the densely collaged wall to his left, covered in a faded yellow botanical print, past the old workhorse TV to his right, a ghostly black now. Peter paused to hold himself up by the teal-painted doorjamb, catching his breath and pricking up his ears. The front door, a pace to his right now, would be too loud, would let in too great a draft, which would go right up the stairs, immediately at his left, and, God, there is nothing he wanted less than a disturbance, a confrontation. The mere thought of having to answer for himself, having to atone for breaking the protocol for an obedient patient, re-rankled him, and so he went on, through a sitting room and into the kitchen to the back door with his determined little hobble.

He didn't look back; he never would, never did. He was always moving, forward, a million miles an hour in whatever direction he happened to be facing, and that was that.

With the door closed behind him, he turned to his left, past the little thatched studio hung with skulls and boat buoys, past the little picnic table where he would have lunches on warmer days, and even on some colder ones. Peter entered the clearing just east of the main house, shuffling into the slight divot in the grass there. The wind from the sea now came to him through an open alley between the thorny trees where the deer loved to linger, whipping through his flannel pajama pants and fleece sweatshirt.

Then, at the eastern edge of his property, where it gives onto the former military base–turned–state park, Peter entered the beginnings of the dense forest, and disappeared.

IN OLD-TIMEY FICTION, PETER MIGHT'VE BEEN CALLED A "MAN of action," a doer, an act-first-and-ask-questions . . . well, *never*, sort of person. When I met him at his house in Montauk, while profiling him for *Interview* magazine in spring of 2016, he described himself, over and over, as an existentialist, like Sartre or Camus. All he believed in was the act, the deed, as he said (and did). He was not a fan of thoughts. Thoughts had gotten him into deep trouble when he had indulged them, in 1969, shortly after his first divorce and a stint in a Nairobi prison for assaulting a game-trapper he'd found on his property. Those thoughts then (whether self-recrimination, self-pity, or what, he did not speak of them specifically) had led him to a kinda-sorta suicide attempt. Oddly, for an existentialist, he was a little fuzzy on the ownership of the action here, suggesting in an interview a few years after the fact that his overdose of sleeping pills in his Manhattan apartment was maybe accidental. During his subsequent stay as a guest of the psych ward at Payne Whitney hospital in New York, he swore never again to spend a single solitary second in his subconscious—an oath he had to reaffirm several times, including when, in 1977, the mill on his property in Montauk, along with all of the artworks by Francis Bacon, Andrew Wyeth, and Andy Warhol, as well as the thirty years of his own personal diaries that were inside it were destroyed in a fire. Both of these events, his first divorce in 1969, and the great fire in '77, seem to have really wobbled him. But in their aftermath and throughout his life, Peter decided that he would never regret, never ever look backward. All there was, he had decided, was what was—and what he was doing. That was to be his mantra, his guiding philosophy, and perhaps his legacy.

There is that wonderful quote by Borges about writers—which easily could be applied to all artists, all people—that we judge others on what they've done but would like to be judged ourselves on what we could do, what we might've done. But there was no might've or would've or could've in Peter's reality. He didn't have that register. There was present tense only. Not that he seemed to care one way or another how he was judged for what he did.

He was himself not one to entertain hypotheticals, what-ifs. The closest he came to having an idea about what *might've* been was such a grand idea, and even then so skeptically suggested, that it hardly even counts as a what-if. It was more on the order of a Utopian ideal, closer to the realm of religion than something like a plan or regret. Peter's one great what-if—wielded mostly in support of his all-encompassing fatalism, because it could never be so—was to wonder aloud at a few points what life might have been like if we'd frozen time in Kenya during the colonial days, when the railroad was bringing goods in and out, land was still plentiful (to some), game was still thriving (in some places), and there was a harmony between (one sort of) man and (a particular kind of) nature. But he knew how many asterisks came with this postulation and acknowledged that it was the kind of Utopianism that has its own cancellation built within it. As he said, once white men had arrived in East Africa, bringing . . . whatever, dental care, I guess, and shotguns, which were to the good in his estimation, they also brought the virus of capitalism, which by definition will always eat up everything for profit, destroying resources and expanding consumption to the point of the extinction of everything.

This notion would lead Peter to the central theme of his life and work, the tentpole on which all the circus of fashion shoots and safaris and debauchery and decadence would hang. His thesis, when he first articulated it, in a beautiful and powerful book on the history of (mostly white) men's metaphorical link and coexistence with the wildlife of Kenya, *The End of the Game*, was incredibly profound, poetic even, and totally devastating. The idea is this: as populations, whether of humans, elephants, or ocelots, rise, consuming all the available resources in their allotted area, be that a mere farm or, in our case, the entirety of Earth, they will reach a point of such "stress and density," that the herd must either be pruned or left to consume everything into arid sterility and witness the die-off of all that is left, all other species, all food, and then die off itself, by starvation, and go extinct. Simply put, thin the herd or it will kill off all life as we know it.

A ghoulish thought—like the plans of a blockbuster villain—but in his close consideration of elephants, Peter believed he saw a foretelling of our own doom in microcosm. In the Tsavo National Park in Kenya in the 1970s, as the elephants, who'd been under protection from poachers, ate and reproduced themselves out of sustainable habitat until they died en masse, by the tens of thousands, Peter felt a foreshock of what he believed was coming our way. From this experience, as well as the teachings of hunters he had known, Peter recognized that, within any finite amount of space, like the one we inhabit, elephants would, like us, necessarily expand their numbers until they exhausted the resources available to them, until their garden became a desert, and they died off in enormous, catastrophic numbers along with all the other creatures who depended on the ecosystem they had ravaged.

Peter believed that we humans had also reached this tipping point and would in very short order consume our own way to starvation and extinction. And to the extent that there is a message within his artwork, it is this—this horrific, fatalist howl from the very near future where our doom is imminent. It was also certainly the subject of most of Peter's great, maniacal monologues, over a campfire in Kenya or carpaccio at Cipriani Downtown, whether trying to seduce potential lovers, charm friends, terrify companions, or just to hear the sound of his own voice. I say "message" and not "warning" because Peter didn't campaign on an answer to the problem. He said *this is what is happening*, showed us his work in evidence, ranted, raved, shrugged his shoulders, and then went and had a few vodkas, joints, and an eight ball in SoHo. He didn't do politics, didn't profess to know the solution—in part because he was so skeptical of the necessary ingredient in any action for the good: humanity. He had no faith in our ability to turn things around, to delay the gratification of immediate consumption for eventual balance and sustainability. So he did as white male aristocrats were expected to do—he just got on with it, in his own signature style of flamboyance and detachment.

Like generations of remittance chums and eccentric second sons of fortune before him, Peter charted his course outside the establishment, outside the expected confines of, in his case, finance, into the realm of art. Animated by his great man-of-action adventurousness, Peter created a life and a lifestyle that became both the subject matter and canvas for his work—a *Gesamtkunstwerk* from which all the other works descended; he was, quite literally, his greatest work of art. I don't mean this in the way we now understand a kind of Warholian performance, a creation of a self as entertainment (for oneself or others), though he was very much that as well, and it is no accident that Warhol was a little bit obsessed with Peter. But Peter's creation was at once far bigger and much simpler than all that. He didn't put on a wig and an accent or play to his own predilections and fetishes to make himself up as a character in a costume. He just imagined himself to be the central character of an adventure novel (or, in his case, a memoir of colonial East Africa), as many adolescent boys do—and then led the protagonist's life as he'd imagined it.

But in the realization of his fantasy, Peter was in every way a proper visionary—insinuating himself into whichever aspects of that imagined (or extinct) world he could find, and constructing from scratch everything else he needed—successfully building himself an actual fantasia. Inspired as he was by the lifestyle he'd inferred from Karen Blixen's book *Out of Africa*, he set about adapting it not for the screen or stage but in real life, directed and set-designed by him, to his own exacting standards and particular aesthetic tastes. The photos he took, documenting wildlife as he was taking on the experiences needed to flesh out the main character—himself—as well as the fashion and art photos of models in the bush, as it were, were mere ephemera, a by-product of the work. They were press releases from the edge, dispatches from and publicity for the ongoing work of art that was his life.

And within this greater architecture of his action, Peter, on a personal level, was completely manic, frenetic. Had he been born a generation or two later, Peter might have been diagnosed with an attention deficit disorder and plied with Ritalin, and it is convenient in retrospect to imagine his liberal use of cocaine as a kind of self-medication to keep himself cool and focused, which it seems to have done. But the irony of Peter's disordered focus was his enormous, almost superhuman capacity for long-term binges of busywork on absolute minutiae—focusing on the needle-tiny detailing of his diaries for hours and even days at a time. When he wasn't talking, or moving, or running around, Peter was busy, always busy, on the gluing, inking, and assembling of his diaries. It was certainly compulsive, obsessive by any definition, and as he was always ready to admit, the resulting work was utterly meaningless. By which he meant there was no there there in the content of the journals. It is sort of astonishing that in the daily diaries of a human male adult, there is, in a recounting of more than seventy years of life, absolutely nothing revelatory of the maker's mindset, nothing exposing an emotional mood, no confessional discursions, no rants, no . . . nothing. Reading them or, more accurately, scrolling through them the way we now do images and ephemera in our various feeds, we may begin to wonder whether if memory and imagination are the impotence of real-life desire and appetite—you know, the overexamined life, spent in a library or in our head with the neurotic voices, rather than out there, *living*— that the reverse could also be true, whether, in order to repress the life of the mind and create a life free of introspection and examination, desire and appetite would grow enormous. But the doing, the making of them was, for Peter, like the construction of geometric shapes that kept Agnes Martin grounded, like a kind of crafty meditation, a really really messy rosary that bound him to the world of things and ink and blood and paper and leather— a tether to reality without which he might have spiraled off into the sky like a loosed helium balloon.

Peter liked to joke, at his own expense, that everything he did, from the densely pasted and lettered diaries, to his photography, and the large-scale collages for which he is perhaps best known, were just the work of an escapist, and his effort, his doodling, pasting, printing, snapping, staging, arranging, drawing, inking, writing, scribbling, and the rest, were just a way to get out of doing something more difficult. *Art*, as Peter loved to say, citing Oscar Wilde, *is all that is unnecessary, superfluous.* If you had to call what he did art, it was merely that: something that didn't really matter. He himself hardly ever made claims to be an artist or even a photographer. Peter regularly described himself as a dilettante, a term that is itself action-based, to describe someone who *does* a little of this, and a little of that.

After chewing on it for several years, testing these claims for irony or as fishing expeditions for flattery, I tend to take Peter at his word. Or at his deed, which is more to the point, as Sartre and Camus surely would agree. Everything Peter did, as he said, was purely and entirely for his enjoyment (adding hedonist to the list along with escapist and existentialist), no matter the implications, the stakes, or indeed the feelings of others. Peter called this pursuit freedom. To a lot of people, this was the very embodiment of rebellion. And, perhaps psychologically, it was a counter-steer away from his doggedly strict mother, and the society that expected him, as a blue-blooded heir to fortune, to grow up in a gray suit, to wear shoes, and sit behind a desk playing with his and other people's money for the rest of his time. Many, many of those who knew, or knew of him found his rejection of that life and his pursuit of pleasure instead to be heroic. In his id-unleashed quest for sex, fun, and consumption of all the drink and drugs in creation, a life unencumbered by guilt or regret, by work, real-world demands, or even, in his safari-tented compound in Africa, by walls, he became a kind of symbol of the male ideal—a James Bond of the jungle in a leopard-skin coat with an Alaïa model on his arm.

His rejection of one life for another, his intense commitment to doing just what he wanted to do just the way he wanted to do it certainly is exceptional. I cannot for the life of me think of a contemporary who so thoroughly indulged his own impulses for purely personal gratification, on such a scale—with such resources, connections, opportunity, unbelievably good luck, and jaw-dropping good looks as Peter Beard. I'd suggest, too, that a good portion of the vitriolic antipathy directed at Peter's third wife and now widow, Nejma, had to do with her attempts to put the brakes on his will to pleasure, to tame the self-fulfillment-at-all-costs mania within him. After a period of estrangement in the mid-1990s, during which Peter had his life-altering run-in with an elephant in the Maasai Mara, followed by a reconciliation of sorts between husband and wife, Nejma took over the management of Peter's business affairs, which, in large part, she did by preventing Peter from fucking everything up, as she saw it. As best she could, she brought a stop to his wanton, random, and frivolous gifting of every single piece and print he'd made, and she even tried to repossess some of the pieces he'd given away. According to friends, she kept him out of town, running up bar tabs in the south of France near where his cousin had established his artist retreat and where Peter felt comfortable, having visited there since his adolescence, rather than in downtown Manhattan where he'd be in the glare of New York media with its appetite for society scandal. And what brought the greatest outcry from his friends was her attempts at barricading Peter from his longtime and even occasional chums, from his ongoing and even prospective lovers, admirers, playmates, and party companions. More than trying to stage-manage his reputation or recoup a collage with which Peter had paid off a debt to a Manhattan restaurant, it was this seeming prohibition of Peter's profligate and exuberant spirit (or reckless and philandering self-destruction, depending on your point of view) that so upset those who knew or even knew of Peter. In blocking him off from his impetuousness, his freewheeling spontaneity, and yes, his drinking and drugging and seducing, Nejma was (at least symbolically) limiting what had made Peter a hero in their minds, what had made him singular, and singularly loved and loathed around the world—his total and absolute commitment to doing whatever he wanted whenever he wanted to do it, and just the way he saw fit. (Several of Peter's collectors, bosom pals, and even family members wouldn't talk to me for fear of Nejma's wrath if they said one word outside of her comfort zone.)

Truly, every single person I talk to about Peter starts by saying something to the effect of *Wow, what a life!*—looking off in awe with a slight shake of the head, marveling at the scrapes, the scandals, the maulings, the lawsuits, the lavish lifestyle, the house, the pictures, the legend. His is an avatar for a kind of teenage boy's fantasy. He was absolutely and utterly fearless, for better or worse. Free from self-doubt, from regret, from guilt, from self-pity (at least enough to make jokes after his pelvis had been shattered by that elephant, while his lungs collapsed, his pulse slowed to a stop, and he nearly bled out while being carted to a faraway hospital), and even free of most insecurity (though I have to speculate that vanity and narcissism come from covering up *some*thing).

And when seen from our neurotic age, maybe Peter's commitment to living his life on a moment-to-moment basis—completely free of neurosis, of any interiority whatsoever—*is* in some way heroic. Isn't that, in fact, the register of consciousness we think of as enlightenment? Isn't that present-tenseness the mode for meditators and yogis?

Still, it is worrisome (for us, who are not free of neurosis), because, if Peter was being all present tense, like some sort of Buddha, he wasn't doing so while in renunciation of appetite, but rather the reverse. And that sort of animalistic existence, moving only on instinct and impulse, without consideration of context, consequence, and repercussions, does sound a lot like sociopathy. Peter's utter devotion to this topsoil consciousness, to existing on the same plane as, say, dogs—his complete commitment to impulses, whether heedless of the consequences or simply inconsiderate of their impact—was, at the very least, startling.

Camus said we're only really free to love people after they're dead. With all the tricky inconsistencies of their actual presence removed, we can re-create the dead into who we wished them to be. That calculus doesn't work as well for Peter, whose greatest gift was his presence and the outrageous charm that caused many of those most adversely affected by his actions to forgive him—even to adore him in spite of his rough patches. His life, and even his work, is much different without him around, without his presence and his enthusiasm breathing life into everything around him. Even at his shows, with grand or intimate displays of his collections and creations arranged around some gallery, what people really came to see was Peter. He was the main attraction, the work of art that made sense of all the rest of the materials.

Was he the truly liberated man, free from superego, self-actualized, a kind of Iron John figure at play in the wilderness of life? Or was he the paragon of entitlement, privileged in every way, living his life in a selfish pursuit of onanistic ego fulfilment? Did he revel just a bit too much in upsetting norms, upsetting other people, like an attention-seeking adolescent who needs you to know his pain? Maybe, yes.

And these were not the extent of his contradictions. He was an outright homophobe who adored Truman Capote. He was a racist whose closest companions were Black and who regularly dated women of color. He was a man who professed to live only in the present but could hold a grudge—mostly against his ex-wives, it seems—for decades.

There were deeper, more subtle contrasts within Peter's character, too, that created funny little rhymes in his life. For example, he made light of his connection to James J. Hill, his paternal great-grandfather, the railroad tycoon who created the trade route by which settlers and capital could flow west to the Pacific. "A robber baron, I hear," Peter said, "on par with J. P. Morgan, E. H. Harriman and Henry Clay Frick. His big thing was hammering out a transcontinental railroad that opened the American Northwest. . . . Ayn Rand held him up as this great paragon of noble capitalism." This from a man who was somewhat obsessed by the stories of the Mombasa–Nairobi Railway cutting through Kenya from the coast to Lake Victoria—a descendant of Manifest Destiny expansionism running off to construct his life and legend along a railroad track where his colonialist heroes had built themselves an oasis, or maybe just a mirage.

I've always been fascinated by the way that Peter's story, both the one he was born into and the one he wrote with his own life, reached back into the previous century. In his genes, he carried a bit of the legacy of the American Empire. And in his behavior he summoned comparison with some of his predecessors in safari and photography, from Teddy Roosevelt to George Eastman, along with the sort of wistful Utopian colonials like his beloved Karen Blixen. From their example, their dreams and values, Peter improvised his own slightly more modern version, then went about reaching into the future, setting the tone for so much of the popular culture and visual media of today. With his high/low heterogeneous sampling of the time and his creation of a vivid self-mythology, or "brand," that was central to his work, Peter anticipated much of the digital mash-up aesthetics and cult-of-personality content of the social-media era. Even at the time, Peter the proto-influencer launched a thousand fashion collections in his image, inspiring the likes of Tommy Hilfiger and Ralph Lauren, Kim Jones, and Emily Bode—all of whom tried to re-create a little something of his ineffable, effortless prep-kid-gone-bamboo style. In his images of the great supermodels of his lifetime—from Veruschka to Donyale Luna, from Iman to Lara Stone—and especially in his self-portraits, he managed, maybe better than anyone, to evoke an entire existence, something so singular, deep, transporting, and, for all we could touch it in our humdrum rat-race lives, almost mythological. I still remember the first time I encountered *I'll Write Whenever I Can*, the picture of a shirtless Peter, hip deep in the belly of a crocodile but still immaculately coiffed, jotting in his journal, the image itself smeared all over with blood and inscribed with his vinous lettering. I was in college at the time, filled to the brim with all of that adolescent brio to *do* and *be* on a grand scale, to travel and experience and create and to matter and be hip deep in life, and this picture said all of that to me in a flash. Even now I'm not totally certain that that picture isn't the reason I picked up a pen and pad rather than . . . anything else, thinking that I too could write wherever and whenever, hoping to look half as dashing as he did while doing so.

But even as he was calling up the ghosts and associations of the past (and living off some of the proceeds they had left him) and forging an image and a mixed-media body of work with a cause behind it, all of which is de rigueur today, Peter was also an extraordinary exemplar of his own times—right there in the thick of the sex, drugs, and rock and roll of the twentieth century, an elite member of the jet set and court jester to Camelot: collaborating with Warhol, touring with the Rolling Stones, celebrating his fortieth birthday at Studio 54, photographing and being painted by Francis Bacon, going to bullfights with Picasso, acting for Jonas Mekas, making a film with the Maysles brothers, modeling for Helmut Newton, and doing a whole lot of waterskiing with Jacqueline Onassis. And he seemed to love an awful lot of it.

Maybe that was Peter's greatest gift, the most valuable asset he had been born with—his capacity for enjoyment. His enthusiasm. That motor that fires up somewhere inside of us when turned on by an idea, an image, a connection, a musical note that chimes with something in our bones. He did everything in his power (and within the reach of those funds and connections, and the deference extended to him for those good looks) to nurture and expand on that enthusiasm. "Do you know what it means?" he asked me, when I spent a weekend with him at his home in Montauk. *Enthusiasm*, he said, means to have a god within. Or a devil. Both, maybe. Probably.

It was this current running through him, almost like a religious possession, that he dedicated his life to, holding it above all other forces—above society's laws and expectations, surely, and above any sort of morality and any of the bonds that existed at the time in which he lived.

NEARLY EVERYTHING PETER DID, OF COURSE, COURTED CON- troversy, or at the very least made for zesty copy. Though he regularly protested to the contrary, he was not a lifelong magnet for publicity accidentally—and his twilight vanishing, the day before April Fool's Day in 2020, did not go unnoticed for long.

By April 2, newspapers, art blogs, and magazine websites were reporting on the police search for Peter. "He was last seen on Tuesday at 4:30 p.m. wearing a blue pullover fleece and black jogging pants, according to a missing persons alert issued by authorities," they wrote. "Nejma Beard, his wife and studio manager, reported him missing two hours later."

A week later, Peter's second wife, Cheryl Tiegs, gave a particularly potent quote to the *New York Post*, when she said she wasn't surprised that Peter had gone missing, characterizing her days and nights with him in the early 1980s as a vacillation between mania and despair. "Maybe someone picked Peter up and he is on a joy-ride across America," she said. "He does pretty wacky things. The night after we got married, he did not come home until dawn." She even recalled that Peter had been diagnosed as bipolar, and seemed to suggest that his running off, running away, was a regular part of their lives together and might be due in part to illness.

At the time of Tiegs's quotes, the local papers reported that Peter's "whereabouts remain a mystery despite an extensive search by 100 police officers, a helicopter, drones and K-9 units," but it was a different illness that seemed to merit further investigation: Peter's dementia. Perhaps it was a factor in his disappearance, they suggested.

On 3/31/20 around 4pm my dad went missing, Peter's daughter Zara posted on her Instagram. If you see him anywhere please contact the East Hampton Town Police . . . or me directly . . . He's so missed and we just want him home safely. He has dementia and a heart condition that he desperately needs medication for so time is of the essence. Prayers welcome. Only a few slides down her profile grid, a matter of weeks prior, Zara had posted pictures of the moment when she had introduced her new daughter, Daisy, to Peter.

Friends of mine—like, I'm sure, friends of Peter's, and people everywhere—speculated about his whereabouts, his reasoning, his state of mind. A good many of them, who seemed to be overnight armchair experts on dementia, assured me that, incapacitated thusly, Peter might have lost his bearings, lost track of who or where he was. Or might have done that which was most primal, most instinctive to him, and gone to hide in the bushes, like a wild animal.

I, for one, could not help but read some symbolism into Peter's disappearance, couldn't resist finding some symmetry in his life mission to re-wild himself culminating in his rejoining himself with nature—as I imagined had happened. I found the mystery of it all sort of fitting, poetic. This larger-than-life guy, dedicated to playing in the mud with the animals he loved, returning to nature to be welcomed back into the wilderness. It was pure Peter.

As much as he talked, Peter didn't accomplish any of what he did in life by talking about it. He didn't get to where he'd been by thinking about it. He was, as he always had been, a doer. And men of action don't end their stories on the cozy couch very often. At least some part of Peter didn't think he should end his that way either.

In his insistence on following his own paths, or at least resolutely refusing to wear the stiff collars of the life that had been expected of him, in the dazzling adventures he'd taken, the better to tell great stories about them around the campfire, and in the images he created, on paper and of himself, Peter lived a life that was entirely his. Why should his death be any different?

CHAPTER 2

Lexington Avenue

F rom a window in his family's ninth-floor apartment at 133 East Eightieth Street, ten-year-old Peter Beard had a great vantage point from which to watch the mayhem he caused as he dropped spitballs down on unsuspecting passersby on Lexington Avenue—a safe remove from which to delight in the splatter patterns of his little projectiles, which would send the pedestrians scattering. Here at this window, little Peter could survey the rooftops of the Upper East Side as if they were part of a great board game laid out for him, counting the pointy-topped water towers and monitoring the local bird life that could at times include the odd owl, hawks, and even an eagle. He could, like a little lord of Manhattan, watch the comings and goings of the silk-stocking corridor, as it was then known, and look down the length of Lex, still a two-way street in 1948, to where it threaded the bigger buildings of midtown, built on better bedrock, and finally gave way in the Village.

This window was the best and most immediate portal Peter had to the outside world. When he was stuck at home nights, forced to do homework, get dressed in perpetually itchy clothes, do chores, clean up, or just keep to himself as the endless hours of adolescence stretched out to infinity and beyond, this window gave him a view of what he was missing, got him closer to the creatures and the natural world where he knew he really belonged.

It was here in this window that Peter had used the Voigtländer camera given to him by Granny Virginia to stage a photo of the family lab, Charcoal, frozen mid-leap in what appeared to be an attack on a stuffed ruffed grouse—a picture for which he won an art prize that year at the Buckley School. Peter shared the prize that year with his classmate and one of his best friends, Michael Rockefeller. Michael's father, Nelson, was at the time about to become the governor of New York (and would later become the vice president), and Peter sometimes went up to stay at the family's home upstate, Kykuit, in Mount Pleasant. Of course, any excuse for an adventure was welcome to a ten-year-old, maybe more so if that young boy happened to be Peter Beard. On the occasion of his first visit to Kykuit, Peter's brothers let their minds go wild as they speculated on the grand opulence he would encounter at the home of a family so famous for its wealth. "We said, 'You're going to have some fun out there,'" Peter's brother Anson wrote. "'They probably have diamonds hanging from the candlesticks; you won't have to make your bed'—we always had to make our beds on the weekends— 'and surely you won't have applesauce for dessert,' which we hated. 'You'll probably have lemon meringue pie or something like that.' Peter came back and reported, 'They live the same way we do. There were no fancy candlesticks. We did have applesauce. But the best thing was they have their own bowling alley in the basement.'"

Like Peter, Michael grew up with an adventurous streak. After Exeter and Harvard, in 1961, Michael took an expedition to Papua New Guinea, where his dugout canoe capsized within sight of land. After drifting for two days, he swam toward shore looking for help and was never seen again. Later, when looking back at his time with his childhood friend, Peter said, "My favorite subject to paint [in those days] was pirates and cannibals. Poor Michael had the misfortune to meet some of the latter while he was off collecting art and researching the Stone Age Asmat tribe in the jungles of New Guinea in 1961. He was due to join me in East Africa right around the time he was eaten."

By the time Peter and Michael were winning their prizes, Peter had already begun his habit of collecting his own sort of art: ephemera, mostly, especially anything having to do with the exotic, the adventurous, or the animal kingdom—and he was already collaging it all together to display it just so. "In his room," Jon Bowermaster wrote, in *The Adventures and Misadventures of Peter Beard in Africa*, "a hand-painted plaster-cast rattlesnake curled up in leaves in a wastepaper basket. An aquarium held at various times salamanders, newts, garter snakes, turtles, tortoises, snails, squirrels, chipmunks, raccoons, and possums, all to the chagrin of his mother, who regularly demanded that he keep his creatures out of the house."

Above the bunk bed he shared with his younger brother, Sam (Peter was on top), he'd hung a mounted, taxidermied deer head, an eight-point buck, and beside it, on a corkboard, pinned-together collages of ticket stubs, photographs, landscape paintings, postcards, and trinkets. "But the animals were all that interested me," he said.

For as long as he could remember, Peter's mother, Roseanne, kept the boys vigilant in maintaining diaries of their daily activities. In the summer, she wouldn't even let them leave the house before they'd completed their written record of the previous day's doings. It was around this time, while visiting a friend's house during a summer vacation, with this habit of journaling drilled into him, that Peter first thought to illuminate his diaries with the tangible trophies and detritus collected in his day's activities—horsehairs from when he'd gone riding, newspaper clippings of the day's current affairs, twigs, pressed leaves, and whatever was at hand that could bring a memory to life and convert the experience into something else, a pattern that pleased him aesthetically.

Just that year, Granny Virginia, his mom's mom, had given him a diary, a leather-bound thing that didn't remind him of the drudgeries of school but instead felt sort of fancy in a tough way, like something a cowboy might have. He had fun doodling in its pages, fattening up this line and that line, curling the teacup handle of a letter P into a spiral design, a pinwheel. He wrote out his name, *peter*, with a kind of swimming script. He wrote out the activities of the day—meals they had, shows they'd heard on the radio, books he was given. And then, this new illumination: he started sticking *things* into the pages of his diary until it became a kind of treasure trove. It was a cabinet of curiosities in which he could store all his feelings of adventure and mystery safely away from his brothers, Anson and Sam, could set the stuff together in a way that made sense.

Already, at ten years old, Peter's ultimate aspiration—if anyone would ever ask him, rather than tell him what he should do or must do or had better think about doing—was to live a life free from underwear and socks. Instead, his everyday reality, from the middle of September to the middle of June, included a scratchy shirt and tie, plus a blazer, per the Buckley School uniform. And don't get his mother started with the fresh suits. All he ever wanted was a nice barefoot run in the park. Or maybe even someplace wilder, like the grounds around Grandma Ruth's apartment on Jekyll Island off the coast of Georgia. There he could set his little trap lines for rabbits, or whatever came through. There were horses on the island, and he could trot around on these, hoping for the moments when the horse's handlers would let him really run them and get up to a dizzying gallop, whomping up and down on the saddle until he felt like he might take flight into the sky and for the rest of the day could feel a little blurry wonderful fright if he thought about it. But summer and escape always seemed an impossible distance away.

Not that the nine rooms of their rent-controlled apartment

on East Eightieth Street were entirely without curiosities, to be sure. The boys weren't allowed TV, which had recently become very popular, though they were sometimes permitted the serials on the radio. But of the many attractions available for the brothers, none was greater than the hallway of paintings, paintings that had come from their great-grandfather, James J. Hill. Hill, as no one in the family tired of reminding Peter, had been one of the greatest empire builders of the American continent—the man who "opened the West," which was probably news to the indigenous peoples there. Born in a log cabin in freezing cold Canada, no place you'd even heard of, really, James J. Hill grew up to make, well, a lot of railroads, but most famously the Great Northern Railway, which, if you thought about it, was Manifest Destiny in one long stretch of steel. The railway, as well as the land it ran on, all of which he owned, and the steel and the voluminous trade that ran along it all, made Hill a very rich and famous man in his day, a symbol of capitalism, expansion, and the American Empire. Indeed, at the end of *The Great Gatsby*, Gatsby's father says that if only his son had lived long enough—and not whiled away his time on parties and Daisy—he would have equaled the great James J. Hill.

Hill's house in St. Paul, Minnesota, cost $1 million to build in 1897 money and had twenty-two fireplaces—which you probably needed in St. Paul in 1897. One of the rooms in the house, a glass-roofed drawing room, is where Hill hung all the art he'd collected, salon style, in much the same way the Royal Academy did their collection at Somerset House in London—and he was a great collector of art, favoring especially work from artists of the Barbizon school. These were painters who often gathered around the area of Barbizon, near Fontainebleau, in the mid-nineteenth century, to create extraordinarily vivid, somewhat romanticized tableaux and landscapes—the most famous of whom, and Peter's favorite artist as a child and perhaps for his entire life, was Théodore Rousseau.

Rousseau's wonderful images of the plains and forests of France have a bit of the same verve, the soft edge focus, the grandeur, and plain majesty of Peter's later pictures. They are even framed similarly and have the feel, if they are a bit pastoral, that they are scenes not from any real countryside but snapshots of some mythic place.

It was tradition that on the wedding days of each of his six surviving children, James J. Hill would give to the betrothed any one of the works on those walls that they selected. Well, Peter's Grandma Ruth eventually got more than just the one she picked on the day she had married Peter's grandfather, Anson McCook Beard, and a few of those in her collection had made their way down to her son's apartment, where they hung in the hallway of 133 East Eightieth Street. The most valuable of these, as the kids were regularly reminded, was Honoré Daumier's *Third Class Carriage*. Peter's dad inherited the Daumier from his mother, Ruth, and after her passing in 1959, he sold it at Christie's in London for $110,000 net. He used the proceeds to buy a plantation in South Carolina called Whitehall, so that he could finally do as he'd dreamed his whole life—just hunt and fish all day every day. He was apparently exceedingly enthusiastic and managed to "overshoot" some fourteen thousand acres of game land, so he had to lease still more land nearby to keep up his daily quail stalking.

Not that Peter could just spend endless hours gawping at paintings in the hallway. As grand as their apartment was, there were still eight whole people scurrying everywhere—Peter; his older brother, Anson, and younger brother, Sam, of course; his mom, Roseanne, and his dad, Anson. Then there was their German governess, Lisa Schaller, who was with the family from before Peter was born until the time Sam went off to college. Every day they were in New York in the spring and fall, she would take the boys to Central Park near the Obelisk, to play and climb on the rocks. There were also the cook, Louise, and a maid/waitress, Annie, who had been with the family since the war. "We liked them so much and they did such a good job that when we moved back North after the war, they came with us," Peter's brother Anson said. "They were like family members. Mother didn't really like 'colored people,' but she loved Annie and Louise."

During the school week, sitting at the breakfast table while everyone else chowed down, Peter would wait for an opportunity to shove away the scrambled eggs he loathed—Yuck!—and make his way to school, hopefully evading yet another nitpicking from his mom about his clothes and general cleanliness. Outside of the apartment, next to the elevator, a smoky glass covered the darkened shaft of the mail chute, and Peter would always catch himself here, or really, allow himself the moment every morning to stare at his dim reflection, a Peter through the glass darkly. Already his face was sharpening into the rough-hewn triangular shape that would make him famous for years to come, his pendulous chin turning into something Gregory Peck–ian, his ears slightly splayed, his bright blond hair bleached almost white by the sun and, forever unto his dying days, firmly parted on the Continental left and finished with a flourish at his right temple. Staring into his ghostly reflection in the hallway, Peter would wonder what *his* life was like, that other Peter, who, as Peter wrote later, looked like "someone else staring back from another time, a darkened continent . . . a stranger wondering why it was so dark, so quiet, so hard to see," and wondering what he must have thought of him, the boring and banal real-life Peter in the shrilly lit hallway waiting for an elevator. No, that's not true, he decided. He didn't wonder. He knew that it was the dark and smoky Peter who actually lived in the real world, the authentic world, closer to dark truths, to some alternative where he really belonged, to a place of childlike freedom and heightened reality—instead of the one he knew of constant and utter boredom, scratchy Oxford shirts and coats and ties, and—Ugh!—shoes! Peter knew that the shadow Peter was safe in his world, looking at the artificially lighted Peter with something like bemused embarrassment. "Then a mad rush of mail would shudder by, an in-house waterfall causing the chute to vibrate and the elevator cables to groan. This was my every-morning school-day routine day after day for seven years."

Downstairs, Lexington Avenue slipped slightly downward, sloping toward Seventy-Ninth Street. The traffic of the city was beginning to heave with postwar ebullience. In 1948, it all seemed alive and bright and shiny. The city "still had trolley cars, open double-decker buses, organ grinders' monkeys running around with tin cups asking for coins," Peter wrote in *Zara's Tales*. "One single Indian Head nickel paid the bus driver," and the cars all looked like futuristic spaceships gliding down the slope of Lex. Some days, as he and his brothers were making their way down the six blocks to Buckley, under the rows of ginkgo trees that lined the streets, beginning to go a shimmering gold in the late fall, they would encounter some other, rougher kids who had hopped off the still-extant El train at Third Avenue and come looking for some fancy-school kids to mess with. Most of the Buckley boys, and certainly the other Beard brothers, wanted no part of these kids off the El, even though Anson was boxing champion of his class at school. Peter, though . . . Peter loved the sense of menace, of adventure, the way he could feel his skin seeming to shrink around his chest and on his forearms as adrenaline pumped through his body, thrilling at the break from routine, and the possibility that *something could happen*!

Physically, he wasn't much afraid of fights, either. He'd always been able to get the best of his brothers and the neighbor kids— even the Sherlock boys, who were their neighbors in Alabama during the war and who once came at him with an axe before mercifully being disarmed. He was tough and quick and his whirling dervish style just sort of out-crazied his opponents, out-willed them unto victory. "Peter kind of reveled in it," his brother Anson said. "One time somebody tried to take his watch. Peter ran, but then stopped in his tracks and smashed the guy right in the face with his fist."

None of those boys were around today, so Peter carried on, making his way toward Lex en route to school. Then he suddenly had that feeling. That clarity, like when he was riding the horses full tilt a-gallop on Jekyll Island. The feeling he had when he went sailing with his dad and they leaned almost all the way over. That feeling of calm. The authentic kind of at-homeness in the shadow that Peter needed always to know. His attention was drawn to one of the big coal trucks that was regularly careening down Lex in those days. Something had snagged in Peter's mind. And then he saw the cyclist. He watched, mesmerized, as the coal truck hit the cyclist, smashing him apart and smashing the moment all to smithereens. In the hush immediately following the collision, Peter ran to the corner where the cyclist was spread out. Peter's ears pounded with the sound of his pulse. And then the noise from everywhere was extraordinary: screaming and slamming of doors and general hubbub. Peter meanwhile knelt over the cyclist, looking straight down on the man's head as it lay on the macadam, cracked like a watermelon. His hair was sticky with blood and dirt and maybe tire tread. The blood seeping from his head made an inky halo collecting all the gutter detritus into a kind of crown. It was horrible. It was wonderful. The sickness, the giddiness, the almost vomiting, almost giggling sensation he had was a kind of wildness, a kind of exhilaration he'd never known before. He knew his mother would say it was sick or just not right. But it was just so *exciting*, he wanted to say. And then his imagined mother's harangue suddenly manifested in his real mother collecting him up by his lapels and feverishly shooing him home, flapping around him like a great bird with its wings, swaddling him, trapping him, flying him away to the nest.

This image of the cyclist, a kind of gutter icon, became a touchstone for Peter throughout his life—an inciting event that he credited with helping him to access his own visionary world for the first time, to explore the grimy glory of life and death, to find beauty in the bloody brutality of existence. It was, too, perhaps, this vision, this artistic point of view, that would lead to his friendship with the painter Francis Bacon, another artist who found beauty in brutality. Specifically, it was the images of desiccated elephant corpses that Peter had photographed from a borrowed Cessna plane—in the same bird's-eye view from which he had seen the cyclist's destroyed body—over Tsavo National Park in Kenya during a massive die-off during the 1970s that brought the two men together. In those images, some of the elephants are shown just moments after their death by dehydration or starvation, swollen like balloons. Others were days or weeks gone, their hides hanging collapsed amid their brilliant white bones and shimmering ivory tusks, like circus big tops sagging off their tent poles. All of them lay in shallow craters gouged out of the tawny Tsavo soil in hysterical desperation, an instinctive frenzy as they lay dying. These circular pits, like the bloody circle in which the cyclist had lain, give the elephants the appearance of being haloed, sainted.

Bacon had wanted to make sculptures of the elephant bodies in these pictures when he had first seen them in *The End of the Game* in the mid-1960s. But when Bacon met Peter a decade later, he thought better of the plan and instead painted several images of Peter in all his own brutal beauty. Among the photographs found in Bacon's studio upon his passing, some 240 were of Peter, many of them self-portraits.

"SCHOOL STARTED IN THOSE DAYS ABOUT SEPTEMBER 15TH and finished mid-June," Peter's brother Anson wrote. "During those nine months we never spent weekends in New York."

The family's commitment to this calendar was total. Extracurriculars be damned. Sporting teams, dances, fairs, art exhibits, and the vaguely martial clubs for young boys, like the Knickerbocker Greys, to which Anson had hoped to pledge, were all no-gos. If it happened on a weekend from fall to summer, the Beard boys were not involved. "Regardless of what else was going on, every Friday afternoon we left New York at three o'clock to try to beat traffic to get to Tuxedo, and we came back Sunday evening. But Tuxedo was no hardship."

Grandma Ruth's twenty-four-thousand-square-foot McKim, Mead and White–designed neoclassical stone castle, Chastellux, overlooking a lake in Tuxedo Park, New York, was built to be the very opposite of hardship. With its little witch-hat tower and endless expanse, Chastellux and its surrounding seventy thousand acres of woodland was like a fairy tale for the Beard boys.

Within the development, there was of course the Tuxedo Club, where these three sporty boys were very much at home, playing their fill of racquetball and tennis. There were also the three lakes, the smallest of which would freeze over in winter, becoming a prime surface for skating and hockey. But most interesting to Peter was, as ever, the wildlife, which he and his father and brothers made a sport of in itself. "We set traps for minks, raccoons and possums," Anson said. "We never got a mink, but we did capture several raccoons. We would kill, then skin them and sell the skins. . . . Each year my father would go out and try to shoot a large buck. Most years he got one . . . the meat was just awful, and tough as shoe leather because the terrain was so rocky and the bucks had to climb up and down all the time. . . . We also went up to the Harriman estate once or twice, because they had big herds of deer up there."

But visiting Harriman territory was fraught. Granny Ruth's father, James J. Hill, had had an epic rivalry with E. H. Harriman, the president and chief shareholder of the competing Union Pacific Railroad. The rivalry crashed the stock market when in 1901 they each bought up shares in the Northern Pacific Railroad, vying for the controlling minority position. "You go on your own," Grandma Ruth would say if the boys were extending their hunting grounds in that direction. "I'm not going anywhere near the Harrimans."

The funny thing is, Ruth should have been more at home in Tuxedo Park than just about anyone. Though she began the building of Chastellux when still married to the Beard boys' grandfather, Anson, she completed it on her own, giving very clear direction to the greatest architects of the day. And two years after Anson's passing, in January 1931, Ruth married a fellow heir to fortune, Pierre Lorillard V, whose father, a tobacco tycoon and racehorse aficionado, had created Tuxedo Park to begin with, using the capital he raised from selling his "summer cottage," a seventy-room Italian Renaissance palazzo in Newport called the Breakers, to Cornelius Vanderbilt. In the wedding announcement, Pierre V was listed as a "socialite" and Ruth, as a "relict," or widow. Nowadays, he is regularly credited with creating the formal attire named after his father's development. Having grown bored of showing up in white tie and tails to dinner every night, the legend goes, Pierre V took a little inspiration from the smoking jackets then de rigueur in the gentlemen's clubs in London, and created a kind of formal uniform for Tuxedo Park, in green silk with yellow piping. The boys didn't really get to know Pierre V, who died when Peter was two. But after her year of mourning, Ruth married Emile Heidsieck, of the famous champagne family—"moving from cigarettes to champagne, you might say," as Anson put it—whom they remembered as being kind and a humble and caring companion to Ruth.

Of course, Ruth, too, was one of the most famous heiresses of her time, never mentioned in the newspapers without reference to her father. And it is a bit curious, in retrospect, to think what significance railroads had in Peter's life. Of course, there was the portion of his inheritance that came by way of his great-grandfather, and from his grandmother Ruth (and each of Ruth's childless sisters, who left trusts to the Beard boys), and the privilege and prestige it had brought his family and the lifestyle in which he was raised—much of it due to the rails James Hill had laid across the American continent. Peter's paternal grandfather, Anson Mc-Cook Beard Sr., who was born and raised in Manhattan, became a two-sport star at Yale, and then a successful lawyer; but *his* father, William Beard, immigrated to New York from Ireland and built Beard's Erie Basin in Brooklyn by filling in marshland with material reclaimed from railroad projects!—primarily "the construction of the Harlem Line and the excavation of the Long Island Railroad tunnel," as Peter's brother Anson would remember in his memoir.

The railroad of money descending from James to Ruth would also go a long way to defining Peter's father, as well as Peter's relationship to him. "My father, Anson McCook Beard Jr. (he dropped the Jr. after his father died in 1929), born on April 23, 1909, was a child of privilege, with all the attendant trappings," Peter's brother, also named Anson, wrote. Raised mostly by Ruth's staff (of nine), and shunted among the family homes in New York, Tuxedo, Southampton, and Jekyll Island, Anson Jr. and his sister Mary had very few friends, no agency, and, beyond being hauled out to entertain their parents' dinner guests from time to time, seemingly no purpose. "As a young man my father was extremely good looking, the ultimate WASC—White Anglo-Saxon Catholic. He was cut out of a mold, and he never learned to think much about anyone except himself. Born in the 'lucky sperm club,' as the expression goes, he enjoyed a life of total entitlement."

As Anson says, their father was a poor student, who, from his earliest days until his hips went out late in his life, cared only about the sporting life. Both Anson and Peter would characterize their father's life as coasting, going to Yale as he was supposed to, and then on to Wall Street to work for a friend of the family and spending his life just managing his mother's money.

With the exception of wartime, every working day from that point on for Anson né Jr. was exactly the same. As Peter's brother Anson wrote,

> His routine was to take the subway (which cost a nickel in those days), to Wall Street, where he worked at Delafield and Delafield after the war. The market opened at ten o'clock, and he'd be at his desk by then, take care of personal matters, maybe read a little more of the paper, do some research, go to lunch at the Chop House with friends (these were not business lunches)—have a drink or two, and return to the office. He called himself an investment advisor but mainly he took care of the family affairs and did a little business with friends. The market closed at three o'clock, and he would go uptown to the Racquet & Tennis Club, play court tennis, get a massage, probably have a drink, come home, fix a martini, settle on the sofa or a chair in the library, read a newspaper, have dinner, go to bed, and start over the next day.

The Beards were incredibly well connected. Everyone they knew was in the *Social Register*, and the families they mixed with were all very well-off Joneses whom the Beards didn't seem to go out of their way to keep up with. Not that they didn't indulge in the perks of those connections. When Roseanne had a pile of speeding tickets she wanted to get rid of, she would call up Mayor Wagner to take care of them. "She'd call and say, 'Hey Wag, I've got another problem. . . .'"

But maybe it's what they *didn't* do from their perch of privilege that so disappointed the boys. Peter's brother Anson went on to become a "titan of Wall Street," in the words of the *New York*

Times, with a long and storied career at Morgan Stanley. And his descriptions of their father are devastating:

- "My father was intelligent and well read, but he had no motivation."
- "He did an adequate job taking care of his mother's money, although he didn't work at it very hard. I once asked why he didn't do more, and he said, 'Because it's not worth working.'"
- "He had enough money that he didn't need to work, and I think in part, he went downtown to have something to do and get out of the house."
- "My father complained that he had spent most of his life doing things he didn't want to do, because he had taken responsibility for managing the family money, while his real dream was to live the life of a gentleman farmer."
- "My father's passive, self-indulgent life motivated me to look back three generations to my great-grandfather," Anson wrote, "and consider what he had achieved."

In Peter's recollections, his father is just a void, an absence, or maybe one of those animals that, to camouflage itself with its surroundings, lies completely still and does absolutely nothing. To Peter, for whom things like duty and obligation entirely contradicted his goals and his mission, his father was a kind of quiet disgrace, evidence of everything he would not do with his own life.

ON DECEMBER 7, 1941, AFTER HEARING OF THE BOMBING OF Pearl Harbor, Peter's father told Roseanne that he planned to enlist in the army. Maybe because he was older than his fellow enlistees and had a young family at home, he was assigned to desk duty. He was sent down to Maxwell Field (now Maxwell-Gunter Air Force Base) in Montgomery, Alabama, where he worked on base for the duration, beginning as a second lieutenant, becoming a first lieutenant, then a captain, and finally a major when he was discharged after the war. Though an uninspired history major at Yale, constantly fielding notes from a disappointed father urging him to bring back better grades or else, Anson was given the duty of writing the history of the Army Air Force. (During the war, both the US Navy and Army had Air Forces; the official military branch was established in 1947.) Upon receiving his orders, he went south ahead of the family, to find a house in Montgomery and set everything up to eventually welcome them. Peter and the family made the first trip sans paterfamilias.

At the time, airplanes were mostly reserved for military use, so the family went by train, "the first of six trips to and from Alabama in a Pullman car," Anson remembered. And that first trip must have been memorable—twenty-four hours from New York to Montgomery, Anson and Peter sharing a cabin, Lisa Schaller and Sam in another, Roseanne in a third, and porters running among them. "In the baggage car were our heavy big black steamer trunks with brass fittings," Anson wrote. "My parents had purchased them for their honeymoon in 1934 when they went across the country and then by ship to spend six weeks in Hawaii."

During the war years in Alabama, the three Beard boys, separated by only three years from oldest to youngest, really began to differentiate themselves. Already, Sam, who would go on to work with eight presidents on financial issues from income inequality to Social Security, was showing himself to be the diplomat, the do-gooder who just wanted everyone to be happy. During the brittle-nerve battles between Peter and Roseanne, it was Sam who tried to bring calm. He "liked peace," Anson says, "and didn't like mummy and Peter going at each other."

Of himself, Anson says, "Basically, I wanted to be a big shot.

I was in the special position being the first child; Sam was in a special position being the baby, and Peter was rolling around in the middle constantly in conflict with his mother. That may be one of the reasons he became so self-involved, and had less interest in others, because he was often overlooked as the middle child."

Even in those early adolescent days, Peter—indefatigable, rebellious Peter—was already in full form, as Anson remembered. "Peter's path was more or less whatever came up. More often than not, he stumbled into something exciting and new, rather than seeking it out. He was always curious and had many hobbies. He started taking pictures when he was a little boy. He began collecting things, like frogs, and kept cocoons in drawers, to see if butterflies would come out."

By far his most meaningful experience during their time in Alabama was a visit to the Ringling Bros. Barnum & Bailey circus that came through town in October 1944, when Peter was six. It must have been quite a sight, at a windblown field just outside of town, when the circus company set up its fading magenta big tops, an entire city of tents and carriages and parades of elephants, walking with their trunks joined to the tail of the preceding pachyderm. Add to the fact that on the day they visited, Peter and Sam and their father, Anson, got tornado weather, with boiling black clouds, whirling cones of sky pouring down on them. But under the big tops, bliss. Lions and tigers and, greatest of all, Gargantua, the famous gorilla who so entranced young Peter that he said he may have set his sights on Africa then and there, knowing that his life was now determined and that he had to go in search of the wondrous land where Gargantuas and elephants roamed, where life was like one of these carnivals and every day carried the same magical, campy, gleeful anarchism and showmanship of the fairgrounds.

But arriving in Alabama also hastened the real conflict with his mother. Peter's relationship with Roseanne seems to have been one of the most frustrating of his life. For her part, Anson said, "Mummy's greatest disappointment was her love-hate relationship with Peter. They were very much alike, yet neither of them saw it that way. When he became famous and was interviewed for magazine articles, he said some hurtful things about her." Mostly he was dismissive of her way of life, her values, and it was during their time in Alabama that, according to Anson, "The conflict between them began to erupt around that educational process."

Having sent her oldest, Anson, off to the ramshackle local schools (and learning, horrified, that his classmates would often attend in bare feet), Roseanne decided that these institutions would be unfit to educate and, crucially, to properly discipline the wild one of her three sons, Peter. So Roseanne opted for the Calvert Homeschool method, a system first established as an offshoot to an esteemed school in Baltimore and claiming as its graduates people as far apart as William F. Buckley Jr. and Barack Obama. Well, Peter took to the art classes, his mind fired up by the personalities behind the great works to the point that, as they played at swordfighting in the pecan orchard out back, he would call his brothers, say, Michelangelo and Leonardo to his Raphael, depending on the era of artists he was studying. Even then, it was the whole world of an artist that he wanted to inhabit. Language and science left him cold, or worse. He was a nightmare of boredom and uninterest for Roseanne to handle, and by the time young Anson was returning from his day at a private school in town, she was regularly describing Peter as "the most uncooperative boy she'd ever met," as if she were meeting lots of five-year-olds.

To Anson's mind, Roseanne was, in all areas of life, too strict, perhaps trying to impose herself, to exorcise her feelings of insignificance. The older of the three boys, the one determined to live up to his august heritage, diagnosed in his mother a lack of self-confidence, feelings of inferiority that he traced to her relationship with her mother, Virginia. Then again, Granny's favoritism of Peter may have made of him a target for tougher grading from Roseanne, a kind of lever for mother and daughter to work up their cold war; the tougher Roseanne was on Peter, the more Granny would spoil him, and vice versa.

"There was a conflict between her innate ability and her lack of self-confidence," Peter's brother Anson wrote of their mother in his memoir, *A Life in Full Sail.* "She was smart and energetic, with great common sense and an extremely strong personality, yet she lacked confidence, perhaps because she didn't have much encouragement from her parents. Intellectually, she couldn't compete with her mother, and I have the impression that Granny made it clear that she was disappointed that her daughter wasn't academically more outstanding." Anson describes their mother's life as being incredibly circumscribed, tiny—even geographically so. "She graduated from Chapin," he wrote, "which was five blocks from her apartment, made her debut at the Junior Assemblies, and was married by the time she was nineteen and a half. After that her career was simple: she had her first child at twenty-two, and dedicated her entire life to raising three boys." Anson says she always felt very firmly the outlines of her life, felt boundaries that she never tried to challenge. "When I was older," Anson wrote, "she confided in me that she didn't know where I inherited such self-confidence. She said, 'Your father has no self-confidence. I have no self-confidence. You walk into a room and you're not intimidated by anybody. I don't get it.'"

Of course, it would have to be the process of education (with its implicit discipline, and its roles of authority and obedience) around which Roseanne and Peter would lock horns. Throughout her life, Roseanne was made to feel her lack of higher education or any particular "talent" in that arena, according to Anson, by her rather extraordinarily accomplished mother. Granny Virginia had gone to Bryn Mawr College and then studied law at NYU. She was among the first women (perhaps the very first one) to pass the bar in New York.

"Rather than having a cat or dog, she had a pet monkey," Anson says, "which entranced Peter and me, although Sam was too young to remember it. She also had a collection of Samurai swords which fascinated us, especially after the war." After the passing of her fabulously named husband, Friend (also a lawyer), Virginia moved a block down from the Beards, to an apartment at 157 East Eighty-First Street, where she became involved in the Lighthouse for the Blind (through her dear friend Helen Keller), supplemented her meager finances by being a card sharp at the ladies' canasta and pinochle tables, and doted mercilessly on young Peter, her kindred spirit. "Peter was her favorite," Anson said, "probably because he was the most creative and interesting of the three of us. Granny and Peter often went on exotic jaunts to the American Museum of Natural History or to see other exhibits in the city." And, in what was to be one of the most important moments of young Peter's life, Granny gave Peter his much longed-for Voigtländer camera—despite the warnings of Roseanne and Anson, who worried that the boy would break it or lose it. On the contrary, the images he made on that camera over the next two decades would begin him on his path as an artist, making up the backbone of his greatest early project, *The End of the Game*, which made his name and set him on the path he was to follow for the rest of his life.

"GRANNY'S BURIAL CEREMONY AT A CEMETERY IN THE BRONX was somewhat disorganized," Anson said later. "Her small family had congregated and the minister was ready to start, but her favorite grandson, Peter, was missing. He had wandered off to look at the names on the gravestones on the far side of the ground. I found him relieving himself behind a tree. Despite the solemnity of the occasion, I thought Granny would have been smiling at Peter's typical curiosity, and would not have taken his irreverence amiss."

Roseanne, of course, was less indulgent of young Peter. Was it because, as Anson suggests, she felt she had something to prove and in the raising of the boys saw her only outlet for expression? The boys were witness to some sweet but heartbreaking scenes, like something out of Cheever's stories, in which their mom would challenge other adults in their orbit, mostly male friends of their father's, to contests of athleticism. Foot races. Tennis. Hockey, of course—Roseanne had been a great young ice skater and loved to show up Anson's friends on the ice, playing games with them, humiliating them as she literally skated circles around them. But it wasn't only on the ice. Wherever there was a contest, especially one in which she would excel, she was in. And perhaps the young Peter eyed this suspiciously, or even fearfully, seeing that will to win in his mother as an expression of her drive to dominate, to rule, to make herself more explicitly the center of attention. Maybe Peter secretly sympathized with someone who was always over-shadowed by the two matriarchs in her family who would not be matched in power and dynamism by anyone.

If she was eager to be noticed for her actions, Roseanne seemed to take the attention she received for her looks with aplomb. Anson remembers that every time the family would go to the movies—and they went to the movies a lot—they would be picked up upon their exit by Ruth's chauffeur in her Packard, and onlookers would all point to Roseanne and cry out, "Look, there goes Lauren Bacall."

"Yeah, I get that a lot," Roseanne would say, seemingly non-plussed. But like most people for whom flattery is little more than expected, their just deserts, Roseanne had a temper when she was disappointed. The best-case scenario for the boys, when they were to get in trouble, was to be passed off to their father.

"As a disciplinarian," Anson says of their father, "he was supportive of my mother. She would talk to him and he would tell us that we had to do something, or stop doing something, but he never raised hell, or got mean, or spanked me. My mother, on the other hand, paddled me so hard one time that she broke my father's DKE fraternity paddle on my backside."

THROUGHOUT THE WAR, ROSEANNE AND THE KIDS WOULD ES-cape the sweltering Southern summers as soon as school was out, heading up to Southampton. "Toward the end of our time in Alabama," Anson remembered, "when Sam learned to talk, he still had a pretty short attention span, and he was always asking, 'How much more miles to U-Nork?'"

At the time, Ruth's mansion in Southampton was requisitioned for military use, so the Beards rented a clapboard house, "fairly near town as you go up Main Street toward Gin Lane." Throughout the summer, the boys would live at the Beach Club, taking swimming lessons, body surfing, and competing in meets, their blond hair going a blinding white in the sun. Their favorite activity, though, was the boxing lessons given by Mr. Monahan in which they'd put on gloves bigger than their heads and learn to hit and to defend themselves. "Peter wasn't much bigger than the gloves, but he could take on anybody," Anson said. "He was very quick and he knew how to bob and weave."

Though parched by rationing, this routine of their summers at the beach would remain intact through the Beard boys' adolescence. After the war, the family bought a stucco house, part of a new development on Bayberry Point, in Islip, put together by their family friends, the Havermeyers (the American Sugar Havermeyers, collectors of impressionist art), and so they traded boxing at the Southampton Beach Club for tennis and swimming lessons with Mr. Gillespie at the Bayberry Beach Club. In

Islip, while Anson sailed and Roseanne golfed, Peter would ex-periment endlessly with his Voigtländer, collecting beach detritus for his journals. More than a hobby, the camera Granny Virginia had given Peter created a purpose. And already, if we are to be-lieve his own reflections, the nature of photography's captured moment—imaging an instant gone by, never to be recovered—appealed to Peter's yen to preserve, to collect moments, things, experiences. What's more, he found, as photographers the world over have found, that in the capturing of one moment, he was not only preserving the past but creating something new, something novel, weird, maybe misformed by technical faults or chance or just pure artistic electricity. And it was in this quantum space, collaging together the past he was hoping to preserve and pin to the wall—in the infinite electric present tense, where he thrilled to his great adventures and discoveries and happy accidents; in that artistic time-out-of-time where he was creating something new, something his own—that Peter found his artistic happy place, not necessarily with any thought of posterity or value, just purely blissed out in the act of creation, in tracing the outlines that his imagination and interests made on the material world. As he would later describe it:

> Photography became a way of life, a way to preserve and to remember the passing, changing, fast-fading fa-vorite things, bullfrogs, woodcocks, ruffed grouse, ducks and deer, weekends and summer vacations with my dog Charcoal. Snakes from the woods, moist neon orange sal-amanders with chartreuse spots revealed like tiny jewels under moss-covered rocks, freshly laid frogs' eggs from the murky swamp, tadpoles, polliwogs—jars full-to-go with ice-picked lids for breathing holes. All were mystic reminders of what people called Natural History. For me it was paradise with campfires, axes, knives, traps, traplines.

I wrote to the Northwestern School of Taxidermy, for a first lesson in preservation.

In the meantime, he perfected his picture taking. Or, really, perfected the art of imperfect picture making—as he loved the accidents more than the perfectly planned results. It was the lens flares, the oopsy-daisy exposures, weird focuses, and blurred appearances in the corners of frames that held Peter's attention, and so he pursued those happy accidents.

"I wasn't old enough to draw," he said of his opting for photography as a form of creativity, and of collecting, "so what could be easier? Click . . . click. I lived for the glossy results, for that moment of tearing open the yellow Kodak envelopes and submerging myself in the frozen frames, the new realities, life-thickening windows on to a captured world that beat the rush of time. Even the accidents were fresh, new and welcome: bad exposures, double exposures, wild movements, high-speed flukes, light leaks, lost focusing—learning to appreciate those exciting mistakes was part of the magic. And, into the bargain, it was a rather tricky way of getting animals into the house."

"WE HAD VERY STRUCTURED DAYS—THERE WAS LITTLE FLEX- ibility," Peter's brother Anson said. "We arose and had breakfast at 8:00—sharp!" And then on to the Bayberry Club for classes with Mr. Gillespie. Only on the weekends and holidays would the family gather, on their little putt-putt boat called *Chica*, which they would pack up for cruises over to Point O' Woods, on Fire Island, or to watch the fireworks on the Fourth of July. "Although my father was essentially passive," Anson said, "to his credit, he was extremely responsive to our mother's 'suggestions,' with a capital 'S.' He could do what he wanted on Saturdays, but Sunday was family day."

It was during one of these beach summers that the Beard boys were to see emotion in their father for the first and last time, on one particularly sweltering summer day, when Roseanne left Charcoal alone in a car with the windows closed. "I came back from sailing and put my boat at the Havermeyers' dock, four houses down from us, where my mother had left the car," Anson says. "I looked inside and saw that Charcoal had almost destroyed the upholstery. He had gone berserk, and was panting and struggling to breathe. It was about 100 degrees. I opened the door and carried him in my arms to our house. By the time we arrived home, he was dead. My father came home about a half an hour later. That was the only time I saw him cry."

Later in their lives, long after they'd left the apartment on East Eightieth Street and sold the Daumier, even long after they'd sold Whitehall in South Carolina and retreated to a place on the North Fork of Long Island, the Beard boys' parents remained consistent—and then some. "Peter used to laugh because the address," of the Beards home on North Fork, "was Misery Road. 'That's the perfect place for those two.'" The characteristics that had raised alarm bells in the boys from a young age grew, in their parents' dotage, to poisonous extremes. Roseanne's cruelty became more pronounced, playing games with her grandchildren that she had with the boys, like asking, "Have you ever seen a match burn twice?" And, "When the grandchildren said no, she would light a wooden match, then blow it out and tell the child to touch it."

But it was her suggestions with a capital S to Anson that seem to have caused the greatest ruin within the family. Their father, already having been conditioned to a high number of drinks a day, drank more and more heavily after the hips gave out and he was more or less confined to the home. "Their relationship had become a vicious circle. The more Daddy drank, the bossier Mummy became, and the bossier she became, the more he drank. They were in the same house, but inhabited two separate worlds."

CHAPTER 3

Scroll & Key

G rowing up in the Upper East Side enclave of Carnegie Hill, the same stretch of real estate where J. D. Salinger had set so many of his stories about the Glass family, and as an almost exact contemporary of the writer's famous mid-century sulk, Holden Caulfield, Peter Beard probably couldn't help but judge most things in his life to be phony. The worst thing imaginable in his cosmos was phoniness. Schools, of course, were the worst. His mom and dad, too, were phonies. They believed in a society, a system, that was totally phony, that, in turn, rewarded phony accomplishments and phony behavior—like wearing shoes and suits and worrying about money and marrying the right person and being a member of this or that club.

What wasn't phony was a little slipperier to get a handle on. He didn't yet have a ton of experience out in the wider world, but Peter knew a few things that seemed real to him, incorruptible, true. Animals, for example. Animals were certainly not phony. The natural world was the polar opposite of phoniness. Animals existed in complete accord with their programming, you might say, with instinct and the pattern of life. What could be more real than that?

If this belief system of Peter's had a house of worship, it was, without question, the Museum of Natural History in New York City, just across Central Park from where Peter grew up. This was the Vatican of *primitiva*, as Peter liked to call it—nature in all of its uncorrupted glory. Or at least that is how it presented itself.

Beyond the imperious-looking statue of Teddy Roosevelt, who at the time was an adventurous adolescent boy's idea of an outdoorsy icon, up on his high horse, literally, and flanked on one side by a Native American in headdress and on the other by a topless African man with braided hair, the museum was like a candy store for the animal-crazed Peter. On his earliest excursions here, with his Granny Virginia, he was spellbound by the delicately detailed dioramas—phenomenally arranged tableaux of animals, from herds of mammoths to couples of leopards, Cro-Magnon men to grizzly bears, in painterly evocations of their natural habitats.

Over the years, and his many visits, Peter began to look a little deeper at these cinematic stagings, and consider more closely the artistry, the adventure, the science, the stories that had gone into making them. He became fascinated with the revolutionary taxidermist Carl Akeley, who had arranged the dioramas and had himself traveled to Africa to bag and then stuff and preserve the many creatures for his creations. The stories of Akeley sliding backward down rain-forested slopes in Virunga while firing off wizard-like shots at three-hundred-pound gorillas quickly vaulted him into Peter's rapidly growing pantheon. But it was the stories around the expedition Akeley took with George Eastman, the inventor and founder of Kodak, through Africa, searching for the very specimens Peter was now so familiar with in the tableaux, that really lit him up. Here was everything he loved and adored in one trip: the origins of photography, represented by a stalwart in the field, in cahoots with the greatest taxidermist of all time, running the width of Equatorial Africa, and, for some of their time, led by the most famous of great white hunters, Philip Percival, who, of course, had been Teddy Roosevelt's guide when he went and shot five hundred–plus animals in Africa in 1909–1910.

Peter's high school days were spent at Pomfret, the boarding school in northern Connecticut where his father had gone, and where his mother had sent him, thinking he needed the discipline its smaller class sizes would provide (as opposed to, say, Exeter or St. Paul's, where Anson went). Peter relished his modicum of independence in Connecticut and spent every last dime of his clothing allowance on big expensive art books. But mostly he felt himself to be on autopilot, just doing what he was told to do. It was a grim existence, and he had pent up his energy like a prisoner waiting to secure his freedom, freedom that arrived for the first time in the form of Quentin Keynes, a fabulously eccentric Englishman. Keynes was in love with sports cars and animals and rare stamps, and, seventeen years Peter's senior, he would become something of a mentor to him, as he would for so many young schoolboys to whom he gave his wildly beloved Africa lectures.

"Everything changed for Peter when Quentin Keynes invited him on safari," Anson said. It was as if his life had begun. And he had made his first, foundational friend—a compatriot in all things Africana and art. Like Peter, Keynes had a whole lot of fancy family members, and this, no doubt, was an enormous bonding point for them. Most impressive to Peter was the fact that Keynes's great-grandfather was Charles Darwin. No less important to Quentin, certainly, his father was a famous book collector and expert on the visionary artist William Blake. And his uncle was the world-famous economist John Maynard Keynes, who brought plenty of real-world gravity, but also substantial bohemian cred, as a true-blue member of the Bloomsbury group.

As an adolescent, Quentin Keynes developed a mania for stamp collecting—driving up some enormous debts that his father had to deal with—and, in the process, developing a fascination with all the far-off places that the beautiful pictures on the stamps evoked, and whence they'd originated. Like Peter, Keynes was the rather rambunctious middle of three brothers and he similarly struggled with his mother's expectations for him. At sixteen, on a visit home for the coronation of George VI, Keynes climbed up on the roof of his parents' apartment building and refused to come down if they insisted on putting him back on the train to his boarding school in Devon. Ultimately, he gave in but discontinued his formal education the following year. On a trip to Zurich that same year, he developed a mild case of polio that later kept him out of war duty.

At the suggestion of his American cousins, Keynes moved to America, where, like Peter, his family connections and irresistible charm opened doors in every direction. At the suggestion of family friend Betsey Cushing, Keynes went to Hollywood to meet Betsey's husband, James Roosevelt (son of FDR), who was then setting up a production company. During the war, Keynes lived in Washington, DC, where he'd gotten a job at the British Embassy—and spent the time mostly going out to parties with the Roosevelts, with Kick Kennedy (JFK's sister, who became Keynes's closest friend), and with Jacqueline Bouvier. At the time, Jackie was working as the "Inquiring Photographer" for the *Washington Times-Herald*, doing a sort of street-style sociology column. Each day she would find a street corner in the capital on which to perch and ask passersby one special question that would be particularly illuminating (she was very proud of her questions). Of "Quentin Keynes, explorer, New York City," when she wrangled him into it on Connecticut Avenue, Ms. Bouvier asked, "When were you the most scared?"

Keynes's reply is certainly something: "Motoring thru [*sic*] Swaziland, South-West Africa, we saw 1500 Swazi celebrating Dingon's day, full of kaffir beer. As I took a photo the chief started screaming. Another Swazi knocked me down with a four-foot assegai [a wooden pole]. I ran to the car and drove away. They might have torn us to pieces."

It was these sorts of stories, delivered with such delectable relish, when given as a lecture or in narration over one of the somewhat crude amateur films he had begun producing in Africa, that made Keynes a wildly popular visitor to schools all along the Eastern Seaboard in the mid-fifties. He traveled a bit like a salesman, though staying at the homes of fabulous friends and driving a particularly wild sports car du jour. Over the years, he had everything from a Hillman Minx to a Gordon Keeble and an Austin-Healey. In fact, he once tried to convince Healey to customize a car for him to drive across the width of Africa, but he eventually had to make do with a Jeep instead. Keynes would pop in at high schools or boarding schools to deliver his talks to great fanfare. Soon he was even leading some of the students from these schools, sons of the best and brightest, on safaris of his own. In 1955, with a commission from *National Geographic* to photograph a near-mythical creature—the coelacanth, in the Comoros Islands, northwest of Madagascar—Keynes set off on his fourth visit to Africa, bringing along seventeen-year-old Peter. And as if Peter weren't already thinking about it, Keynes would've made sure that he secured a good camera for the trip, no matter how well he knew how to use it.

As he no doubt would have told his new mentee, Keynes's own first journey, an overland trip from Cairo to the Cape (with his then brand-new Leica in tow), was as life-changing for him as their upcoming voyage would be for young Peter, and not just because of the dangerous scrapes and wild adventures. On one memorable occasion, Keynes had the composure to photograph a charging rhino as he climbed up a tree to escape it—and the picture he took won an award after being published in *Country Life* magazine. That same year, *National Geographic* published a whole series of pictures he took of elephants at Treetops Lodge in Kenya—the same canopy-high game lookout where, a couple of years later, Princess Elizabeth learned that she had ascended to the throne of the British Empire. Keynes's elephant story began his long relationship with the magazine, a relationship that provided the basis for the journey that first propelled Peter to Africa.

Along the way, as they crossed the Atlantic, the two photographers talked excitedly of their destination. Having given up on stamps in his teens, Keynes's new collecting obsession was books, specifically anything having to do with the nineteenth-century explorers of Africa—Livingstone, Burton, Speke, Stanley. Burton was his prevailing fixation, and he would even propose the idea of a biopic about him to Peter Ustinov and Mrs. David Lean. But each and every one of these Victorian gentlemen explorers lit him up. He was distantly related to Speke, "the Nilotic Psychotic!" as he described him, and had, on his most recent visit to Africa, gone in search of a single, particular baobab tree that Livingstone had described in detail. Livingstone had been in awe of these mammoth-trunked towers with their funny T-rex-arm branches way up at the top, making particular mention in his journals of the way the trees grew new bark over wounds and fire damage and crevices, so as to prevent further weathering. Knowing these writings as well as he did, Keynes not only found the tree—one specific tree, in all of Africa—he also found a "Kilroy was here"–style engraving Livingstone had made of his initials in the tree's (newly regrown) bark, within a cavern-like crevice. One expert called it the greatest Livingstone discovery in thirty years.

Obviously, all of this was music to Peter's ears. Being with Darwin's great-grandson on a journey to find and document a species believed to have gone extinct ages before, a journey in the footsteps of outsize personalities whom he so desperately admired and whom his companion was an absolute world-class expert on . . . Photography! Adventure! And animals! The perfect combination.

On their crossing, Peter read Karen Blixen's memoir of her time growing coffee and having a love affair—tragedies, both—in colonial Kenya between the wars. He devoured *Out of Africa*, making copious notes in the margins and underlining virtually the entire book. Once around the Cape of Good Hope, the two adventurers made stops in South Africa, Zimbabwe, and then out on Comoros Islands off Madagascar, where Keynes hoped to find traces of the rare dinosaur fish, the coelacanth—which looks as pretty as it sounds, with its speckled rock-like complexion, ghostly eyes, and almost elephantine jowls. Their search was ultimately unsuccessful, as were the two by Jacques Cousteau that followed soon after. Not until 1979 did David Attenborough's team from the BBC finally manage to film a coelacanth that had been caught by a local fisherman, just as it died in the shallows off the Comoros.

Peter and Quentin continued their journey on to Kenya, then only recently removed from the most eventful skirmishes of the Mau Mau uprising. Beginning in 1952, the Kenya Land and Freedom Army led an armed insurrection in an attempt to evict the English and end colonial rule. In response, the British Army, along with nearly twenty-five thousand local Kikuyu, who had been loyal to the Crown during wars against other colonial armies, put down the rebellion, ultimately capturing Field Marshal Dedan Kimathi in 1956, which effectively ended the war. But what would become of great interest to Peter in his many years there, a fraught subject during otherwise boastful drunk chats in the bush, was how the British had employed native trackers and Western hunters to seek out the rebels in the very same way they did game—something Peter would later describe with some of the horror and awe it deserved.

After that first trip, Peter made his way to the English preparatory school Felsted, in Essex, where he was sent "to gain a little old-world polish," as his host's son said (though perhaps the polish was needed for his educational résumé, to make up for credits missed at Pomfret, or a CV that underwhelmed the admittance teams at the Ivy League schools where a male Beard simply had to go). On the advice of Keynes (weirdly, since he had staged a sort of suicide attempt in protest of his own boarding school), Peter boarded at Felsted, and there he met Clive Fiske-Harrison, with whom he would spend his off days and holidays, at the "grand old family house" in Layer de la Haye. "My family were a wild bunch with a penchant for gunplay," writes Clive's son, Alexander Fiske-Harrison, "nominally hunting duck in the marshes but frequently 'peppering' one another, by accident or design. Peter shot my father. But then again, so did my uncle."

Of his school days at Felsted, like those at Pomfret, Peter said little other than to talk about his little rebellions. At Pomfret that rebellion had taken the form of the reallocation of clothing allowances for art books. At Felsted, Peter had staged his defiance in the ring. He joined the school boxing team and faced off with blokes several stones larger than his scrawny self. And still he remained fearless, or maybe just a little hell-bent on blood and destruction.

When Peter finally did make it to New Haven and Yale in the fall of 1956, he was still doing essentially what was expected of and assigned to him. He started by studying medicine, with the idea, perhaps, that he would go on to become a doctor. With his appreciation for blood, his more than toleration of gore, and his interest in the material interiors of critters large and small, this could conceivably have worked out for him. But no way was Peter going to invest the seven-odd years of study to complete a degree in anything, let alone medicine, which would then require years of grunt work. On top of which, as Anson so aptly put it, Peter never really managed to be interested that much in the well-being of others. Not individuals, and maybe not even humanity at large, as a species. Looking back on his decision to switch to the art department, Peter loved to say that he had determined that curing people was an oxymoron because "humanity was the disease."

But no one, he said, really majored in art, at least not at Yale and not up to that point. It just wasn't done. Art History, yes, but what was the future of someone who just . . . made things? Here again, Peter happened into one of those fortuitous moments that so colored his whole life, walking into an art department absolutely stacked with glitzy names and dedicated to a philosophy perfectly aligned with his sensibilities. A few years earlier, the great artist of graphic abstractions Josef Albers had left his position at Black Mountain College in North Carolina to head the newly formed Department of Design at Yale, and he immediately made an impact.

Perceived by students as "a cross between Otto von Bismarck and Santa Claus," according to one biography, Albers in the classroom could be intimidating, going around confiscating erasers (so as to ensure boldness and surety of line), inspiring his students to tenacious effort and almost pious reverence. But he was also wildly spontaneous and even gregarious, dancing about gleefully on sidewalks when greeted by students. And he was a stickler for fundamentals, believing college ought to be a rigorous time of instruction—but also when students learned to follow their own instincts. His exercises were aimed at cracking open the way aspiring artists saw the world, their media, and the work.

This holistic element of Albers's philosophy might have been the most important for Peter, who really would make of himself and his life a vessel for art, so that everything he did, everything he touched, was in fact a part of his oeuvre. With some later dissatisfaction, Peter described how he had attempted "Old Master"–style painting and just wasn't very good at it. Peter didn't love his own attempts at sketching and drawing and didn't think he had real genius there—or the will to dedicate himself to the years in perfecting his craft. One of his teachers at the time, a graduate assistant, was Alex Katz, now a wildly revered painter with devastatingly assured opinions on his contemporaries, and perhaps Peter was a bit intimidated by the in-crowd of the then burgeoning art world, just as he would have been magnetically repelled by academia. He simply wasn't a joiner, wasn't going to do anything that had been done before. And he knew very well that he wanted to get in the dirt with the wildlife he loved. For this, photography still couldn't be beat as a medium. And his particular adventuring style and predilections for Africana were, for the work, the secret spice that would set him apart. For him personally, of course, it was something else, something greater—as if he had found his identity, his real home in a vanishing outpost in colonial East Africa, and it was only there that he could be himself.

In short order, Peter dedicated himself to photography with his zealous misunderstanding of due dates, project costs, timelines of any sort, and even other people, producing more of what he wanted to make than what was assigned. His classmate, and later his publicist, Bobby Zarem, remembered Peter chaining himself in the photo studio and darkroom for days on end so that he could work undisturbed by sunshine, the rhythm of classes, or the reality of his fellow photographers who were locked out of their workspace.

Now free from the close watch of his mother and the discipline of Pomfret, Peter began really indulging his mania in sustained jags of work. Later, of course, when putting together the final draft of *The End of the Game*, Peter camped out in the offices of his editor, buoyed by whatever chemical assistance was then available, to work for days at a time as he regularly did when putting together shows and books, and even while working on individual pieces. His capacity for focus and busywork was almost superhuman, and Yale was where he created some of that habit.

However, apart from a whole lot of alcohol, there were no other intoxicants around at the time—so says Anson, who was a couple of years ahead of Peter—or at least Peter wasn't interested in looking for them, not having any experience with drugs at all until a few years later. But if he was looking to burn off a little steam and adolescent hormones, Yale seemed an accommodating place for that—providing, of course, that you were white and had the right last name.

Though he would fairly limp through the completion of his degree—in fact, Anson speculated that Peter wrote an essay about Africa many months after completing his studies and only then was grudgingly granted a diploma—he was still invited to one of the exclusive seniors clubs at Yale, supposedly reserved for exceptional members of the graduating class. Surely it was just coincidence that Peter's mother was friends with a board member of the Scroll & Key club and they invited him to be among the mere thirteen inductees that year based on merit alone. "Scroll & Key is one of the most beautiful buildings on campus," said Anson, in his fact-of-the-matter style. "You enter the Hall with a code, there's a lot of ritual, you sing songs, some of them are fun, some of them are serious. There is a very rigorous program; it is time consuming and we took it very seriously. We met Thursday and Sunday nights. There were formal presentations and informal ones. Sometimes there was a previously assigned discussion topic. . . ." None of which seemed to square with the recklessly independent Peter.

Still, the middle Beard brother took to the fraternity's atmosphere of recklessness and entitlement; he would later say that his membership in the group was the only thing that had made his college years bearable. As part of his welcoming ceremony, Peter was let loose to channel all of his puckish impulses and even a little vandalistic rage on the fraternity's rivals, the famous Skull & Bones. "Sixty-six years after my grandfather graduated," Peter's brother Anson recalled in his 2012 memoir, "during Peter's senior year at Yale in 1961 . . . he broke into the Bones 'temple' on High Street. That was hardly unique, it was traditional for members of the seven senior societies to occasionally attempt to enter each other's halls and remove artifacts, keeping them as trophies. Peter pilfered a skull that had the names of several well-known Bones-men engraved on it, including that of our grandfather. The graduate authorities at Scroll & Key decided the raid had gone too far and returned the skull and other loot to High Street. To this day, Peter believes they overreacted."

Looking back, maybe Peter's yearning to escape the strictures of society and the proscribed life of a stockbroker was a kind of wisdom. Maybe he knew that he just wanted to go on raiding parties and gleefully entertain himself playing with beasts of the wild. In the particular postcolonial Africa he'd found, a remittance chum like him could pretty much get away with any sort of behavior this side of murder and pillage (those had gone out of style the century prior), so maybe the move there was just a square peg finding its right and true fit.

Not that Peter was averse to sophistication. He liked the Scroll & Key's stalwarts around him—like *New Yorker* writer Calvin Trillin and cartoonist Gary Trudeau, who were his near contemporaries. He wanted a little literary flair and artistic panache in his playtime. He wanted, in other words, to find—or make—a real and proper bohemia. In this, Peter's cousin Jerome Hill proved invaluable, the ultimate kindred spirit.

Jerome Hill, a grandchild of James J. Hill, just as Peter's father Anson was, was everything Peter's father was not. He was artistic, cultured, dynamic—and while Anson slumbered through his job protecting his mother's money at the bank, grumbling about what a waste of time and money the New Deal's Federal Art Projects had been, and making visits to the club and the beach house for a reprieve, Jerome Hill did and tried *everything* in the arts, and left, as part of his legacy, artist fellowships in the States and in Cassis in the south of France. It was in Cassis, at a tumbledown old *bastide*, called le Batterie, where Jerome had first set himself up as a painter, soaking himself and his canvases in that Côte d'Azur light that had so intoxicated the cubists, impressionists, and, well, everyone. And everyone who was everyone came to hang out with Jerome, who made it his business to be a friend to artists.

As a kid, growing up in a house next door to his grandfather's grand mansion on Summit Avenue in St. Paul, Minnesota, Jerome wrote, set-designed, and acted out elaborate plays. He loved to watch films when his family screened them at home (as they avoided theaters for fear of germs), and he was allowed and even encouraged to indulge his artistic interests, while his two older brothers were tapped by their father for banking and industry. As a young man, Jerome put together a massive document titled "Synoptic History of Civilization," gathering together momentous occasions, eras, and developments in human history from the fifth century to the 1920s into a single chronological timeline, so that all of the threads can be seen and viewed in context.

After studying music at Yale, Jerome moved to the south of France to study painting in the mecca of the medium. After his grandfather's passing in 1916, Jerome had inherited many of the industrialist's incredible paintings (several by Corot, who had been James Hill's favorite, as well as by Delacroix, and many from the Barbizon school), and with them the means to begin collecting of his own accord. The works of Ed Weston were a particular favorite, and Jerome began to play with photography too, and soon, with filmmaking—and Peter always loved to describe his cousin as an inveterate shutterbug like himself. Though Jerome would far surpass his cousin in this arena: one of his films, about the French doctor and missionary Albert Schweitzer, won the Academy Award for Best Documentary in 1958.

Throughout the late 1950s and early '60s, Peter visited his elder cousin in Cassis, where he was introduced to the likes of Picasso and Brigitte Bardot (both of whom he made absolutely sure to photograph), in whose company he felt utterly at home and free to go the full Peter. Picasso was at the time living and working at his Belle Époque mansion La Californie in Cannes, married to his second wife, Jacqueline Roque, who had the unenviable job of controlling access to the artist and keeping at bay the hordes of hangers-on, fans, friends, and floozies who wanted to spend time with her husband.

Through Jerome, Peter also met the photographer and collector Lucien Clergue, who was a great friend of Picasso's. Clergue was, like Jerome, a bastion for other artists, building a great network of communication for the artists' mutual benefit and setting up the now legendary Les Rencontres d'Arles photography festival in his hometown. "Everyone remembers Peter in Arles, this irresistible being, full of talent and free as a bird," Clergue's daughter, Anne, says. On one of his visits to see Clergue and the family in Arles, Peter managed to get to a bullfight with Picasso. "He wanted to jump into the arena during a bullfight and kill a bull," Anna says, "but the former bullfighter Pataroni opened his shirt and showed him the terrible scars caused by the bulls."

When, in 1984, Clergue invited Peter to exhibit his own work at Rencontres, Peter stayed at the Arlatan, and established his headquarters (for morning orange gins and rants about art) at Le Tambourin café in the Place du Forum. "As soon as he arrived," Anne Clergue remembered, "his room was immediately transformed into an artist's studio: photos, collages, fake blood for making up his notebooks, the famous UHU glue, a thousand incongruous objects littered the floor and occupied all the space." He and his second wife, Cheryl Tiegs, had just divorced, and Peter showed up with a new girlfriend, the English actress and photographer Marella Oppenheim, who had broken off her own wedding to be with Peter. (In one of those very weird little chimes of history that happened around Peter, one of Oppenheim's later acting credits would include her performance as Lee Radziwill in the 1988 TV movie *Onassis: The Richest Man in the World*. For some of the time during which her sister Jackie was married to Onassis, Lee was Peter's girlfriend, so it was a case of one girlfriend playing another.) "He was not afraid of anything," Anne said, "he had a crazy charm and seduced all women."

On a walk with Marella and Anne, "in the footsteps of van Gogh," Anne says, Peter marched the girls up the steep slopes of Montmajour Abbey, making a beeline for the forbidden areas, the roped-off areas, areas even guarded by barbed wire. "He entered wherever he wanted, especially in places where access was prohibited. [His] was a bohemian life where everything was simple, nothing mattered, it was a time of carelessness." For example, he didn't care about the five-hundred-franc notes flying out the back of his shopping basket. "The only thing that interested him was the long discussions about the artists, Van Gogh, Bacon, Picasso and the others."

A few years later, Anne moved to New York and became a curator at the Leo Castelli Gallery. When she and Peter would hang out, they'd go to Jezebel, the absolutely wild soul-food restaurant at Ninth Avenue and Forty-Fifth Street run by Alberta Wright, a woman from South Carolina who worked in fashion sales before opening a beloved women's vintage clothing store on the Upper West Side, also called Jezebel. At Jezebel the restaurant, which ran from 1983 to 2007, there were Warhols next to swaths of wild, exotic fabrics, downtowners next to all sorts from the Upper East and West, all there for the martinis and deep-soul Southern cooking. In a review of the restaurant for the *New York Times* in 1983, Bryan Miller could have been describing Peter's later decorating efforts at Hog Ranch and in Montauk. "Palms and assorted foliage sway under the breeze of big room fans . . . antique furniture mixes with white wicker chairs and porch swings suspended from the ceiling . . . Oriental rugs, vintage posters, lace-covered tables and crystal chandeliers . . ." Such a Peter place.

Back in New York in the early sixties, where Peter was already starting to collect his own eclectic mélange of characters, he was only really beginning to discover that other great passion of his life—women. It wasn't until just after college that Peter, one of the most celebrated Don Juans of the twentieth century, lost his virginity, presumably to his longtime sweetheart, the model and actress Dorothy McGowan. But if he took his time in showing up to the party, he certainly spent the rest of his life making up for it. "He dated the most extraordinary women . . . all of them," Ali MacGraw told me. She also said that she did not date Peter but was always in awe of his girlfriends.

The first very serious relationship seems to have been with the actress Astrid Heeren, who played Steve McQueen's girlfriend in the beginning of *The Thomas Crown Affair*. Peter and Heeren were even briefly engaged, and she joined him on a trip to visit Jerome in Cassis in the early sixties. Pictures of the couple from that time are remarkable in that Peter already looks fully formed, if youthfully skinny, surrounded by animal skulls, wearing safari shorts and plaid shirts with his golden hair parted just so. Heeren looks as though she's just realized she's taken a powerful drug— a thrilling and intoxicating drug, perhaps, but who knows how toxic and what sort of tears it might hold in store for her.

I think it is probably a bit too easy to assign this or that Freudian reading to a seducer's behavior, but in his seductions, as in everything he did in his life, Peter was obsessive, insatiable, so perhaps it is only natural to see certain psychological mechanisms at work. It seems clear, for example, that Peter went out of his way to court affection, attention, praise, and maybe even love, which he so expressly says he did not receive from his mother.

Vanity, too, must have been a big part of the equation. Because no one who's born looking like Peter, who goes through life being told at every turn just how astonishingly handsome he is, can fail to place *enormous* value on their looks, on everyone's looks. Throughout his life, Peter professed to value nothing at all above beauty; maybe even nothing *but* beauty, in all of its manifestations.

"And he was unbelievably handsome," the great New York wit and social critic Fran Lebowitz told me. "I mean, he really looked like a young Gary Cooper. He was dazzling. And let me assure you if he was an ordinary looking man, you would not be writing about him. What really set him apart from the other beautiful boys was he was straight. I mean, he's one of the most handsome straight men I've ever seen in my life. And all the other stuff he did that people found so mesmerizing, I assure you they would not have [thought about him one way or another] if he'd looked just like any guy." In fact, Fran says, Peter's work, and his behavior—"that kind of very showy eccentricity," as she calls it—"was the kind of stuff that girls did. He was like a beautiful girl in lots of ways. His behavior was the behavior of a very beautiful girl. Kind of crazy upper-class girls trying to get back at their parents for not paying attention to them or whatever. Usually they can get away with everything until they're not very beautiful."

Fran's not the only person to frame Peter's personality this way. One young woman, who had a romantic relationship with Peter later in his life, a model who would ride out to Peter's Montauk house in a limo he had sent for her, described his enormous conversational activity, his utter self-absorption, and his court-jester animation as a great relief. For her, being a beautiful woman in a culture and economy that prized her youth and beauty above all else, having been placed on a pedestal and gawped at her whole life, getting a break from all of that was a joy. Peter's doing all the work, gobbling up all of the attention, keeping all eyes on him, his Tinker Bell–like effort to keep everyone else charmed and amused lest they lose interest for one moment and he fade away—all that provided her a glorious break.

Peter did nothing to discourage the reputation he was getting as a rake and a ladies' man. He was even getting credit for girl-friends who were not girlfriends—like MacGraw, whom he could conceivably have met in the late fifties when she was a "part-time model," as she called it, or when she worked as an assistant to Diana Vreeland, in a very *The Devil Wears Prada* sort of engagement, or else during her time as stylist and collaborator with photographer Melvin Sokolsky, though the two never even met until forty years later. Another rumored girlfriend of the time was Candice Bergen, who did shelter at Peter's house when fleeing a different relationship. She told me that she and Peter didn't really know each other all that well. But besides a lot of smoke, there was also a lot of fire. Barbara Allen, while working with Andy Warhol at *Interview*, met Peter to do a story on him and basically ran away with him for the summer, away from her husband, Joe, who then owned a quarter of the magazine. Eventual Bond girl Carole Bouquet (*For Your Eyes Only*) sat for a portrait with Peter and seems to have stuck around for a while thereafter.

But none of the women with whom Peter is most closely associated—the models whose images are in some way tied back to him, from Iman to Beverly Johnson to Donyale Luna, as well as Janice Dickinson—had romantic relationships with Peter. ("I don't know how I missed that opportunity for romance," Johnson recalls, while reveling in memories of Peter's boyish beauty at the time.) He did seem to love to bask in their reflected glory, though, just as he loved being in the company of Veruschka in the late 1950s in New York.

After returning from Africa on his first trip with Quentin Keynes and the Voigtländer his Granny Virginia had given him, Peter very ambitiously brought some of his pictures to the attention of Alexander Liberman, the all-powerful creative director at Condé Nast at the time, who on the strength of those pictures, immediately gave him assignments. And very soon he had a contract with *Vogue* and then with *Harper's Bazaar* and Diana Vreeland, to photograph society ladies (like Lee Radziwill) as well as fashion stories. One of these, perhaps the very first, was a story featuring the German model Veruschka, born Countess Vera von Lehndorff-Steinort, in what was to be her first shoot ever.

"I did my first *Vogue* shoot in June 1963—14 pages, with Veruschka and my then girlfriend Astrid Heeren on this big Arabian horse farm in Moline, Illinois," Peter said. "I'd done some photos of Veruschka on the beach at Coney Island the year before—her first pictures. In Moline I had her jumping up while a horse cavorted around her, occasionally getting all of its legs into the air—it was like one of Eadweard Muybridge's pioneering motion photographs which he reportedly invented to support his bet that the four legs of a horse could be off the ground at the same time."

After the horse shoot, the two rookies, Peter and Veruschka, seemed to hit it off, and Peter kept in very close contact with the model, whom Richard Avedon would shortly describe as "the most beautiful woman in the world." Peter and Veruschka were friends, surely, but they were something else besides. Peter's relationship with the model was almost like that of a manager. Of course, they did continue to work together—creating, a few years later, one of the really great images of her career, on an expedition to round up rhinos in Kenya, in which she is wearing the same acid-yellow python-print jumpsuit by Arnold Scaasi that she had worn in the Michelangelo Antonioni film *Blow-Up*, a film inspired by the life of Peter's friend the photographer David Bailey. But then Peter also booked her on jobs he wasn't shooting and ran communication for her. He acted as a sort of intermediary, or an agent.

When Salvador Dalí wanted to hire Veruschka to model for a *Vogue* shoot he was arranging at his home in Cadaqués, he called Peter to set it up. Peter had first introduced the surrealist to the model in the early sixties, and of this strange arrangement around the shoot, Veruschka said, "[Dalí and I] did not speak about it at all. Dalí didn't call you. At that time we were in contact through Peter Beard."

Ever the gentleman, Peter opted to tag along on the all-expenses-paid trip to the Med and loved every minute of it. "We had a lot of fun in Port Lligat," he said, stating what would be the obvious. "We had a lot of amazing meals and Dalí was such a generous person. He was an incredibly generous person." It's interesting that Peter singles out Dalí's (and his wife Gala's, of course) gifts as hosts, as if one wouldn't expect such a thing from such an elaborate narcissist. After all, Peter and Veruschka were there to do a shoot for an issue of *Vogue* with, as Dalí said, "the aim of glorifying the cult of his own personality and that of Gala." It is a combination—of seemingly enormous generosity with a kind of selfishness unto the point of solipsism—that flourished within Peter as well.

Peter said that he and Dalí had first met through Jerome Hill, and they began hanging out at the King Cole Bar at the St. Regis, where Dalí and Gala were living. Like many of the wan young beautiful butterflies Dalí seems to have attracted and caught to put under glass for further study, Peter was attracted by the artist's flamboyance and flattery. For his part, Dalí was absolutely convinced that Peter was his dead brother.

"He was the idea man of all time," Peter said. "He kept insisting, weirdly enough, that I was his dead brother. He said I was a dead ringer for him and that he had used my face for his portrait. People like to think Dalí was crazy. Believe me, he was never crazy—he was just inspired."

It is unclear, of course—Dalí being Dalí—if he believed in this reincarnation scenario, if he was pulling Peter's leg, or if all and both and none of it was true and he was just arranging a scenario that pleased him aesthetically. One thing does seem clear of their relationship: Dalí believed himself to be in a mentor role, responsible for imparting to the young artist-aspirant some advice about how to manage his image, above all else. "He loved going through my diaries; he used to say, 'Mr. Bird, it's the quantity!'" Implying perhaps that they lacked quality.

"One of our extravagances uptown," Peter explained, "is we would go around in a limo with Dalí and do these things. The limo delivered us back to the King Cole Bar and two or three people got out and then Dalí and I was the last person to get out. And he turned to me in the limo and said, 'Mr. Beard,'"— or as Peter liked to say in doing his impersonation—"'Mr. Bird, one thing, if you ever do any drugs, don't tell anybody.' I had no idea what he meant but I could sort of figure it out because we did some extremely exciting and dynamic filming and I guess he thought that I had done some coke. I had no idea what coke was."

Dalí was famously abstemious throughout his life—"clean," Veruschka called him, saying he hardly even had wine. And of course he curated this aspect of his image as carefully as all others, bragging in the third person, that, "Dalí is the only painter of LSD without LSD . . . I have never taken drugs because I am the drug." Which is a wonderful line. "He was giving me a secret there," Peter said, of his lesson in the limo. What Peter inferred from this warning was that, if Dalí were known to have taken drugs, that would "in some people's eyes, lessen his accomplishment in painting because they would say he cheated, he did drugs, it wasn't his idea." At any rate, it doesn't seem as though Peter heeded this particular advice too carefully.

And if Dalí was Peter's first great introduction to the art of merciless self-promotion, around this time he also met the other great practitioner of the form, Andy Warhol, at a Luis Buñuel screening. It is perhaps telling that, at the time, Peter thought of Andy as "a freak," and stayed away from him. Only a few years on, he would say of Warhol and Dalí that, "They were in the same ballpark, so different but so similar. I don't like the word *genius*, but of course we do have Picasso. I would say they were both geniuses. . . . One of their genius elements was to exponentially exaggerate the originality that they each had."

If, as Lebowitz explains, photography wasn't quite the most

esteemed medium in the late fifties—"you cannot imagine how *not* seriously it was taken," she says—the art of personality was quickly becoming the main practice of the day, as it is now. And, for a time, from the late sixties into the early seventies, Peter was to sit at the feet of two of the medium's most famous practitioners. Dalí and Warhol are the artists we most closely associate with making of themselves their greatest work and making the public consciousness their canvas—and we can't help but see where this rubbed off on him.

AS PART OF THEIR EXTRAVAGANCES DOWNTOWN, PETER IN-troduced Dalí to the artistic demimonde, bringing him around the film-society gatherings that he was arranging at the time with his friend Jonas Mekas—the Lithuanian refugee and poet laureate of the East Village who later presided over the Anthology Film Center. Dalí told Mekas that he "wanted to do some happenings/performances himself." And it was Peter who became the manager of these odd events. As Mekas says, Beard was "always with the *Vogue* magazine fashion crowd, so he provided willing models." Veruschka chief among them: Dalí created a "shaving cream performance" in which she covered her body with shaving cream, a concept that has been imitated approximately a zillion times since. But Veruschka was not always available. In one case, when Dalí was putting together what he called *Major Accident*, a happening around a crashed car on 125th Street, Veruschka was under the weather and Peter improvised by calling on Nena Thurman (mother to the actress Uma), née von Schlebrügge, a model who had been discovered by the great photographer Norman Parkinson in her native Stockholm when she was fourteen. "It was Sunday morning and I was luxuriating in bed," von Schlebrügge said, "when the phone rang. It was Peter Beard, and he was most insistent that I get out of bed to meet him and Salvador Dalí for a special photo shoot. . . . He had Dalí right there and if I could just please do him this favor, they would come right over and pick me up in a car. I could not resist his plea and gave up my peaceful morning."

The happening happened, Peter captured the moment, and smeared a print in blood for posterity. In his image, von Schlebrügge lies atop an utterly destroyed—Buick? Who can tell?—in snowy Harlem while Dalí stares at the camera and points off to the sky, a conductor about to begin his opus. (Interestingly, the next year, von Schlebrügge married her first husband, a man who may not have been "the drug" but was perhaps the most famous proselytizer for LSD, Timothy Leary.)

Maybe the most celebrated of the Dalí happenings of the time, a continuation of the situationist work he had been doing for more than twenty years in Europe, was the protest of the *Mona Lisa*, which he arranged with Peter to take place outside the Metropolitan Museum. "We got up at four in the morning and picketed *Mona Lisa*," Peter said, "which had been brought to the Metropolitan, because Dalí just really wanted us to do it. And we had these Mona Lisas with the heads cut out and stuck our heads in. . . . We were very obnoxious." The assembled mob of Peter's friends, models, Jonas, and others were given protest signs that, rather than bearing a slogan, had an image of the Mona Lisa with the face removed and a hole through which the protestors could jut their own jaws. Not quite *The Thomas Crown Affair*, but funny—even if both Peter and Jonas later lamented the whole operation.

Far more fulfilling for Mekas, at least, was the film he was planning to make with his brother Adolphas, and for which he would ultimately cast Peter in the lead, *Hallelujah the Hills*. In the film, Peter and another man pine endlessly for a woman who eventually runs off with someone else. In despair and hilarity, the two rejected men run off into the woods to play out a survivalist fantasy of romance and heroism. In the *New Yorker*, Richard Brody describes the performers as "the two loudest silent comics," and Peter specifically as "a sort of East Village Buster Keaton." And "Mekas puts them through shambling but surprisingly snap-timed routines that teem with cartoonish, bittersweet whimsy. These cinematic idiots savants come off as the self-aware worshippers of clichés that everyone else in their eccentric orbit lives out blindly."

Later Peter would downplay the whole thing, saying essentially that he was tagging along with his girlfriend at the time, Dorothy McGowan, who was one of the leads, when Mekas had him audition for the part. Footage of his screen test appears in Jonas Mekas's film *Walden*—and Peter certainly passes the test, looking a bit like a young Montgomery Clift. The better to woo Miss McGowan of course, who was herself a legendary beauty. "Seventeen *Vogue* covers!" Peter said, more than anybody else up to then.

After Peter had gotten the contract from Alex Liberman at *Vogue*, he says, "Dorothy was my first job. She was Irish from Brooklyn, with a perfect, round and cute little freckled face. And she had these Arctic-wolf eyes, the lightest blue. She was only my second real girlfriend. I'd never even had sex until I was out of Yale."

In *Hallelujah the Hills*, the East Village Buster Keaton, Peter, runs stark naked through the Vermont snow (performing what Andy Warhol would call the first "streak"). A still frame from this scene ran alongside reviews for the film everywhere, including in *Time* magazine—making something of a star of Peter, or at least of his backside, for part of 1962. From virgin to sex symbol in the blink of an eye.

Of course, by then, he was creating a kind of survivalist fantasy of his own halfway across the world.

CHAPTER 4

Paradise Lost

Why is it that we think of Kenya the way that we do, as the birthplace of humans, and the last place to see *Lost World*–like wildlife? How is it that cosmic history and a kind of *Jungle Book* fantasia can comingle here in the way that they do in our imaginings?

East Africa, in the Western mind, is home to what Peter liked to call *primitiva*, the unspoiled evidence of existence before the fall—before Eden and Genesis even—and this, for generations prior to the Leakey family making their discoveries of early hominid skulls in the Great Rift Valley in the 1960s.

Beginning in the nineteenth century, English fantasists projected onto the "dark continent" all that they feared and fetishized about humankind and the natural world. Writers like H. Rider Haggard and Edgar Rice Burroughs sent their sage Quartermains and dexterous Tarzans into the savannahs and the jungles to play out picaresque derring-do, firing the minds of their young readers with precisely the kind of romantic fervor then animating the would-be heroes of the Empire, the Victorian explorers looking to make their names, and fortunes, in like manner in just such a magical place. Lone white men, usually of the ruling classes, but often from much more modest beginnings, as in the case of David Livingstone and Henry Morton Stanley, were at that time wandering around sub-Saharan Africa, financed by scientific and geo-graphical societies, or else by newspapers keen on their Romantic stories, trailed by hundreds of porters laden with tons of gear, food, and camping supplies, most of the time lost, dying, looking for the sources of the Nile in vain, killing most of their employees through attrition, and spreading God and Queen wherever they could. In the stories of their exploits, these men would become the greatest celebrities of the day—demigods of a sort, partly mythic for having crossed over into an otherness so alien as to be halfway make-believe.

But their real purpose was to be scouts for the machinery of empire to follow. At the Berlin Conference in 1885, Queen Victoria and William I of the newish empire of Germany (whose son was married to the daughter of William's cousin, Victoria), met to divvy up this land they were hearing so much about, the better to most effectively plunder and rule it. And the straight-line ruler with which they did it, dividing British-held East Africa (Kenya) with its highlands and Mount Kenya to the north, from the German Tanganyika (Tanzania) and Mount Kilimanjaro to the south, isn't as arbitrary as it appears on a map. As Robert Redford, playing Denys Finch Hatton in the film *Out of Africa,* so memorably says, "Victoria and the Kaiser were relatives, for God's sake. Do you know where there's a border? Because she had two mountains and he had none, so she gave him Kilimanjaro."

But once settled on their allotted territories, the competition for resources and control was even greater than before. Feeling pressure by the patent ambition of the German railway then underway, Victoria wanted her own line from the interior, Uganda and Lake Victoria, that could bring resources to Mombasa, where they could be placed on ships and sent off to be converted into treasure. So, in 1896, construction began on the "lunatic express," as its detractors called it, and it went about picking up outlandish stories and infamy every step of the way.

The most famous chapter in the railway's progress, memorialized in the book by Lieutenant Colonel John Henry Patterson, and the movie it inspired, *The Ghost and the Darkness*, is the now nearly mythic tale, beloved by Peter, of the "man-eaters of Tsavo." On December 1, 1897, about 120 miles in from the coast, in the thorny stretch of baobabs and *Commiphora* called Tsavo, thousands of rail workers threw themselves onto the tracks in order to halt all work until something was done about the two maneless devil lions attacking the construction convoy. "Since March they had been feasting with brazen regularity on the occupants of camps near the railhead," Peter wrote. And so Patterson, the chief engineer of the railway, set himself to catching the marauders—camping in trees nearby hoping to catch a glimpse and get a shot at the lions as they approached camp, only to discover they had hunted elsewhere down the line, taking one or more workers into the bush. "The terrible thing was to feel so helpless," Patterson wrote. "I have a very vivid recollection of one particular night when the brutes seized a man from the railway station and brought him close to my camp to devour . . . I could plainly hear them crunching the bone, and the sound of their dreadful purring filled the air." Traps and poisoning schemes failed, so Patterson resumed his vigil, and on the night of December 10, "from his rickety ten-foot-high platform, Patterson fired four shots at a dun form," and got one. Eighteen days later, he shot the other, and life and work were, for a time, restored to the railway.

Two years and more than two hundred miles later, at the last possible point to pause work before track climbed the perilous slope of the Kikuyu escarpment on the Eastern edge of Great Rift Valley, the railway halted at mile 357, near a swamp that the Maasai called "Cool Waters," or Nairobi, and a camp was established. "Tea was taken at Naivasha station, the beginning of the highlands," James Fox wrote in *White Mischief*, "[and] the promised land was slowly revealed, in all its immense variety and beauty. After some miles of thorn and red rock, you emerged into thousands of acres of rolling English parkland, a haze of blue lawn rising and falling to the horizon, untouched by the plough and apparently uninhabited. Some of it resembled the landscape of the west of Scotland, with the same dramatic rock formations, grazing pastures, dew-laden mists. Streams rippled through the valleys, wild fig (sacred to the Kikuyu) and olive grew in the forests; the air was deliciously bracing, producing an ecstasy of wellbeing, and the quality of light was staggering. There were scents too, the indefinable flavour of peppery red dust and acrid wood smoke that never fail to excite the deepest nostalgia."

And yet what was the point of getting people here from the coast or getting them back, if the land wasn't profitable? "It had been built for prestige and super-power competition, and its only effect was to drain the Colonial budget," Fox wrote. "The development of the Colony was a secondary consideration, indeed almost an accident."

A recruitment drive was launched, and in 1903 a very rough bunch of "fugitives, wasters, speculators" arrived, according to Fox's memorable description, looking like "'Forty-niners' from the Yukon. Nevertheless, there were many peers among these first arrivals . . . and victims of the English system of primogeniture . . . there were millionaires too."

Bror Blixen, his wife, Karen, and friend Denys Finch Hatton were part of this first wave of "settlers," if you will. And then there was Hugh Cholmondeley, Third Baron Delamere, who had arrived in Kenya after a two-thousand-mile camel ride through Somalia. In 1903 Cholmondeley was awarded the first million-acre parcel of land (where he remained until his death in 1931 as the unquestioned and official leader of the colonials in Kenya). Still, much of this generation of colonials managed only to eke out tiny returns on their experiments with farming. Blixen, with her coffee farm, like Delamere, ended up burning through her fortune.

Which is how this group could consider their efforts a sacrifice, "to open the country," whereas the next generation was just looking for a place to play.

IN 1909, THEODORE ROOSEVELT LANDED IN MOMBASA AND, outfitted by the Smithsonian, made his way all the way across Kenya to Uganda, killing 512 animals as he went. His hunting guide was a man by the name of Philip Percival—revered by many as the greatest of all the Great White Hunters—who was later immortalized as the character Pops, in Ernest Hemingway's fictionalized memoir of his hunts through Kenya. It was with Percival that Bror Blixen launched his safari company, taking clientele into the deepest reaches of the bush for the greatest shooting experiences. But it was Peter's spiritual ancestor Denys Finch Hatton who, on trips in 1928 and 1930, led the Prince of Wales on safaris that would shift the focus from shooting to photographing the wildlife. During that time, the inventor and founder of Kodak, George Eastman, and Carl Akeley, the taxidermist responsible for Peter's beloved tableaux in the Museum of Natural History, took a collecting trip throughout East Africa (taking, along the way, a good many of the animals now in those dioramas) that pretty much combined all of Peter's favorite pursuits (photography, collection, safari).

Although the first wave, generally speaking, were of the hearty and heroic sort, farming in unthinkably treacherous conditions or hunting wildlife for sport and money, the next batch were slightly different. "Many of the new arrivals," James Fox wrote in *White Mischief*, "looked down on harshly by the pre-war generation, had money to spare and no great interest in making a profit, earning themselves the disparaging description of 'veranda farmers.'" Fox, who researched and reported some of his classic on the colonial era in Kenya while working as a newspaperman in Nairobi, goes on to describe this new bunch as, "A few socialite settlers—whose exclusive interest was the pursuit of pleasure, although there were a few veranda farmers among them." In the 1920s, this bunch settled in the area north of town known as Happy Valley, a place that would become synonymous with outré behavior and utter decadence. "In New York and London, the legend grew up of a set of socialites in the Aberdares whose existence was a permanent feast of dissipation and sensual pleasure. Happy Valley was the by-word for this way of life. Rumors circulated about endless orgies, of wife swapping, drinking and stripping, often embellished in the heat of gossip. The Wanjohi River was said to run with cocktails and there was that joke, quickly worn to death by its own success: Are you married or do you live in Kenya?"

Meanwhile, politically, the Colonial Office was continually making moves—it will surprise no one in retrospect—to displace and disenfranchise the people who had lived on these lands, in an ecological balance with the flora and fauna, for hundreds of years. And in every case, the motive, the justification, was profit: to better and more efficiently extract and consume resources or convert them into treasure. Seen this way, grazing lands used now and again by the migratory Maasai and their cattle were put to better use as farms, where the Maasai then had to pay a hut tax to set up their seasonal encampments, converting them to systems of capital, debt, wages. The race for space, too, in a desperate scramble to pull any profit possible out of the tenable land, squeezed wildlife into tighter and tighter territory. Left unchecked by poaching, which had been outlawed, the animals reproduced to a point that exhausted the resources of their now limited landscape, and they died off in cataclysmic numbers.

These measures were the symptoms and effects of the expansion and consumption of resources that Peter believed would be the end of the human experiment, and in short order—we too, he believed, had overfilled our territory and were consuming it to the point where nothing would be left, and we too would die off. He could be cosmically fatalistic, and was fond of quoting Tertullian, who wrote that "our numbers are burdensome to the world, which can hardly supply us from its natural elements . . . [so] pestilence, and famine and wars, and earthquakes have to be regarded as a remedy for nations, as the means of pruning the luxuriance of the human race." But from the beginning he had a clear idea—granted a wildly chauvinist, neocolonial idea—of what he thought was going on.

"As the century turned," he wrote, "Africa began to emerge from a Dark Age stretching as far back as life on earth, into all the years that lay ahead—years of Renaissance, Enlightenment, Industry, and, if you will, Anxiety." Or violence, cultural annihilation, and capitalistic feudalism, depending on your perspective. All of which came in on the railroad,

> . . . the means through which foreign capital, the paraphernalia of technology, and foreigners themselves would enter. But because an incision is also a wound, the railroad was also the means through which the old life suppurated and poured out of Africa.
>
> This then is the tragic paradox of the white man's encroachment. The deeper he went into Africa, the faster the life flowed out of it, off the plains, and out of the bush into the cities, vanishing in acres of trophies and hides and carcasses. The coming of the white man, who imposed his steel tracks, his brains, and his will, on the great continent was attended by glory and courage, ennobled by sacrifice, enriched by science and law. But it marked the beginning of the end in a land where nature herself had always been sovereign: at once sickness and cure, crime and punishment, beginning and end. Not the least of the signs of decay and dying was the gradual, remorseless end of the wild game.

This is all very obviously to ignore the actual human beings—their brains and their will, their law and their medicines. Clearly, Peter was far from a bleeding heart, and what he knew of the Maasai, the Kikuyu, the Waliangulu, at the time he arrived in Kenya the first time, was next to nothing. But Peter was a quick study—or, rather, he was obsessive, not always toward an end, but when he found a passion, he dove in quickly, wholly, and deeply (deeply within the limited range of his interests, obviously). And from even before he read *Out of Africa* while sailing across the Atlantic, maybe even before he'd seen Akeley's taxidermied tableaux in the museum, before he'd seen Gargantua and Barnum & Bailey's, maybe as far back as when he was a toddler, looking up at the stickers of Disney's Dumbo and the gang that were pasted above his crib, he was obsessed with the idea of Africa. When he finally did arrive, he made it his mission to swallow the entirety of Africana, to absorb it in his cells.

Not like some scholastic memorization and analysis of dates and times, Peter's research project was utterly immersive, and he absorbed particular stories, or characters' biographies, arcana, facts, romantic apocrypha, and personal remembrances almost as if they were his own memories, reciting them for the rest of his life as a pedant might a yard of Byron at a dinner party. He made that lore and legacy a part of him because he so badly wanted to be a part of it.

From his very first visit to Africa, in 1955, touring around with Quentin Keynes, Peter knew how he wanted to frame his African experience, knew even the project into which he might fit it (if not the form that project would take). He was going to join in, to make himself a part of the legacy of white hunters and wildlife enthusiasts, a last link in the chain of immigrants and colonists to go absolutely wild there—to live entirely as they wished to do, in a garden of Eden of their making.

The first step in this process, and typical of how Peter would proceed in every venture, began with the charm offensive, by which he went about insinuating himself with the remaining Great Whites still prowling about the Continent, or indeed, beyond—and first and foremost among the high holies to whom he made pilgrimage, at her home in Denmark, was Karen Blixen.

Securing an audience with Blixen was no sure thing. Legend had it she received no visitors whatever and had rebuked even William Holden. But here again we find Peter, perpetually favored by the gods of good fortune and possessed of a tenacious persistence, skipping on in where no others were permitted. Looking back at it, friends of his and biographers of hers could only scratch their heads at it, why she was happy to welcome him rather than another. "The entree was mostly through my cousin Jerome Hill, who was a friend of hers," Peter said later.

"I had written her before," Peter said, "about my first visits to Kenya and gotten a very poetic and thoughtful letter back, but she didn't say come visit me or anything." Shortly after eking out a diploma from Yale, and en route to Kenya for a walking safari with his college pal William Du Pont III, Peter gave it another go. "I was taking the Bremen to Southampton on my way to Africa and sent her a radio telegram from the boat, asking if I could stop in for a visit. I got no reply." And so he just went—got a plane to Copenhagen and struck up a conversation with the Dane sitting next to him, who recommended the Angleterre Hotel. But when he arrived, the hotel was fully booked. "Disappointed, he turned to leave, but as he neared the door he was stopped by the hotel's manager, who asked him, 'What did you say your name was?'"

The manager had a note for him, "It was from Karen Blixen," Peter said. "She had guessed that I would go to the Angleterre and had arranged a room for me. It was incredibly heavy." Within the note, Blixen explained that she would be happy to welcome him the next day, "at Rungstedlund, her family estate near Copenhagen," Peter wrote. He was shown into a hall to wait. And, he wrote, "I just stood around, shuffling and fidgeting, for four or five long minutes. Finally I caught a sight of this eyeball— a very old eyeball, made up with kohl. It was staring at me through the hinge crack of the ever-so-slightly-open living room door, and that's when I realized what the Honorable Baroness had done: she had set me up to be spied on."

And though she apparently found Peter "exhausting but endearing" in that first meeting, according to her biographer, they seem to have gotten along. At the time, Blixen was terribly infirm, only eighty-five pounds with "advanced syphilis of the spine," which made it difficult for her to stand, and she survived mostly on vegetable juice and oysters. Still, she put out a fabulous lunch of grouse for Peter, and what's more, consented to a little impromptu portrait photography session—the results of which he later showed her, and she hated. Peter stayed in Copenhagen for two weeks, at the home of Blixen's brother, Thomas Dinesen, returning to visit the baroness another couple of times, to tour her office, heavily stacked with Maasai spears. But maybe the greatest gift of the trip was a little insight into his lucky connection. As Peter said, "Clara Svendsen meanwhile had confided to me that normally anyone who had any connection with Africa didn't get in to see the Baroness because it was just such a brutally painful memory for her. But then Clara added, 'I think you remind her of Denys Finch Hatton.' You know, her great love."

This clearly hit a very happy mark for Peter, who was enormously flattered by the association. And, looking back at Blixen's descriptions of Finch Hatton, and even more so, at Robert Redford's portrayal of him, it is eerie how often Finch Hatton does or says something that seems oh so Peter—which, of course, is a bit of a chicken and egg situation: Did Peter model himself on Finch Hatton, consciously or otherwise, adopting his feeling about, say, monogamy, or politics, or did he see in Blixen's rendition of this man something like a kindred spirit?

Arriving again in Nairobi in 1961, Peter found the city to still have about it the feel of a dusty set from a rather exotic Hollywood Western. Less than ten years before, it was not uncommon for lions and leopards to stroll down the streets—nor for the old-timers to take the odd shot at the passing big game from their living-room windows. What hadn't yet changed from the great old days he was looking to re-create was that the New Stanley Hotel's Thorn Tree bar was still the nerve center of the nation's wildlife-adjacent white folk, where the hunters, guides, misfits, and mountebanks gathered to tell exceedingly tall tales, to rustle up the means for some safari or another, and then complain about their clients. Having taken a room at the hotel, which would serve as his headquarters for the mission, Peter would "come down in the morning, get a small table at the Thorn Tree, and buy the papers. Before long several tables would be piled together, and fifteen to twenty people would be drinking coffee, eating, and sharing their most recent escapades." And most of the people he met this way and spent his mornings with would become his greatest friends in Africa, the people with whom he created his life, took adventures, and formulated his thinking about Kenya, about the landscape, wildlife, and his part in it all. Crucially, on this visit, he made fast friendships with Bill and Ruth Woodley, who became something like a second set of parents for Peter. Bill was born and raised in Nairobi and had begun working as a game warden in what was then the Tsavo Royal National Park in 1948. On their honeymoon near Mount Meru (south of Kilimanjaro) the previous year, Bill and Ruth had run into John Wayne and Howard Hawks filming their bizarre wildlife romp *Hatari!*—a sort of signature Hawksian screwball situation, portraying cheetahs, elephants, and rhinos as sort of cartoonish cuddly (if sometimes a little scary) characters, which was, even then, the most profitable portrayal of the local wildlife.

At the time, Ruth was working for Ker & Downey, one of the

oldest and most esteemed safari outfits, selling packages from her kiosk in the New Stanley Hotel. With her expertise in the arena, having gotten to know Peter's interest in something far more advanced than the odd game drive, she put him together with an eccentric hunter out of Peter's wildest dreams. Douglas Collins, whom everyone called Ponsumby though no one knew why, a former district commissioner of Somaliland, proposed that the two men and Collins's tracker partner, Mbuno, take a little trip down around Kilimanjaro, through Tsavo, and then eventually head north into what was then known as the Northern Frontier District—what Collins called "the greater shag," the wildest of wild places one could visit, and, conveniently, on the way to Somalia, where Collins was planning to go.

"Thanks to our hand-written Somali visas, we were to have a small footnote in history." Peter wrote that "these were the last visas of their kind ever issued by the Italian Consulate, Somali [*sic*] having declared her independence the next day." Not that the expected upheaval would deter the two men. "As Uhuru [independence in Swahili] could always be counted on for a certain amount of mayhem, everyone to a man urged us to bypass the new nation—which was yet another incentive for us to reach it."

At the big festive send-off feast at the Banda School, the night before they set out, "Beard spent much of the night talking with Harold Prowse, an American who come to Kenya as an 'in-transit tourist' during the Mau Mau days and never left. A Harvard Business school graduate, Prowse was the first to suggest to the young Beard that 'the end of the game' was approaching." Lest he miss out, Peter bought a Husqvarna 9.3 mm gun from an elephant-control officer in the Long Bar at the New Stanley for fourteen dollars, and then a fourth-hand Land Rover that Ponsumby had found for him, which he then loaded up with food (well, canned spaghetti, fig Newtons, and a few sacks of rice), and the guys set out. They were gone for three months.

Having learned to shoot as a kid, Peter had faith in his marksmanship, but when they were out on their own, hunting for their own survival, he really got to test himself. And at their first stop, near Donya Sabuk, "a giant mound of tropical vegetation not far from Nairobi," he made his first kill, a hippo with Mbuno's .375. "It wasn't a hard shot," Peter said, "but it had to be done right, within about two inches of the ear. Up came the head of the cow with its distended eyes. A rifle crack ruptured the silence; a thud and a monstrous sinking. Not a bird or anything stirred. The kill had been too quick for me to know exactly how I felt; it was strangely exciting. The result was two tons of meat, which was carved up for workers on a nearby estate."

Beyond the initiation to blood sport, this particular hunt underscored for Peter another stark reality—call it a quirk of conservation, hypocrisy, a hangover from colonialism, or plain racism—that was crucial to the way Kenya policed the killing of animals. In Donya Sabuk, Peter and Ponsumby were guests of Major Ray Mayers, a former colonial fighter who had a coffee and sisal plantation on what had been Juja Farm—auto-heir Northrup McMillan's spread where Teddy Roosevelt stayed and shot hippopotami when he came to Kenya, an association not missed by Peter. As he writes, "We discovered that meat had been promised to 300 plantation workers, forbidden by government decree to hunt the animals they had once depended on for food." Because, see, that would be poaching—a grave crime, just like owning unlicensed firearms or even having in one's home anything like a zebra-skin rug or a cow skull over the fireplace, because that was illegal collection of trophies. But a hunter, with a license to kill paid for at a government office, was merely engaging in a totally legal sport, usually a meaningless one in terms of his own survival. So, while gleefully following in the footsteps of Teddy Roosevelt, Peter could frame his first shot in Africa as something like honorable white-savior redress to right a wrong. "If their life with the game was over, ours was not, and it was now up to the licensed gun-holders like us to provide for them."

We were eating lunch in the shade of the porch when Buno came up and announced that the kiboko was "on the water" [having finally expended all of its gases] and that we could "come now and let the meat be cut."

There must have been a hundred pair of hands helping us there at the river's edge. Many dogs, too. We hauled the hippo against the current into the shallow water and hacked the two tons of meat into portable chunks. We made out, in the middle of all the slimy waste, the rubbery form of a fetus, unfinished, never to be born. The dogs worried at it as if it were a great delicacy, but the natives disdained it as spongy and tasteless and left it as food for a nearby column of army ants.

While we were butchering the meat, a garden boy at Donya Sabuk had speared a python between a row of cabbages and, when we returned to pack up, presented the skin to us as a going-away present. Stretching to almost twenty feet, it was wide and beautifully patterned.

Of this scene, Peter made one of the most compelling images of his young life. Around the hippo, arranged in beautiful accidental symmetry, are Ponsumby and three children, sons of the factory workers, perhaps. And the emotion on their faces is mesmerizing, transporting, testaments to the wild, cascading feelings brought on by such an enormous event. Ponsumby, slightly out of focus, looks to be himself in a bit of a blur, in between activities, perhaps about to get up from what he was doing and head off elsewhere. The boys meanwhile, of varying ages, from about twelve to five, all seem to know that Peter is up to something with his camera, all seem on the point of rancor, even, though this could be a pantomime of anger, a kind of bluff to look like tough little guys for posterity while they are mid-hippo-hack on a sisal plantation outside of Nairobi. There is a kind of surging energy about the children, whether they are suspicious or just pretending, angry or performing anger, they are fully committed to the feeling, in a kind of young adolescent intoxication that comes from proximity to such a sight, to the rivers of blood and ambient ecstasy of the workers who were then probably already fantasizing about the meals to come from this haul, that high you get by osmosis, feeling all the drama and momentousness taking place around you.

It is a wonderful picture and clearly demonstrates that, whenever it was that he found his eye, his talent, whether it was in the hours he had spent cooking up shots with Anson and his sailboat in Islip, or during an assignment for his classwork at school, or by chance, just realizing something innate, Peter had something. And he was putting it to use in a singular and profound way; very few people on the planet who were at that point in time possessed of the same training, equipment, infernal passion, and dedication were at that moment knee-deep in muck and blood taking pictures of such intimacy, delicacy, and brutality (it is always the beauty and the gore together).

From there, the guys traveled south to Amboseli, and Peter could again feel his connection to the generations past. "We laid out our bedrolls in the tall grass. A sky of stars stretched over Africa from one end of time to another," he wrote. "They were the same stars that had watched over the travellers, traders, and engineers who 60 years before had slept fitfully among the wild game as the Mombasa railroad was being pushed through, who had shot the rhinos that charged the trains, and who had earned their living selling in Nairobi for a pound a piece the lion skins they had risked their lives collecting."

Clearly, he was in full flood, feeling the Hemingway and Blixen pumping through him. "The mornings at Amboseli were among the most beautiful I had ever known," he wrote, "cold, opaque mornings when Buno or Morengaru would murmur some friendly Swahili and bring in the delicious kahawa [coffee]. This was the country of the Masai—herdsmen, aristocrats, warriors, carriers of tall spears, drinkers of blood and milk, lion-killers." And here he turns to his hero, Blixen, whose description of the Maasai supported what he was then seeing all around him: "fighters who had been stopped from fighting, a dying lion with his claws clipped, a castrated nation . . . They will bear us all a grudge, which will be wiped out only when the tribe is wiped out itself."

Even as he began to create his own voice, beyond what he was borrowing from Blixen, Peter would look back on this time, traveling around like a wild, invincible kid (he was only twenty-three)—without a fear, less than two years from Kenya declaring its own Uhuru—with the same sort of wizened, elegiac tone, as his own halcyon time. In a way, this perspective was implicit in his project, which tracked the lineage of the white immigrants and adventurers in Kenya in parallel with the wildlife there . . . and ended with him. So, as he and Ponsumby traipsed around, nearly starving to death, getting rammed by rhinos and nearly trampled by stampeding elephants, shooting the odd leopard, and photographing little dik-diks. Peter sought out the keepers of the flame, interviewing them, ingratiating himself, and recording all of it for the project. The highlight of the trip may have been when he met the famous great white hunter J. A. Hunter, who "larded with legends, showed himself to be open and courteous—and a fine host. It struck me that what he was a host to was nothing less than the past, his own and part of Africa's." And, "J.A. gloried in rekindling the old days for us."

When they had made it deep into the sand of Somali, Peter made another picture significant for its glimpse of what could have been, what might have been. It is a picture of a beautiful Somali woman in quarter profile, her head and shoulders draped in a fabric that might be cobalt blue, but for the black-and-white film reads somewhere between charcoal and ash. Her look at Peter or, more accurately, into the open aperture of Peter's camera and right at the viewer of the image all these years later, is direct. Not open, not unguarded, by any means, and not quite stern. It is a look that meets you where you are, giving nothing, not asking to gain anything. A kind of sudden icon, very reminiscent in fact of *Afghan Girl*, an image that the great photojournalist Steve McCurry would take more than twenty years later in a mountain village in Afghanistan, an image that when it ran on the cover of *National Geographic* made a star of McCurry and became a kind of avatar for the conflict in Afghanistan at the time (and which would later be called the most famous photograph of all time). The similarity of what Peter and McCurry were responding to in making their pictures makes me think of the photographer Peter didn't but perhaps could have become, if his adventure to Kenya had been but one leg on a journey to other elsewheres, putting the craft and the lens in front of him, perhaps following wars as McCurry did, or in search of something mythopoeic like Sebastião Salgado, say, photographing man and the land in extremis. This picture is a little crack, one of many that marble Peter's life and work, giving us an idea of the decisions he made along the way, artistically, perhaps, but more broadly, aesthetically. It gives us a glimpse into what he might've done but chose not to pursue. Even if the results of this picture were positive, they clearly did not encourage him to deviate from the plan, his project. Didn't send him in search of other styles, other angles. Didn't cause him to go after political ideas and portraits of personalities the way, say, Priya Ramrakha was then doing in Ethiopia, did not compel him to go to North Africa or document combat the way, say, Don McCullen would do, or make him want to become a traditional *National Geographic*–style wildlife photographer. When it came to his work, his life—as if one could differentiate between them—

Peter didn't have doubts, didn't question the burning drive to throw himself bodily and spiritually into his Africa project, and so he did precisely that, precisely the way he wished to.

At that moment, Ponsumby received a letter from the man who had been his clerk during his tenure as district commissioner in Mogadishu. The former clerk was now prime minister of the young country, and he was writing to invite Ponsumby to stay at the Palace, and "although he had officially closed the new nation to hunting for a few months, welcome 'Abdi Melik' ('the bastard') [Ponsumby] and his friends to take as much ivory and as many trophy skins as they wanted." Peter's elation at the prospect was quickly dimmed by the idea of committing another several months to this excursion, when there was so much else to do, to learn. And so Ponsumby carried on, to his own safari in Somalia, and Peter, the Land Rover, and Mbuno made their way back to Nairobi—and in a way, Mbuno stayed with Peter from that point on, working with Peter at Hog Ranch until his death in 1992. But Ponsumby left Peter with one last gift, a letter of introduction to a hunter friend of his, Bryan Coleman ("Here's where you'll find him when he's not slogging down *wompos* at the Thorn Tree"), who pulled him into his next adventure.

"With an interloper's enthusiasm and a sense of curiosity," Peter wrote, "I joined Doug's friend Bryan Coleman on his control scheme on the 172,000-acre Boran cattle estate belonging to Gilbert Colville in Laikipia." And yes, for those wondering, "game control" is as euphemistic a term as it appears to be. In Kenya, after the myriad struggles faced by the first generations of colonials in farming the land, some of the heartiest of major landowners were still heavily invested in livestock—cattle, in Colville's case. But in the year of our lord 1961, one's 172,000 acres of livestock land was never very far away from a whole lot of hunters—big cats, mostly—never mind the rinderpest and tick-borne diseases, Cape buffalos knocking down the paddock fencing in their nightly grazing, elephants steamrolling miles of fencing seemingly out of spite, and zebras grazing to exhaustion the same fields meant to feed the cows.

"The problem has always been that there is no easy way to raise stock on the same land as wild game," Peter concluded. "When space becomes a problem, as eventually it does even on estates as large as [Colville's] Lariak, the value of each acre increases, and the only course of action left to profit-minded farmers is to exterminate the wildlife they have been protecting."

The plan, then, if it can be called that, was to eliminate the cow's competition, more or less at random. Not that there weren't qualified professionals among their number—seventeen in all. The Turkana skinners and trackers would prove invaluable, for instance. But the haphazardness of heading out, in a Land Rover or on horseback, into the thorny warrens of bush around Lariak, hoping to happen on a large enough grouping of zebra, oryx, and the like to tilt the scales in the cow's favor, did lead to some rather madcap adventures. For one, you could never really get very close to any number of the animals without spooking them, and by the time you'd taken the first shot the whole scrum had scattered to the wind. Atop his one-eyed horse, in a sort of makeshift saddle, Peter was more regularly run straight into trees and thorns than in the direction of their prey. And when he did manage to crack off a shot from his Husqvarna 9.3 mm, his horse would buck and rear, "making a bloody pulp of my nose and lip."

But persistence pays, and setting out every morning before dawn, following their trackers and their trained pack of dogs who, "living on an all-zebra diet," expelled rather noxious gases behind them, they were able to stack up significant numbers of kills—maybe eighteen creatures on a good day. Throughout his time on Lariak, hunting lions, skinning zebras, and even with the bloodied lip and a broken ankle he sustained while running after an impala he'd shot, Peter was in a kind of bliss, having his full

Hemingway experience, spending every day in the bush, learning the landscape and the wildlife, and putting his marksmanship to the greatest of tests—for what he understood to be a good cause. And he was really absorbing the various contradictions of keeping a farm and being conservation minded, attuned to the delicate balances they were toying with. Of the owner of Lariak, his employer, Peter writes,

> It was only as a last resort that Colville, himself a great sportsman and trophy hunter, turned to game control. At first he tried to eliminate only the lions, after they had made kills that not even an estate on the scale of Lariak could sustain. But then the hyenas came in, and they too had to be eliminated. With the destruction of the hyenas, the plains game began to proliferate. And so on until even the most delicate zebra foal might have to be passed sentence on. . . . On another estate, the owners had to shoot their giraffes not only because they spread rinderpest, but also because their height and keenness made it difficult for control hunters to work. But there was a danger in eliminating them, which the owners of the estate had not reckoned on: the acacia thorn trees, without the giraffes to nibble from them, became so thick that the movement and grazing of cattle was seriously impeded.

It was during this time too that Peter seems to have made, or accepted, the long-held link between man and elephant, "the beast that passeth all others in wit and mind and, by its intelligence, it makes as near an approach to man as matter can approach spirit." And, what was crucial to Peter's ongoing understanding of conservation, preservation, and man's existence on the globe, he saw that in order to "protect" elephants, they needed to be controlled, restrained, and kept away from the great farms, which they would bulldoze. He understood that, "if left on his own in a given area, the elephant would eventually destroy not only its own food supply, but also that of the other animals," he wrote. So, what to do?

With these important learning experiences under his belt, Peter looked forward to what he had planned to be the capstone of his great Africa project, the final chapter to what he was now thinking of as the book *The End of the Game*, a walking safari with his college friend (and an heir to the Du Pont chemical fortune) William Du Pont III, in which he would follow in the footsteps of Teddy Roosevelt, Bror Blixen, and Denys Finch Hatton. The plotting and planning of the adventure had been done by Peter's new friend, the Harvard Business grad–turned–elephant enthusiast Harold Prowse, who'd first given Peter the phrase "the end of the game." Peter wrote, "Over the years, Harold had assembled one of the surest hunting teams in the business. His four trackers and gunbearers, Ndende, Heekuta, Gala-Gala, and Kiribai, were members of the Waliangulu (a Giriama word meaning "meateaters") tribe celebrated for its skill in firing carefully made poison arrows into elephants' spleens."

The two heirs to American fortunes greeted their comrades "at the foot of the Nguruman Escarpment, in Masai country," amid the Athi Plains. When Carl Jung came to this very spot, in 1925, inspired as he was by the immensity of the silence, he had a rather famous and frequently referenced revelation about man's place in the world. "This was the stillness of the eternal beginning," Jung remembered thinking upon arriving, "the world as it had always been, in the state of non-being, for until then no one had been present to know that it was this world."

Having thought about what it meant, then, for him to be in this place, contemplating a world before contemplation, before man, Jung contemplated still further. "Now I knew," he said, "that man is indispensable for the completion of creation; that, in fact, he himself is the second creator of the world, who alone has given to the world its objective existence without which, un-heard, unseen, silently eating, giving birth, dying, heads nodding through hundreds of millions of years, it would have gone on in the profoundest night of non-being down to its unknown end." Which sounds as if Jung doesn't in fact believe a tree falling in the woods quite makes a sound. Or at least it wouldn't matter. Here we have Jung quite literally *othering* nature. Here in this birth-place of man, Jung had a vision that seems to set man outside of and apart from nature, making the human perspective of nature a phenomenon that brings nature into being, or at least into mean-ing. Apart from being the original sin in Peter's way of thinking—the misunderstanding of ourselves that gives us the belief that we are not part of nature and so are above its rules—Jung's insight would also seem to suggest that we do not exist until we look into a mirror.

"Human consciousness created objective existence and mean-ing," Jung says, "and man found his indispensable place in the great process of being."

Anyway, it is that kind of a landscape, and you understand why Peter and his friend were thrilled to be there, with such an all-star crew, to boot. Pulling out all the stops, as was his way, Peter even arranged to have a cameo appearance by the greatest living legend of the game, the hunter who had led Roosevelt on his expedition, and been immortalized by Hemingway, Philip Percival. "Percival himself flew in and joined us," Peter wrote, in an area that he "preferred to all others . . . for what would turn out to be his last safari."

It was the completion of a circle, tying his project ever so neatly together, and Peter could not have been happier, sitting at the feet of his great guru: "At five each morning he would sit down by our campfire, take some tea from Kiete, his Makamba safari helper for 50 years who had taught Hemingway to box on that very camp-site, and reminisce with the modesty appropriate to someone who had been elected to 34 consecutive terms as President of the Professional Hunter's Association."

For hours, days, they talked—or, well, Percival, "who made history sound as we had never heard it," talked, and Peter listened, rapt—about Roosevelt, about Hemingway, about Percival's military service, and his encounters (several and sometimes harrowing) with lions. He told the young men about his home, a little hunting lodge that had been built to accommodate Roosevelt on his visit in 1909, and which, at that moment in 1961, was "overflowing with priceless memorabilia," Peter wrote, eyes popping, "including . . . one of the original Eastman Kodak cameras from the George Eastman–Carl Akeley safaris for the American Museum of Natural History in New York; innumerable photos taken by Akeley and Martin Johnson; the skin of a Kapiti man-eater; Sir Alfred's 1911 drawings and diary account of George Grey's fatal mauling on Wami Hill, a few hundred yards from where Roosevelt shot his first lion; stacks of letters and books from Hemingway, who was a frequent house-guest; . . . a photograph of Percival on safari with King George V . . . all potent reminders of a half-century in Africa that began for Percival in September 1905 when he came out to Nairobi from England to join his brother."

Percival told Peter his life story, and summed up the wisdom he'd gained in the process, giving Peter "the feeling that we were on better terms with the old tyrant, Africa," and everything he needed to make his book. And whether the ideas were new to him or were first introduced to him during this visit, Percival would lay out for Peter his great concerns, the obsessions and laments that would define Peter's life and work for decades to come. "Of all the evolving losses," Peter wrote, "Percival most lamented the situation of the small Waliangulu tribe which he and Bror Blixen had grown to know—perhaps more intimately than they would their English friends. 'No people could ever have been more compromised in so short a time,'" Peter wrote, quoting Percival. "'A group that coexisted with elephants for hundreds of years, and that in its own way played an important role in the "dynamic mosaic" of the Tsavo lowlands. They were helping to keep the age-old balances—practicing a form of game control, if you will. . . . You cannot just interrupt a whole system of life and expect things to work out smoothly,' he said." Which is everything Peter said, in his book, in interviews, in his work, from that point on.

When *The End of the Game* came out, Peter's former dean at Yale, John James Ellis Palmer, told him, "I've been thinking about this book of yours and I think you could do the 'end of the game' for the rest of your life." And in so many ways he did, repeating the stories again and again, of the Mombasa Railway, of J. H. Patterson, of Percival and Blixen—but also of his own adventures on his first visits to the continent. Peter's revelations from this period, his experiences, and the lessons he carried from this time only deepened over the years, like grooves in a record he played over and over again. Once he'd woven together this one tapestry, he didn't up and move on, looking for another story to tell, another life to live, different legacies to try on. He had found his place, his way, his home, and a style to match.

The pictures Peter took during this time, of zebra skinners in Laika during his work on game control, of lions, cheetahs, and giraffes on the Athi Plains, would remain among the principal images in his ongoing collage work for the rest of his life. He just kept printing out new copies to paste into his work. Not to mention that he literally continued to work on and re-create the book *The End of the Game* itself over the years, putting out new editions in 1977, 1988, and then, on the occasion of its fiftieth anniversary, in 2015. It was in many ways his own mythopoeic Genesis story, and perhaps he felt that he never topped the experiences, never felt again as naïf an adolescent among the ghosts of Old Africa as he was then.

CHAPTER 5

Life-Thickening Thing

L eaving his last great safari with Philip Percival had been such a letdown—the feeling of "funga safari," packing up and heading home, so crushing—that when Peter was finally back "home" at the New Stanley Hotel in Nairobi, he was determined to never let it happen again. "So what to do?" he said. "To solve this problem pickle, to fix it so that I was never *off* safari, never indoor or far from a glowing campfire, I put up some tents in a patch of bush twelve miles outside of Nairobi."

Thanks in part to the American ambassador at the time, Peter heard that Mervyn Cowie, the founding director of Kenya's National Parks, was looking to sell a lot of land. And as soon as he saw this "patch of bush"—some forty acres of virgin forest land—at the end of a dirt track on the southwestern edge of Nairobi County, about two miles from Karen Blixen's house, Peter knew right away he'd found his permanent vacation spot, his escape from "those repulsive realities" of the real world, "like looming lists of things-to-do, licenses, permits, dentists, lawyers, immigration, insurance, supplies, repairs." Standing on the roof of his Land Rover at the edge of the property, he could just see the four ridges of the Ngong Hills, knuckles in the fist of a fallen giant who once haunted the region, as the legend had it. And here, outside of the city center as he was, the land still teemed with wildlife—"giraffe, warthogs, dik-dik, bushbuck, waterbucks, leopards, guinea fowls, tree squirrels, mongoose, and a hundred varieties of exotic birds." He would come to find that the land had quite a history of its own, having "been the site of the last great battles between the Kikuyu and the Masai; in fact a Masai *laibon* (holy man) is buried on the property in a stone grave next to an age-old cattle path."

But buying property in Kenya was a little tricky just then, with the country in the throes of independence. To begin with, the piece of land was too big to be considered residential and so was not available for a foreigner to purchase. Peter and his lawyers applied for a special presidential dispensation, making the claim that the land would be used as an athenaeum, a kind of hub for artists of all stripes. "Beard envisioned a kind of Kenyan Yaddo," Jon Bowermaster wrote, "an artist's colony set on the outskirts of Nairobi." In 1963 he was granted permission to proceed by Jomo Kenyatta, the first president of Kenya.

With some of the $25,000 his parents had seeded each of the boys on finishing their schooling, and a little of the money he'd been paid by Coca-Cola for helping to wrangle animals in a commercial directed by Nic Roeg, Peter purchased his Hog Ranch (for $20,000)—so named for the various Pumbaas roaming the property—and began making a little garden of his own in Eden. "After clearing a view of the Ngong Hills, Beard put up a string of safari tents along the ridge," from which to watch what he called, "the greatest show on Earth."

Conscious of keeping the lineage firmly linked between himself and Baroness Blixen, Peter next set out in search of one of the heroes of *Out of Africa*, the badly wounded boy taken in by Blixen who grew up to become her cook, Kamante. With a letter of introduction from the baroness, given to him on his last visit with her a few months before she died, Peter made his way out to a village on the Kikuyu reserve. "There we found Kamante, or Kamande (depending on how one pronounces the words of a language that was never written down). I presented him with the letter from Baroness Blixen and received a rumpled chicken in return."

That day, Kamante joined Peter for a trip to Mbogani House on the old Karen Coffee Farm, where he had lived and worked with Blixen more than twenty years prior (he hadn't been back since). As he was wont to do, Peter invited Kamante to join him on a project—one that would last for more than a decade—the creation of a kind of parallax-view version of *Out of Africa*, with the stories recounted from Kamante's point of view, nourished with the context of his insight, and accented by folklore fables that had informed his way of thinking about life on the farm. "Over a period of twelve years, sometimes casually, sometimes scrupu-lously, and sometimes with grand propriety, as if divesting himself of his possessions, Kamante put down the extra dimensions of truth which are at the heart of *Out of Africa*," Peter wrote. It was a passion project for Peter, both in memoriam to his hero Blixen and as a celebration of his new friend. Unfortunately, it wasn't until the early seventies, when his then bosom buddy Jaqueline Onassis agreed to write an afterword, that he could convince a publisher, Knopf, to take on the book.

His other invitation to Kamante that day was much simpler—to come live with him as he had with Blixen, to keep the old glory fires burning still. Kamante accepted. "Kamante and his wife Wambui lived with me at Hog Ranch from the very beginning and brought to it a real feeling of the Old Africa," Peter wrote in *Zara's Tales*, and he goes on to articulate a kind of manifesto of nostalgia and aesthetic value that would illuminate his life in Kenya for decades to come, his life in search of and homage to Old Africa, to:

. . . the early days, when things were simple. Not easy, but simple. And this is all I ever longed for: the atmosphere and natural pace of the old days, which show up so clearly in those scratched and faded early films; haunting exposures of savage enormity, Stone Age space, sepia-colored "authentica"—worked on by specks of dust and the scratches of time. The feeling still shows up sometimes, in the darkness of dawn, in the great quietness and loneliness of the tropical nights when hyenas come and the wild dogs howl. The feeling of standing out there, alone under the nocturnal enormity—the shooting stars, like tears on cheeks, run down from the sky and disappear. This endless sky, where the Southern Cross hangs above the iron gray wasteland of the plains, the plains of midday mirages at Ongata Rongai. Darkest Africa, which means only that its timeworn roots were not exposed to glaring, blazing, blinding lights, pitiless as the sun, aimed at darker, calmer eyes. Such thoughts come to you in the deep, intoxicating, isolating nights of Equatorial East Africa.

Thus ensconced, and ennobled by his partnership with Kamante, Peter felt it was time again for some adventure, more collecting of experiences to be spun out over future campfires on the ranch. He had heard about another wildlife crisis, a need to redistribute exceedingly rare white rhinos in the wild, a project that seemed appropriately outsize and epic for his appetite. "Farther down in Zululand," he wrote, in South Africa, "Umfolozi's park warden was constantly talking about having far too many of an animal that was far too rare—too much of a good thing. On one moonlit night on an open plain, he [the park warden] saw sixty-four white rhinos standing together in the silvery glow—a horny mob scene under the full moon."

Having visited rhino reserves on his trip with Quentin Keynes in 1955, Peter was aware of the animal's scarcity. (And as of this writing, it appears that there are, in total, worldwide, only two remaining Northern White Rhinos, a mother and a daughter at a preserve in Kenya.) "These nearly extinct relics of the early world," Peter wrote, "were so protected and were multiplying so fast it was getting scary. They were overgrazing the limited land, overeating it, slowly but surely exceeding the carrying capacity of their shrinking territory. If something wasn't done soon, there wouldn't be enough for any of them." A constant refrain.

The warden's plan was to move a number of his white rhinos from South Africa to Kenya, where they might thrive in all the wide-open spaces. And after years and years of negotiations between the two countries, it was eventually decided that, at some vague, undetermined point in the future, Kenya would welcome some of South Africa's white rhinos, endangered but now too numerous for their setting, in exchange for some of its own black rhinos. For this latter trick, Kenya's black rhinos would have to be rounded up, roped, allowed to relax after the experience, and ultimately shipped south as part of the exchange. The rounding-up stage could begin at once, and the rhinos could wait in Tsavo National Park before being sent south. For the job, the game department hired, "by pure luck," Peter wrote, "the most eccentric animal trapper in the history of this eccentric calling—my next-door neighbor, Ken Randall, a gnarled and weather-beaten veteran of Old Kenya." Peter would later call Randall, who would go months without bathing but knew his craft better than anyone, "the craziest man I ever met," and the months they spent roping rhinos together in Tsavo, "a gift to me and my camera."

The job, as Peter described it later, was "conservation at its loony best," by which he meant idiotic, and he could only laugh at the absurdity. Their mandate from the game department was to go in search of young black rhinos to be rounded up for safekeeping before they could eventually be sent south in the trade. The work was wildly difficult, first, because rhinos are almost impossible to spot within the "hunting blocks" areas of Tsavo, which were their remit, and because Randall refused to use any light aircraft to spot them. And second, because they are rhinos, and when you are not shooting them or incapacitating them with tranquilizers so as not to completely traumatize them, you are in essence trying to run down a wild tank with a lasso. And, still, the guys made progress. When eventually the game department extended the mandate to include bigger, adult rhinos to be let loose in Tsavo National Park, they had fun running down the big Moby Dicks of the hunting blocks—all the while reveling in what Peter called, sardonically, "the logic of bureaucracies and politicians heroically engaged in 'saving the game' from their fund-raising offices." The irony as they saw it was that these rhinos, though they had been disinfected and de-wormed, were actually being "rescued from a lush, green hunting area," only to be set free in "an overeaten, windswept wasteland, and man-made Elephants' Graveyard." Mercifully, they noticed, nothing was stopping the "rescued" rhinos from heading home the eighty miles to return to their lush hunting grounds. "The waste of time was immense," Peter said, "but the life was rich." He called it his first and best job in Kenya.

It was also during this time that he would meet and begin his close association with Galo-Galo Guyu, "the once great Waliangulu poacher and Mau-Mau tracker," as Peter described him, shortly thereafter correcting himself to say, "Waliangulu is the Giriama word for 'meat-eaters.' They were traditional hunters, renamed 'poachers' by us." Over the generations, the Waliangulu had famously used the tacky sap of a compound they would brew from the roots of *Acokanthera* plants to coat their arrowheads when hunting elephants. The tips themselves, of course, were not forged metal, as the Waliangulu had no need for metallurgy, counting on the sheer ballistics created by their astonishingly powerful longbows to penetrate even the often bulletproof hide of an elephant. The trick they had found with their serum was that, if it could make its way into the elephant's bloodstream by way of the spleen or the area around the belly, it would take almost immediate effect and drop the seven-ton beast in moments, not far from where it had been struck. All of which is to say that later accusations of inhumane practices, poisoned arrows causing their victims a long and slow suffering unto death, were a perhaps unintentionally misleading (or else a kind of biased propaganda) part of the campaign to have traditional hunting outlawed in Kenya. Which it was—preventing Waliangulu and Giriami, for example, from practicing their livelihoods while allowing trophy hunters from Texas who'd paid for a license and a shotgun from Sears & Roebuck all the opportunity they needed for a souvenir to go on their mantel. Indeed, if a traditional hunter had so much as an old hide, for decoration even, he could be hauled in on poaching charges, while a busload of tourists with the right permit can pull up on a pride of lions and shoot them for sport. This was a grave injustice in Peter's eyes, not only for the racist hypocrisy that it was (and not only because of the cartoonish corruption of officials who would themselves profit from the collection and export of ivory), but because traditional hunters had lived among and alongside these herds maintaining a delicate balance, as Peter saw it, a balance that was irrevocably thrown out of whack when traditional hunting was smeared as poaching and outlawed.

Because he was so good, at hunting and at everything else ("games and puzzles, traps, snares, bows, bags, ropes, fires in the rain—he knew and could make them all," Peter liked to brag), Galo-Galo became a kind of bogeyman for the conservationists. In the film *Blood Ivory*, about the life and work of David Sheldrick (which, it is crucial to note, was completed and assembled after Sheldrick's death without his input and point of view on these things), the Waliangulu in general are made out to be some sort of wildlife mafia, murderous outlaws running the underworld of the ivory trade, and Galo-Galo, the greatest hunter of his generation, the Al Capone of Tsavo.

Galo-Galo was born near the town of Voi, a short way from where Denys Finch Hatton died in a plane crash, an area that had historically been home to the Giriami and Galo-Galo's Walian-gulu. When Randall put the rhino roping on pause to take some time off and restock their supplies, Peter and Galo-Galo would head down into that region, walking for miles among the roaming elephants. At the time, Peter's friend Glen Cottar, a Kenyan-born guide whose father had come east from Oklahoma, was setting up fly-in camps for a new generation of more rugged, mobile safaris. In order that the guests on these trips had safe hides from which to observe passing elephants and lions in the area when they arrived, Peter was helping to set up some of these bolt-holes, digging and disguising little nooks in the bush. Along the way, taking advantage of these incredible lookouts and the serene intimacy he found there among the passing wildlife, Peter took some of the most remarkable images of his career during these months—lush landscapes of long-tusked elephants among the palm trees and baobabs in the sandy dry streambeds of Tsavo. In such close-ups, against the faded blue of the skies and seafoam greens of the trees, the elephants look a lot like figures out of Akeley's great tableaux back at the Museum of Natural History. There is a vividness to the motion, a grandeur to the scale, and yet a great poise, almost a distance, a restraint in the composition that set these pieces apart from the rest of Peter's work. There is something incredibly paint-erly, calm, and optimistic about these—like comfy cozy versions of Peter's beloved Rousseaus.

When these groundbreaking images of elephants did finally reach the Western world, it was in a cover story for the special edition double issue of *Life* magazine, accompanied by an ode to the elephant by the legendary writer Romain Gary. Gary, who had written the Goncourt Prize–winning novel *The Roots of Heaven* about a man's impassioned crusade to protect elephants, was in real life too a passionate friend of elephants. The association with such an esteemed artist-activist, along with the sensational images, firmly established Peter's reputation as the American elephant man—and a master of his own artful version of wildlife reportage.

One night, on one of their sojourns through Tsavo, after a long day unearthing a half-buried elephant skull and tusks (and coincidentally discovering "ancient ochre-clay cave drawings on the eastern face of the Yatta Plateau"), Peter and Galo-Galo had a surprise visitor, a traveler friend of theirs who'd lost his way and couldn't believe his luck at coming across the two men. To celebrate, Galo-Galo pulled out a bottle of sake the guys had been saving, but had forgotten entirely to drink at New Year's Eve. Over a fireside feast of Ritz crackers, bread-and-butter pickles, and Hellman's mayonnaise, they got to talking shop—wildlife tales and the lore of Africa, of course. Chatter that night was focused primarily around one of Peter's favorite subjects, J. H. Patterson's experiences with the man-eaters of Tsavo—all of which took place just a few miles from where they were sitting right then. After every glass, Peter's glee at the devilish details of the lions' attacks on the railway workers and even passengers in their Pullman cars, grew more and more toothsome, ghoulish, until, inevitably, he had to pee.

As one does at a campfire, he stood up, making excuses, and stumbled to the fringe of the firelight, "staring blankly into space," aiming to relieve himself in the dust, when he saw it. "It came in slow motion," he remembers in *Zara's Tales*, "like a bullet train erupting out of a tunnel, soundless, without any sense of reality at all. The fireball express at midnight. Like an ancient force, a primitive power, bigger and more powerful than you or I can ever imagine—an unnamable and unbelievable flow of silent *SPEED*—a mental nightmare before I knew about it, like when you get burned and snap back before the pain registers—and so much more." Peter was paralyzed as he watched this lion come screaming toward him from dark night. Until, of course, Galo-Galo came to his rescue, came up screaming at the lion to the point that the giant cat stopped in its tracks—a "man-eater . . . with brakes," as Peter wrote—and, "as quickly as it came, the glorious gray devil was gone."

LIKE ALL YOUNG MEN WHO HAVE COME FACE-TO-FACE WITH death and survived, Peter came away from the lion experience somehow emboldened. If not exactly convinced of his luck or something like invincibility, he was certainly amused at the effect of the night's retelling over Hog Ranch campfires. And, like all inveterate hams, lovers of garish yarns, and narcissistic men really beginning to feel their oats, Peter now needed to top himself. So, how does one top a meeting with a ghost, a devil, the darkness? One can only from then on go straight to hell.

If Peter had imagined his adventuring in Africa as some sort of hero's journey, the deepest, furthest, most desolate place he could go—and, thus, to his way of thinking, the place where he explicitly *had* to go—was what was then called Lake Rudolf. In the bleak and cosmically barren northwest of Kenya, a landscape almost Martian in its profound heat, desolation, geological strangeness, and windswept hostility to most life, this massive saltwater lake was once named for Austrian Crown Prince Rudolf by a bumbling explorer who led an expedition there in 1888 and managed to capsize all his boats. Now named for the local peoples, the Turkana, it was a kind of uncharted netherworld for scientists and adventurers, and so an ideal expedition site for Peter.

This was in the mid-1960s, but even as recently as the turn of the millennium, the region was still thought of as a kind of wild terra incognita. In *The Constant Gardener*, John le Carré's great 2001 novel set in Kenya, his optimistic, crusading heroine is murdered on the shores of Turkana, and the horror the region evokes in every character is palpable throughout the book. It is a barbarous wasteland, as far from civilization, safety, or comfort as can be imagined. Incidentally, Richard Leakey's first great discovery (a complete *Homo erectus* skeleton, "Turkana Boy," found in the mid-1980s), setting him at competitive odds with his more famous archaeologist parents but beginning in earnest the narrative of Kenya as the cradle for mankind, took place on these rocky shores of Lake Turkana.

Beyond its end-of-the-earth reputation, what made this a desirable destination for Peter in the mid-1960s was that Lake Turkana boasted the largest collection of Nile crocodiles in the world, and the Kenyan Game Department had just commissioned the biologist Alastair Graham to conduct an in-depth study of the population. So it was in the service of science that Peter made his many visits there. The built-in irony of conducting wildlife research on Nile crocs is that, while they are among the most ancient species inhabiting the earth today (and thus well worth considering for their profound experience of life), they are probably the world's least-loved creature, with terrifying armored lizard bodies, stretching up to some eighteen feet long and nearly five feet wide, along with those reptilian eyes and great big chomping jaws. Peter, of course, throwing himself body and soul into everything he did, loved the adventure of Turkana, the biting sandblasting winds and unbearable heat, the constant sinking of their vessels in the violent soupy waves of the lake, even, and maybe especially, his actual wrestling with the killer crocs. And their mandate—to study, document, and perhaps number the crocs in the region—also meant not a little hunting, shooting, and slicing up these militarized monsters out of the Pleistocene.

In the time it took them to capture, kill, document, and study in detail the nearly three hundred crocodiles deemed a necessary minimum count from which to draw conclusions about the whole population, their expedition ran into every conceivable detour. To begin with, the living conditions were extraordinarily difficult. "Hot dry winds blow day and night," Peter said, "first from one direction and then, after lunch, from the other. Temperatures reach 120F." Though they treated it with tablets they'd brought in for the purpose, the water they drank turned their teeth brown: "We ate gale-blown volcanic sand in every mouthful of food: catfish, perch, turtle, zebra, whatever." Bandits passed by on more than one occasion, and apparently found nothing of interest in their camps, which were merely tarps tied over aluminum poles dug deep into the earth, with the sides left open so as not to contend with the ferocious winds that never stopped blowing through.

Graham was bitten (glancingly, mercifully) by a spitting cobra. One of their number was bitten by a croc and had to be flown out to Nairobi to be treated for his wounds. Another team member nearly drowned when he caught a six-foot, two-hundred-pound Nile perch that dragged him down under. And their boat, which they had taken to calling *The Curse* for all their troubles, sank four times—the final time with Graham, Beard, and a skinner they called Wildman (who spoke neither Swahili nor English, nor "anything we knew or understood," and on top of it all, did not know how to swim) aboard. After a twelve-hour stalk that had netted them the final three crocodiles in their survey, they ran into a sudden storm kicking up five-foot waves on the way home. Quickly they ditched their quarry but *The Curse* took on too much water, flipped, and went down. "We were down in the middle of nowhere," Peter said, "bobbing around like surprised corks in the wilderness." They were about a half mile from Shingle Island (now Central Island) and began their desperate swim, settling Wildman up with an empty tank can as a floating device and setting him kicking away toward relative safety. "I stayed behind to find my diary in the submerged hull," Peter said, in the hopes of preserving something of their past months of study, notation, observation. "After three or four fruitless bang-about dives, groping amongst the ropes and bags and boxes of supplies swimming below in the metal cockpit," he found it.

In his book-form letter to Zara, Peter cataloged the specifics of his unique log, giving a little idea of the value it held for him. In *Zara's Tales*, he wrote:

> For years I'd been keeping journals, saving mixed-up scraps and clippings, dawdles and dipsy doodles, in daily diary layouts for the sheer pleasure of it, escapism: snapshots of buddies from school, snakes eating rats, rampaging rhinos, old photos worked on by the passage of time, bits of cloth, dry things, Captain Marvel and the Phantom, clippings from the *Nairobi Standard*, Picayune cigarettes, hog hairs, my hair, teeth, and claws, run-over toads, fish scales, elephant tales, lizard tails, bits of bullets, bugs, twigs, seeds, plants, scorpion carcasses, snakeskin sheddings from lakeside lava rocks—all manner of miniscule jottings, scraps for a scrapbook—a homework assignment that nobody asked for. . . . It meant nothing to anyone else but me, myself and I. But now, for the first time ever, it contained something irreplaceable: all of Alistair's croc data, markings, measurements, and tail-scale sequences.

On their stormy sodden crawl toward safety at Shingle Island, Graham very nearly drowned, came so close in fact to drowning that he all but gave up on life, surrendered existence, went well past any fear of death, and only kept swimming, he said, "for something to do."

All three men made it to the island, in disbelief, but then had to contend with the greater notion that they were now stranded on an island within a body of water the size of the Caspian Sea, and still two miles from the actual shore. Of course, they had no radio or means of contacting anyone anywhere. No one would come looking for them. There were no other vessels or means by which they might craft something floatable on the island. And so, having just nearly died, Graham and Peter decided to do it all over again, swimming an additional two miles in the most densely croc-infested waters you'd ever want to be in, with the unpredictable currents and all hellacious tides that had already caused them and every other expedition to the lake such trouble. Well, they made it. And Graham immediately flew off to get a boat to pick up Wildman, who, unable to make the swim, had stayed back on Shingle Island.

When, the next day, Wildman had been collected safely, Peter and Graham immediately turned their attentions to the diary, repository of all the precious data they had come there to collect—assuming of course that the water and mud, the incredible alkalinity of the water and the salt, would have destroyed the pages, glued them together in irreparable blobs of meaninglessness. But it was all there, better than there. As Peter wrote later, in *Zara's Tales*, "Every waterlogged page had been turned, over and over for all those hours on windy Shingle Island, the work of the Wildman. Each soggy diary day had been kept apart from the next with bits and pieces of this and that; strands of seaweed, bones, and Shingly sand got fitted in between the pages. Methodically, systematically, in my friend's calloused wood-hard hands, all was separated and dried with great care and saved."

The resulting texture, density, and stained appearance of the diary pages was like a thunderbolt in Peter's creative life. "It was a gift from the gods," he wrote, "the ink-stained photos never looked so good. . . . Nine months of hoarded scraps had fossilized themselves together. . . . All my photos peeled and dyed, dried differently from anything I could have dreamed: bleached out on top, fermenting underneath, all nice and rotten and runny and dry. A liquid tapestry bled to the edge. I seemed to be seeing those ruined pictures for the first time. The scales fell from my eyes." The effect caused by this accident and Wildman's meticulous care gave Peter the look and feel he would try to re-create in his diaries and collages and prints forever more. It became his undeniable signature, for which he is recognized more than probably anything else.

I HAVE NEVER SEEN AN EVEN HALFWAY DECENT PRINT OF ONE of the zillions of images Peter took while in Turkana—most of them so blasted out and overexposed as to register almost like etchings, line drawings in their drastic contrast and graphic form—and yet, among these are three or four of the greatest images of the century. Important for science, sure—one bird's-eye view of a crocodile, taken from the top of a ladder looking down at one of their quarry, was even selected by Carl Sagan and his team to be among the 277 images on The Golden Record, the ultimate guide to life on earth, shipped out to whomever it may concern on the Voyager II in 1977—but so too an expression of the time and Peter's role in it.

Another of those taken ostensibly for purely scientific purposes of two men holding up a crocodile they have caught, and against whom its size can be gauged, is probably Peter's most astoundingly grand composition. We usually see it as he hangs it, upside down, a photo, taken from across a puddle of crystalline water (in contrast to the sea-like tidal churn of the lake beyond) of two men and a massive lizard. The men stand on either side of a tripod atop which they have mounted their coiling catch in front of the lake, creating a perfectly mirrored image. A picture of a scale, with scales and balances within. And Peter seems hip to all the material summoned by these symbols. He called the image *Reflections on Natural History.*

The most famous picture from this time is, of course, *I'll Write Whenever I Can*, made near Ferguson's Gulf, of Peter half submerged down the gullet of an enormous croc, appearing to scribble away in his journal. In that one incredible frame, Peter somehow managed to capture all of the glamour and danger and fun and humor of the image he was cultivating and projecting.

At an opening for a show in SoHo in the early 2000s, Jonas Mekas stopped in front of a print of this picture, chuckling to himself at the legendary life and times of his old friend Peter Beard. "Did he tell you about this one," he asked, "that it snapped? You see, he thought it was totally dead but crocodiles retain some of their muscle electricity and this one was only dead a short time and it snapped and he was badly hurt."

All of which is great gossip and a complete and utter fabrication. A moment's study of the image shows the careful staging to make it appear that the croc, with its jaws open and its head twisted toward him, is in fact swallowing Peter whole, when it is merely lying beside him. He is not inside of the animal (thinking about the anatomical impossibilities of this too are a bit of an impediment to the fourth wall). But the fact that he continued, for more than thirty years, to pull the leg of one of his oldest friends is quite telling both about his puckish sense of humor and his delight in the image he was projecting.

BACK AT THE LONG BAR AT THE NEW STANLEY HOTEL, CATCH-ing up on the town gossip and his beloved bullshots, Peter met the arrestingly beautiful, "tall, hazel eyed" Mary Cushing—"Minnie" to her friends—who was there on safari with her family. Minnie's dad, Howard, was a painter, of landscapes, and portraits, who had a studio in Manhattan. But the family's main residence was in Newport, Rhode Island, at the white cottage-style mansion built in 1850 on the cliffs, the home they called the Ledges. And the family history was as grand and wild as Peter's own: the Cushings had been in the tea trade in China, where they were called the Ku-shings for generations. Minnie's grandfather had been a notorious smuggler, of opium, among other things. In the mid-1960s, she and her brothers were the athletic swans of the society pages. When Minnie wasn't at work, as assistant to Oscar de la Renta, she was being photographed surfing out in front of the Ledges by Slim Aarons.

The chemistry between the two young beautiful people seemed to be instantaneous. Later, though, Peter would suggest that they were both merely succumbing to society's pressure, that they were pushed together by expectations—maybe even unconsciously, as they'd been coached from the earliest age that their lives would follow just these kinds of contours, toward just such a mate. Swallowed up by the machinery of wealthy families and pedigreed institutions, then, the young couple were engaged to marry before they even knew what had happened to them.

Their wedding, in Newport, on August 12, 1967, mere months after they'd met, too, seems as if it were preordained, a performance as much for the benefit of others as for themselves. "Historic Trinity Church (Episcopal) was lighted with candles, decorated with white delphinium, stock and carnations and jammed with people today for the wedding of Mary Olivia Cochran (Minnie) Cushing and Peter Hill Beard, a writer-photographer she met on African safari." The bride was "a tall, hazel-eyed member of one of this aristocratic resort's oldest families," in the words of the *New York Times* report. "After the ceremony in the small 241-year-old church, the wedding party and 416 guests drove to The Ledges. . . . 'We didn't ask Peter for anything special,' the bride said before heading down the aisle, 'and we aren't having any special champagne or anything. Just the usual Heidsieck or whatever it is and some hot and cold hors d'oeuvres.'"

In video of the event, filmed at Peter's request by his friend Jonas Mekas, the groom looks a bit adrift, a deer in exceptionally high-wattage headlights. When Minnie turned to find him for the first dance, he was gone—apparently taking pictures on the lawn, where no one could find him. Still, that wasn't the extent of his rebellious behavior on the day. After the cake and dancing at the reception, in a great big green-and-white awninged tent beside the main mansion, Peter led his new bride down to the edge of the cliff, with all the guests watching and making *aw*-faces at her wonderful couture Oscar de la Renta gown—"a long white organdy dress with appliques of organdy flowers, crystals and chalk beads on the hem and long sleeves"—made just for the occasion. On the count of three, they were going to make the leap together, into the sea, a symbol of their embarkation on a thrilling adventure of their lives together. But one, two, three . . . Peter let go and only Minnie jumped, soaking the gown and probably spoiling her mood a million different ways.

Then, at sunset, as the sky over the cliff cove south of the house turned pink and mauve, the freshly reclothed bride and the groom climbed into a helicopter that had landed on the lawn—one of those helicopters that is just a clear bubble of a cockpit. And then they floated off into the sky. It is one of the most beautiful images imaginable—and still, all you can think of is how angry Minnie must have been over the cliff-jumping stunt.

For their honeymoon, the two well-traveled newlyweds returned to Kenya, at first holing up at Hog Ranch, before going very very deep into the mountainous Aberdares rain forest, to spend their days shivering, soaked to the bone, and silently awaiting a glimpse of the wildly rare bongo, for Peter to take a picture of. "They are like Tarzan and Jane," Carol Bell said of the couple, before she eventually took Minnie's place in Peter's affections. "He's strong and brave, she's beautiful. They're both beautiful."

If Minnie had been an ardent enthusiast of life in Africa, eager to spend more and more time deeper and deeper in the bush, this was to be her trial by fire. And you can almost read, in retrospect, the kind of flippant aggression in Peter's suggestion of the Aberdares as a honeymoon spot, as if he were testing her, or even punishing her for something. For her part, Minnie took the adventure like a champion. Better than just being a good sport, she seems to have thrilled at their honeymoon, and for the rest of his life expressed great affection for Peter and their time together. "What we had was special," she told me, special beyond the tabloid stuff that she so detested (and he perhaps didn't detest quite enough). "There were times I almost felt I was losing a personality," she said, of life with her often domineering partner, "but really it was a blossoming. I'm still very earmarked," she said. "I still have a lot from him." A lot even beyond her memory of being bitten by a snake during the trip.

"Peter loved the bush and living in it the way the Africans did," Carol Bell said, thinking perhaps that all Africans lived "without tents or even sleeping bags. He could go for weeks and months into the bush. That changed after marrying Minnie. She tried," Bell said, "but couldn't live like that. She got sick, and Peter had no patience for such 'weakness.' Still the breakup with Minnie really hurt him—and he never really went back to the bush. The society side of his life had won him back."

What is remarkable is that, looking back at this time, Peter would sound both forever besotted and unconscionably cruel about his first wife, saying, "She is the greatest. Always was. But ultimately her 'love' for Africa turned out to be just an act. . . . A very nice act, but basically just fear-oriented and it's at the very heart of America, at the heart of spoiledness and all the disadvantages that come with having advantages." Which makes him sound like the wounded one here, after having made such extraordinary demands on his new bride, and then offering no comfort when she'd been hurt and fallen ill. Instead, flailing, selfishly wanting to wound back, he insulted the one who has hurt him by letting him down. There is, in his comment, attempting to gouge as deeply as he can, a violent pettiness that one finds sprinkled throughout Peter's insults, most of them directed at women (at his mother, at Minnie, and later at his second wife, Cheryl Tiegs).

Back at Hog Ranch, alone but for his staff, Minnie having flown back to New York, Peter fell into the first deep legal trouble of his life. From our vantage point now, looking back, it is almost impossible not to link the frustration at his wife having left him (though he made every cruel and dismissive claim to the contrary, to any and everyone who would listen) to the violence that would land him in a prison cell.

As he would explain the incident, downplaying it as best he could, Peter would say later that, in April 1968, he and Galo-Galo came upon a poacher's trap in which was snared a small suni. Deeming this now suddenly "poaching" and not a livelihood, and a wire-noose trap inhumane, Peter and Galo-Galo lay in wait for the trapper to return for his quarry. The reports, even by Peter's own admissions, of what happened next vary wildly from Peter merely punching the man and performing what he called a citizen's arrest, to punching him and tying him up in a tree with his own noose. After which, Peter either went on the lam, or to a bar for bullshots, or into Nairobi to report the perpetrator.

"We didn't know who it was at first," Peter said. "We were clearing bush at Hog Ranch and kept running across snares, nearly forty in all. So Galo-Galo staked out the area and waited for the poacher to come back." When he did, the man, Peter says, walked right up to the trap, knowing right where it was because he was evidently the selfsame man who had set it there. "He was a Mkama, carrying a *panga* [machete] and a *rungu* [club]," Peter wrote to Zara. Galo-Galo confronted this man who, according to Peter, became aggressive and claimed he happened on the snare by chance. So Galo-Galo let the man go on his way and went to tell Peter. Peter and Galo-Galo knew the man worked on Mervyn Cowie's property adjacent to his own, so they walked over and confronted the man, who still denied everything. "It was obvious he was lying," Peter wrote later. "So I hit him, once, as hard as I could, to sort of bring him back to reality." But the blow did not have the desired effect, so, Peter said, he escalated things. "Since the blow didn't achieve its objective," he wrote, "we put him in the snare and gagged him with a glove. I photographed the suni and the guy in the snare and then went off to have the films developed—and have lunch." And that was that, Peter maintained. "Any other story you hear is *fitina* [gossip], and there are a million versions: that I tortured him, strung him up between two trees 'in a dangerous part of the forest'—that's what the local papers wrote. In fact, he was in the snare for an hour and a half. I went into town, had the films developed, had lunch and came back. By then it had started to rain and Galo-Galo had undone him and returned to camp. My Africans had let him out."

In the aftermath, a furor began to mount around town. Richard Leakey, the archaeologist, conservationist, and now politician got involved, phoning friends of Peter's in a fever to find him. In November 1969, charges were pressed, and police came to Hog Ranch and arrested Peter and Galo-Galo. After a short trial, Peter was sentenced to eighteen months in Kamiti Prison and twelve strokes with a cane; Galo-Galo was given nine months and six strokes. Peter's head was shaved and though he joked about missing tasty food and a comfy mattress, and the horrors of having to use the loo in an open room with "a thousand other guys," his prospects were bleak—or would have been had he not been Peter Beard, on whose behalf no less a personage than Jackie Kennedy prevailed upon the American ambassador to intervene.

Carol Bell, who was by that time Peter's girlfriend, said, "Whenever Peter got in trouble he thought it was no big deal, just another 'experience.'"

AFTER TEN DAYS, PETER WAS ALLOWED BAIL—$2,500, WHICH had been put up by Jack Block, owner of the New Stanley and Norfolk hotels and a friend of Ruth and Bill Woodley, who had pleaded for his intervention. Block had also appealed to a friend of President Kenyatta's, hoping for greater favor. And pressure soon started to mount from the American State Department, at the urging of Jackie O, and Peter and Galo-Galo were soon granted another hearing. In January 1970, a new judge granted the men conditional discharges and fines (£500 for Peter and £25 for Galo-Galo, half of which was to be paid to the trapper). Peter's welcome back to the ranch and his Kenyan community was mixed. He was still on the outs with some of the old hunters who hated the way he'd sounded the death knell for hunting in *The End of the Game*, and the Leakeys of the world would forever look upon Peter as a kind of dangerous trickster figure in their midst. But Peter reveled in the reaction of others in the Langai and Ongata Rongai, to whom from then on he was "The Hangman," giving him a reputation he credited with keeping Hog Ranch free from other interested parties for decades.

IN THE LEAD-UP TO THE FIRST TRIAL, MINNIE FLEW BACK TO Nairobi to be at Peter's side, but the experience seems to have been harrowing for her, and she declined to talk about it. Since her first flight from the marriage, she had begun a romantic relationship with Michael Butler, then the producer of the musical *Hair* off-Broadway, and while she was in Nairobi this last time, she called Butler and poured out her heart to him. He arranged a return flight for her (and helped her later get a divorce from Peter in absentia in Mexico). She never returned to Africa.

When Peter too finally made it back to New York, while he was on bail and awaiting new sentencing from the courts in Kenya, the gravity of the previous months seems to have caught up with him.

"See, all the cast of *Hair* had moved back from Mexico to continue their pursuit of their newfound leader, my wife, the hippie's hero coming down from the Establishment to join the hippies in their rebellion," he told Doon Arbus, Diane's daughter, in a *Rolling Stone* interview a few years later, "and the place was full of all those *Hair* actors and producers and god-knows-what." The place being his apartment, which he still then shared with Minnie. (Neither Minnie nor Michael Butler remembers this event.) "I was really wrecked at the time" Peter said, "and so short on sleep I just super-OD'd, and was heading for the ultimate relaxation, copping my final zees so to speak." But, somehow, while he was in his stupor, Peter managed to hear the phone ringing. Somehow he answered, and the police were called (Peter is vague about who contacted them). "The police brought me into the emergency ward of New York Hospital on a chair stretcher in one of those last-minute special deliveries," Peter told Arbus, still sounding rather pleased by the drama of it all, "and I was out for four days, didn't wake up until January 22nd, my birthday as a matter of fact, feeling really good, too." Eventually, when the doctors deemed him fit enough to be moved, he was transferred to Payne Whitney for psychological evaluations. "And, just to show you how suave and advanced the whole field of psychiatry was," Peter said, in his puckish mode, "on my first interview with my doctor . . . the supervisor turned around and said to me, 'You're one of the most suicidal people I've ever met. You're going to be down here a long time.' And then he slammed the door. Well, I was actually only there a few weeks, locked, you know." And then, almost as an afterthought, Peter did as he did throughout his life, reframed the experience for the purpose of pushing a narrative, one that places him in supreme control, utterly at ease, and having a laugh. "After that I kind of used [Payne Whitney] as a hotel for a couple of months; otherwise I would have had to move back in with Minnie."

CHAPTER 6

Land's End

I n the summer of 1971, Peter's friend Jacqueline Onassis invited him to join her and her new husband, Ari, on his private island in Greece for a few months' vacation. As two Upper East Siders who ran in the kinds of crowds that summered in the Hamptons and skied in the Alps (and, both, friends of Quentin Keynes), Peter and Jackie had known each other socially forever, and she knew him to be a great entertainer, an enthusiastic storyteller who might be a great summer companion for her children, Jack Jr. and Caroline. So it was ostensibly as a babysitter, "to amuse her children," that Peter packed his bags and made his way to Skorpios. But upon arriving, the former first lady's real plan must have been crystal clear: Peter was a blind date of sorts, a blue-blooded boy toy whom Jackie had beckoned for the amusement of her younger sister Lee Radziwill.

Peter was always purposefully vague about how he and Jackie had met, perhaps because she seemed to think of him as a babysitter and boy toy, but he didn't seem to mind too much and happily accepted her invitation. At the time, Lee was drifting apart from her second husband, the Polish prince–turned–naturalized British citizen (and real estate developer, like her father), Stas Radziwill, and was recovering from a recent hysterectomy. So Jackie's invitation to a little island retreat where she could rest and relax with her kids in a house of their own—as well as, perhaps, have a little summer fling as a diversion—was very welcome.

Thirty-eight at the time, to Peter's thirty-three, Lee was of a familiar social circle for Peter, groomed by the same sort of schools and deb balls as Minnie had been, and her proximity to Camelot along with her formidable ambition was clearly intoxicating to Peter. Lee was yearning, struggling with her role as the second sister to perhaps the most famous woman on Earth, even as she was widely regarded as one of the world's great beauties. As the *New York Times* reporter Charlotte Curtis had written in 1961, Lee was "the epitome of all that is considered chic, and therefore elegantly understated, in the world today." Her best friend, Truman Capote, described "Princess Dear," as he called Lee, as beauty, outside and inside—her eyes "gold-brown like a glass of brandy resting on a table in front of a fireplace." She was then, as she was her entire adult life, an alluring muse to fashion designers, like her sister, a living icon of style, taste, and beauty.

It is possible that she didn't remember meeting Peter twelve years before, when he was still an undergraduate at Yale and had been assigned by Alexander Liberman to photograph her at her apartment in New York. Peter certainly did, and it seems to have been a momentous occasion for the young and ambitious photographer. As he would later recall it, "The first job I ever had as a Yalie from New Haven was for *Harper's Bazaar*: a portrait of Lee Radziwill," he said. "When we first got together at her seriously impressive art-filled apartment, she fell, almost immediately into a miracle vision in front of my pathetic Voigtländer bellows camera." With some of the stars still in his eyes from the encounter, Peter said, "It couldn't be called a job, and actually I never bothered to pick up the fee. The one or two Tri-X films that we took came away with the easiest total winners of simplicity and taste. It's hard to forget a flash performance like that. I've always said the most essential approach to a good photograph is subject matter. Here it was: pure and simple innocence staring, without concern, right into my amateur glass-eye camera (totally at home). It was one exposure after the other, asking nothing, totally silent, conveying something deeply different, fresh, original, surprising, ingenious, Bazaar! As Salvador Dalí liked to say: diveeen. That was and is Lee. It is important in life to hold out for elegant miracles."

If he sounded as though he fell a little in love with his subject in 1959, he seems to have gone whole hog on Skorpios in the summer of 1971. And Lee reciprocated. "He was superb looking," she told Sofia Coppola, in a 2013 interview for the *New York Times*. "Had a body of a Greek god that was always the same color tan. Always an opinion. An extraordinary costume that only he could get away with. He just gave me so many more interests, and so much more curiosity about possibilities." If Lee had initially been comfortable to perform a version of herself for his camera, to embody the mystique of money and breeding that Peter seemed to fetishize (even as he claimed to loathe it in himself), it was her insatiable energy, curiosity, and appetite for life that would in the summer of '71 bring them so close.

Watching him water-skiing with the kids—who Lee said just adored Peter—running around the beach, endlessly at play, and then sprawled all over the floor with his inks and glues and mad swirls of prints and general detritus, she was certainly enamored. "There is no question that he hastened my recovery enormously with his enthusiasm and joie de vivre," she wrote in her scrapbook memoir, *Lee*. Even if that joie was simply all over the place. "His mess was everywhere," she said, marveling at this incredible person who came spilling into her life just then, "his collages, photographs, just all over the floor. He was always on knees, gluing, or rubbing a pen into his arm to get blood to put on his paintings. And then we'd go off and waterski for hours when the heat had gone down. It was just paradise. You had at least 100 beaches to yourself."

Not that everything was bliss that summer. Relationships on the island were incredibly complex. To begin with, *it was Lee* who had first begun an affair with their host, Jackie's new husband, the shipping tycoon Ari. Almost ten years prior to their Skorpios sojourn, Onassis had left Maria Callas to be with Lee, but even then he seemed to always be biding his time for Jackie, as if she were the real prize. In August 1963, when Jackie's infant son, Patrick, died shortly after birth, Lee invited Jackie *to join her* for a cruise aboard Ari's yacht—the *Christina*, named for Onassis's daughter, who famously disliked the Bouvier sisters. After her father's death, Christina bought Jackie out of her prenuptial agreements for $25 million so as to have nothing further to do with her, and she never spoke to Lee and Jackie again.

It was to be a recuperation, an escape, as only Onassis could provide, whisking the sisters away from the swarms of paparazzi that were then stalking them. But Ari's attempts to lift Jackie's spirits went a little further than Lee might've hoped. At the end of the cruise, Lee was destroyed to see that their host's parting gift to Jackie—a gold necklace with rubies—was so much more grand than her own—bracelets that, she said, her own daughter would be embarrassed to wear to her birthday party. Nor could Lee comfort herself in the generosity of the land Onassis had given her in Greece, as she suspected that he had only given it to her in the hopes that Jackie would build a house for herself there.

The balance of power—the pecking order, as Peter would surely have called it—was something that had always been in flux and was of great sensitivity to the sisters, then as ever. When they were children, it was Lee who was always being fussed over and singled out for her beauty, while Jackie buried herself in books, whether by design, in calculated contrast, or *just because*, she could no longer tell. "Lee was the pretty one," Jackie said. "So I guess I was supposed to be the intelligent one." But soon after Jackie became the first lady, Lee would ask people, protesting a bit too much, perhaps, "Why would anyone care what I do when there are so many more interesting people in the world? I haven't done anything at all."

Even in 1971, on Skorpios, Jackie the hostess, the grand sister then and forevermore, did not seem to be having a great time of it. The newlyweds squabbled like an old married couple, according to Peter. At every group gathering, Ari seemed to seethe with venom and resentment of his new wife, going out of his way to make an awkward scene. "I can't tell you how many meals I sat through when Onassis would scream at her," Peter said. "He used to make insulting comparisons right to her face between Jackie and Callas," whom Onassis regularly recognized as the great love of his life. "He said that Jackie was superficial and Callas was a 'real artist.' Jackie sat around and took it."

According to biographers of the Bouvier sisters, Peter "also noticed that Onassis was nicer to Jackie when they were in London, visiting Lee, or in Manhattan, but on Greek soil, 'all the macho in him came out,' Peter said. 'When he exploded, everybody ran for cover.'"

For the entirety of his life, Peter would brag that Onassis had bet him $2,000 that he couldn't hold his breath for four minutes and delighted in taking money off the tycoon with his feats of physical prowess and determination (Jackie timed him at 4:20, and the $2,000 he won in 1971 money is a little over $13,000 in 2021). Onassis's joke, as he must've seen it, was of course the perfect lure for the young buck Peter, who could push himself to herculean ends with his outsize will, and not a little extra urging from his vanity in wanting to show off for the sisters. But if Peter was having a great time, counting himself the young, virile winner of these exchanges, one can't help but imagine Onassis finding some wicked pleasure in making the blond boy (and lover to his former lover) do tricks for his amusement. To Onassis it was good sport either way, and maybe the messy American playboy wouldn't bob back up and they could finally have some peace and quiet around the island.

One wonders what Jackie made of all this. Surely a lot of time and media attention have been spent seeking insight into Jackie's love life. Amid all that speculation over the allure Jackie's husbands held for her and the ways in which they may have reminded her of her great dandy and financial ruin of a father, one wonders where Peter might fit into this mold—where his life and image chimes with Jack Bouvier, a clotheshorse who would come even to the girls' riding practices with his hair pomaded, a pearl tie pin and a flashy pocket square at his breast, a gregarious man about town who loved to ham it up with the fellas at his various clubs, and an inveterate philanderer, always on the prowl. Peter differed in just about every imaginable way from Stas Radziwill (and perhaps that was the initial point of him), who was staid, polished in the way of European aristocracy, taking great care over his tailoring and personal contacts. Peter seems to have brought a spark that Lee was looking for—he was "life-enhancing," as she had described her father.

The phrase that was dear to Peter, in fact, who always described his diaries, and anything that might aspire to the heights of art, as life-enhancing, or life-thickening. The only other person in his milieu who used this term frequently was the writer Terry Southern, who spent a good deal of time with both Peter and Lee on the Rolling Stones' *Exile on Main Street* tour the next year, and it seems that Peter picked up that little saying during his life-enhancing romance with Lee (who, in turn, received it from the aesthete, wanderer, and Renaissance art historian Bernard Berenson, who was for a time her instructor, and for many years a pen pal. "Berenson said so many wonderful and memorable things," she wrote later, "chief among them that there are two categories of people: life diminishing and life enhancing. To this day, I think that is so true, and I still apply it in my life.").

She certainly seemed to count Peter and their summer fling as the life-enhancing sort.

Summer flings end with the fall, though, and what Lee and Peter had found on their private island kept right on. "Back in London with Stas, Lee missed Peter Beard terribly and wrote him passionate letters," her biographers wrote. "They would meet again in February of 1972 when Lee decided to accompany Stas on safari in Kenya, something she normally would not have done."

"Stas loved shooting," Lee later wrote, "which I hated."

But she wasn't there for the game when she came, a week in advance of Stas, with a girlfriend who provided cover for her real purpose, to continue her fling with Peter. Even when Stas did join them, Lee and Peter carried on, in secret. From Kenya, Peter accompanied the Radziwills back to London, where he stayed with them in their house, and then on holiday in a villa in Barbados, where Jackie and the kids rejoined them.

The audacity is quite spectacular, but, "if Stas knew that Lee and Peter were in love he did not let on, nor did he make a scene," according to Lee's biographers. From Barbados, Stas flew home to London while Lee and Jackie and the kids flew to New York on Onassis's private plane. "And that was how Lee's thirteen-year marriage ended. Lee had had enough, not just of her passionless marriage . . . but of her life in London . . . she was lonely. She was homesick. . . . She wanted to be with Peter Beard. She was thirty-nine years old, she had recently undergone a hysterectomy, and she felt strongly that it was time for a major change in her life."

BACK HOME IN NEW YORK, PERHAPS EAGER TO STEP OUT OF his role as cabana-boy entertainment, Peter put on his tour-guide hat and showed Lee the sights and scene that she'd been missing while she'd been off playing Princess in London. He invited her to the round-table salons hosted by his cousin Jerome Hill at the

Algonquin Hotel, where Jerome stayed while he was visiting New York. At one of these gatherings, Peter introduced Lee to his new bosom pal Andy Warhol, and to Warhol's companion, Paul Morrissey, who invited Lee and Peter to visit them at their new beach cottage in the sleepy fishing village of Montauk, out at the very tip of Long Island.

Warhol and Morrissey's "cottage," called Eothen, composed of one main house and five cabins spread across five and a half acres, had been built as a fishing camp in the 1930s by the Church family of Arm & Hammer baking soda fame. Warhol had paid $220,000 for it, and in 2015, former J.Crew CEO Mickey Drexler sold it for nearly $50 million. It was a kind of raw and elemental seaside paradise a few hours from Manhattan. But a beach house, especially one as remote and rugged as Eothen, is a very odd thing to have for an indoor cat like Warhol—a man who thoroughly hated sun, sand, and the sea breeze kicking up his wig—and so, by the time Peter introduced him to Lee, he had yet to even spend a night at the house.

Figuring she would put it to better use, Lee rented the main house from Andy for the summer, giving him all the excuse to come visit (and then leave), to attend gatherings of famous friends but stay a bit removed. Which was perfect for him, and he even got to love playing in the sand with Lee's children. But for Lee and Peter, Montauk was a revelation. "It was really roughing it," she said, "but it was *in* the sea and I adored that." Here they could enjoy each other in the sun, on their own turf, in their own time. They could encourage each other. Comfort each other. Indeed, Peter seems to have recharged Lee's creative aspirations, which had to still be a bit sore after the critical response she'd received from her acting debut (a debacle into which she'd been coaxed rather aggressively by Capote, who perhaps liked a little too much to see his grand friends knocked down a peg). As all new couples do, they started making plans.

Lee and Peter both struggled throughout their lives with wanting to be taken seriously, on their own terms, without always having to lug around the baggage of the family name and legacy. Part of their connection was the bond over their conflicted relationships with their image in the popular culture, the gap between what they hoped to project and how they were habitually received, the myriad opportunities afforded them by their families, money and entrée, and how all of those things clouded their accomplishments. Peter hated being called a socialite (though he loved being on the scene, and being seen, well into his seventies), as well as being counted among the jet set (a Space Age advancement from café society into which he fit squarely—being in fact the poster child for the group, along with his pal Mick Jagger). He had an uneasy relationship with the word *dilettante* (though over the years he tried to wrestle it back for his own purposes, away from any pejorative connotations). Lee, too, wanted to be recognized for her style and interior design sense, and now, of course, in our era of influencers, when individual taste is accorded not just aesthetic but also commercial value and given pride of place within the culture, Lee is held up to be one of her generation's highest holies of taste. Her attempts at photography and at acting had been dismissed, but beginning with her initiation of the film that would become *Grey Gardens*, Lee got back to work in a way that can't help but have been encouraged by Peter, strengthened by their bond.

"It was my idea to go back to East Hampton," Lee said, "for which I had this great nostalgia as a child and have my extremely eccentric aunt be a narrator for my memories." Lee's aunt, Edith Bouvier Beale, and her daughter, also Edith, but known as Little Edie, were then living in a decrepit old house in East Hampton and facing threats of eviction. Lee waded into this fray, using what power and money—and lawyers—she could summon to support the Beales, all the while mining them for their memories, the family stories. And she put them on film. At first, Peter suggested hiring his pals the Mekas brothers to film it, but as the project began to sprawl beyond anything they could have imagined, they brought in the Maysles brothers to film, edit, and direct the whole thing. And the delicate portraits the Maysles brothers made of mother and daughter in their crumbling old pile became a kind of cult phenomenon, and then a classic of American cinema.

BACK IN TOWN, PETER WAS EXPLORING THE COMMERCIAL OP-portunities for his style of work, partly with the aid of his cousin Jerome Hill, who was at the time an investor in Andy Warhol's *Interview* magazine. A few years prior, Jerome arranged for Peter and Warhol to connect properly for the first time, over drinks at the bar of the Algonquin Hotel, which had been made famous a few generations before as the watering hole for the greatest wits and media mavens of the twenties and thirties, the setting for more than a few of Dorothy Parker's *mots*. In his biography of Andy, *Holy Terror*, Bob Colacello, who was then the editor of Andy's magazine and was present at this first meeting—which would have been in 1969—famously described the Peter he met at the Algonquin as "Half Tarzan, Half Byron." Lord of the jungle and of excess.

"I was quite taken by him at first," Colacello writes of Peter. "And Andy was like, 'Oh, Bob's falling for Peter.'" But the impression Peter made on Colacello was similar to that which he made on everyone he met, at once seducing and overwhelming them. "He was a dazzling conversationalist," Colacello wrote, "or a monologist actually. And he seemed to know so much about everything, from subjects I knew something about like Nietzsche and Kierkegaard and existentialism." One subject that would never be far from the minds of this bunch was art. And Colacello's quip about Peter's guiding aesthetic philosophy—"that beauty was more beautiful when it was in danger"—is quite good, especially as he notes that "some of the women who modeled for him found [that this philosophy of beauty] meant hanging from branches on cliffs, over the ocean in Montauk."

If Colacello was taken by Peter, he was far from the only one. The model Barbara Allen, whose husband, Joe Allen, had (along with Peter Brant) recently purchased half of *Interview* from Jerome Hill, had been asking Andy for something to do for the magazine. When he sent her out to Montauk to interview Peter, she basically stayed for the summer (much to the consternation of her husband; of Lee, who was then still dating Peter and living next door; and of Andy, who feared she was jeopardizing his relationship with Joe).

Even when he wasn't literally seducing people, he was making friends with any and everyone. One of the funnier bits in *Holy Terror* is when Peter shows up to the Factory with Leni Riefenstahl, who had just finished her book *Last of the Nuba*, "and she sat with Andy for like half an hour going through it page by page," Colacello wrote, "pointing out the beautiful arc of a great black man's thigh or arm. I mean, she was so into bodies."

So maybe this should not seem so odd. The Factory was, after all, the ultimate mixing place for people from Uptown and down, for people of all politics and persuasions—in a time of colliding cultures making very strange bedfellows. And there is perhaps a lot in common between the legendary propagandist Riefenstahl and Peter, who called his portraits and nudes "living sculptures," about their objectification of bodies. Not that politics would have gotten in the way for Peter. "Peter was kind of apolitical in the sense that Andy was apolitical," Colacello says. With those guys, he says, "It was art for art's sake, but yet with a heavy dose of social consciousness. Peter didn't see a contradiction in appreciating the work of Leni Riefenstahl, which today wouldn't probably be called a progressive world view."

But if there were symmetries in Peter's and Andy's outlooks, their interactions were not always the smoothest. In Colacello's words, "Andy read him as a hustler, as if there were some ulterior motive to his doing things. I wouldn't say that Andy had the greatest rapport with Peter. He always said, 'Oh, Peter has a problem.' He always thought Peter had to be gay or part gay or, and I'd say, 'Well, no, Andy. He really loves women.'" But as Colacello notes, Peter was narcissistic, and narcissists need to feel attraction, love, adoration in everyone they can. "I mean, he had to be aware of his beauty, but he was attracted to beautiful women," Colacello says. And Peter's constant romancing of women, he says, "was never *womanizing*, in the sense that he forced himself upon women or tricked them into going to bed with him. Women lined up to be with Peter. His work had two subjects, beautiful women and wildlife in Africa. Those were his two subjects. So you can't really separate his love life from his work life. It was one and the same thing."

On the strength of the first meetings, Colacello commissioned Peter to shoot for *Interview*, and he recounts with growing horror Peter having buckets and buckets of blood delivered to the Factory prior to the shoot. Then, when the buckets of blood he'd had delivered were deemed to be of the wrong sort, he ordered many more buckets besides.

Peter sort of cackled about this later and told me, half defensively, "I've always liked blood. Everybody thinks I am very sick, but the thing is, blood is better than any ink or paint."

ONE PERSON WHO DEFINITELY DIDN'T THINK IT WAS SICK—OR if he did, thought it was also great—was Peter's fellow fan of gore, the Irish-born English painter Francis Bacon. During a show of Bacon's work in London at the Marlborough Gallery in 1971 (during the time Peter was staying with Lee and Stas), Peter introduced himself to the painter and the two struck up an immediate and deep friendship. For more than twenty years, until Bacon's death in 1992, the artists kept up a correspondence. Peter sent florid and elaborately illuminated letters to Bacon, encouraging him to take up and then continue his triptych inspired by Van Gogh, for instance, flattering the painter incessantly, and spouting off about nature and apocalypse, as was his way.

When the two were together, in London and New York, they would photograph and paint each other and have long, rambling, probably drunken conversations about life and wildlife, some of which Peter recorded, Warhol style. He later transcribed and edited these to be included in the catalog for Bacon's show at the Metropolitan Museum in New York in 1975, calling them, rather grandly, "The Dead Elephant Interviews." Bacon was obsessed by the pictures Peter had taken in Tsavo, saying, "Dead elephants are more beautiful because they trigger off more ideas in me than living ones. Alive, they just remain beautiful elephants, whereas the other ones are suggestive of all types of beauty." But he may also have been a little bit obsessed with Peter.

When Peter hoped to commission a portrait of himself by Bacon, knowing he could never afford it, the two of them agreed to a plan: Bacon would paint three portraits of Peter, sell two, and Peter could have the third. In the 1990s, after Bacon's death, Peter said, "My genius wife sold [the Bacon] for half a million bucks and then it sold right away for two and a half million."

"The work reveals Bacon's complicated feelings for a man he loves but cannot have, at least not physically," according to an assessment in the *Guardian*. "The photographer's renowned good looks are still there in the portrait, despite the disfigurement," a Bacon-eque grotesquerie, inspired perhaps by images of World War I soldiers who had suffered terrible injuries. "The black void in which Beard's face is isolated invades part of his face. His left cheek has gone and his mouth is a gory mess."

These particular images, made in 1976, were just a few of the more than two dozen Bacon would go on to paint of Peter, who became his great muse at the time, even inspiring some of the work not explicitly about him—including the great *Triptych 1976*, which Bacon told friends was inspired by *Heart of Darkness*, and in which the unnamed figure holds an elephant fetus in his lap.

"A friend observed that Bacon had 'a thing' for the photographer," Jonathan Jones writes. "But you don't need the gossip. The portraits say it all."

Even when they weren't making pictures of each other or talking about art, but especially when they were, Bacon and Beard seemed to share the same sort of thirst. Andy Warhol once wrote in his diary, "Mick [Jagger] arrived so drunk from an afternoon with Peter Beard and Francis Bacon that he fell asleep on my bed."

After Bacon died, more than two hundred of Peter's pictures were found in his famous studio.

"I FIRST MET PETER IN '66 OR '67," JANN WENNER SAYS, "WHEN Jackie Onassis had a Christmas luncheon at her apartment, for her kids and Peter and us. He seemed funny and, of course, in that situation, you're being witty and fun and relaxed. But I thought no more of it. I didn't really meet Peter again until I had signed Truman to do the Stones tour. Truman wanted to bring Lee along, and then Truman said he wanted his friend, Peter, to come to take the photographs. I knew who he was, and I said, sure, of course."

The tour for which Wenner engaged Capote to report, and Peter to photograph, was of course the famously, fabulously libidinous 1972 Rolling Stones *Exile on Main Street* tour—maybe the absolute worldwide historical apogee of sex, drugs, and rock and roll. It was the perfect subject for Wenner's magazine *Rolling Stone*.

For the purpose of the journey, Ahmet Ertegun, the founder

of Atlantic Records, had provided the band and their ever-changing entourage with a private jet, even painted it with their hungry mouth logo. "The 1972 tour included Truman Capote, Terry Southern (would have included William S. Burroughs if the *Saturday Review* had come up with Bill's price), Princess Lee Radziwill, and Robert Frank," Stanley Booth later wrote in his book about the Stones guitarist Keith Richards, *Keith: Standing in the Shadows*. "Featured sideshows on the tour involved a traveling physician, hordes of dealers and groupies, big sex-and-dope scenes. I could describe for you in intimate detail the public desecrations and orgies I witnessed and participated in on this tour, but once you've seen sufficient fettuccine on flocked velvet, hot urine pooling on deep carpets, and tidal waves of spewing sex organs, they seem to run together. So to speak. Seen one, you seen 'em all. The variations are trivial."

That may be the case in retrospect, when speaking broadly and generally of orgies, of the enormous and deranging power disparity between rock gods and mortals they encounter along the way. Except for the fact that there is film documentation of some of these "orgies," these displays of power, wealth, and fame, its gravity, the intoxication that surrounds it and with which it bends the world around it. The great photographer and documentarian Robert Frank, above mentioned, was not just along for the ride here. The creator of the landmark photographic survey of the States, *The Americans*, had been engaged by the band, after designing the album packaging for *Exile on Main Street*, to make a film of the tour, a film which he eventually titled *Cocksucker Blues*—after a throwaway song Mick wrote to get out of a record deal; the film was immediately bought up, buried, and scrubbed from the record by the band, who felt, rightly, that it cast them in somewhat of an unflattering light.

In one particularly harrowing scene from the film—which has now surfaced online and on streaming platforms—mute, somewhat delirious-looking young women are stripped for spectacle, in front of all those aboard the plane, to be made pleasure of. And then chucked overboard, presumably. "Roadies grope seemingly compliant women like grapes on a withered vine," Terry Southern's biographer writes of the scene. "Their chauvinistic behavior culminates in a notorious midair gang bang on the Stones' touring plane (with Mick and Keith providing impromptu musical accompaniment)." The feeling of jet-set buccaneers on a pillaging rampage is very strong throughout the film. As is the unbelievable boredom behind the scenes. "As the rich and famous drop by to chat backstage, they are greeted with varying degrees of ennui. *Cocksucker Blues* is a film about people seeing how close they can skirt despair and death and still survive."

Capote, for his part, echoed this feeling, claiming a lack of inspiration in the proceedings to excuse his failure to file his piece. Rather than send along another writer to join the melee, *Rolling Stone* invited Andy Warhol to interview Capote about his experience on the tour.

The novelist Richard Elman, too, was a part of this menagerie, covering the tour for *Esquire* magazine, and his portfolio report, *Uptight with the Stones*, is a rich exercise in hipster drollery, affecting the greatest apathetic boredom from the very center of global pop culture. It's kind of a riot, and not just for his descriptions of "Mick's society friends," as Keith called them, but for that as well. Elman's thesis is that Mick does everything he can, even encouraging Keith's drug use, to maintain control; that Mick needs to be seen as cool but is the opposite of it. And he is no more forgiving toward the band's audience. Elman writes:

> If some Martian were to come to a Stones concert somewhere in Middle America and be told that what he was hearing was a group of deracinated Englishmen asserting their identities by pretending to be Delta blackmen before

a largely redneck audience who, being somewhat in rebellion against their own culturally-enforced identities, are into pretending they are hip international freaks so that they can somehow relate better to that part of themselves which has been living cheek by jowl with black culture for three centuries and largely ignoring it, he would surely wonder if this was an act of cultural synthesis, or just some entirely synthetic put on.

There is little doubt which conclusion Elman favors. Here he is on his fellow artists on the tour:

> Looking like a grizzled Lincoln Brigadier just having made it across the Pyrenees after the Fall of Barcelona, writer Terry Southern enters—seemingly from one of the wall lockers on the side of the room, as if he'd been stuffed inside there the night before and only now just released. . . . Mick Taylor gabs with Princess Lee. There are assorted handshakes, sniffles, and snorfels from the cocaine caucus. Truman Capote again appears, flanked by a pretty lad, his photographer, a wild-life man from Kenya. They look like they prefer a well-aged Vicks VapoRub for inhaling purposes.

According to Elman, this pretty wild-life "man from Kenya," as he now calls him, explains: "You mustn't think Truman is prejudiced. He's just very angry. He didn't come here for the money. Didn't have to make this trip. He had better things to do. . . ." At which point Truman says it is a pity that William Burroughs, who had been invited, couldn't make it. Or, rather, it is suggested, didn't deem the financial offer made to him sufficient.

"That's why Terry is here," Truman says, according to Elman, sounding as cutting and petty as can be. "I'm wondering why not

Jean Genet, or Jorge Luis Borges, or Aleksandr Solzhenitsyn," Elman writes. "Shlock such as this should be fittingly memorialized."

Keith's view of it all seems to follow a similar tenor. At various times in his autobiography, he refers to Lee as Princess Lee, Princess Radziwill, or just Princess Radish. Richards writes:

> We had some sport with Truman Capote, author of *In Cold Blood*, one of the group of Mick's society friends who had attached themselves to the tour and who included Princess Lee Radziwill, Princess Radish to us, as Truman was just Truby. He was on assignment from some high-paying magazine, so he was ostensibly working. Truby said something bitchy and whiny backstage—he was being an old fart, actually complaining about the noise. It was just some snide, queenie remark and sometimes I don't give a damn, other times it just gets up my nose. This happened after a show and I was already on cloud nine. Mother-fucker needed a lesson. I mean, this snooty New York attitude. You're in Dallas. It got a little raucous. I remember, back at the hotel, kicking Truman's door. I'd splattered it with ketchup I'd picked up off a trolley. Come out, you old queen. What are you doing round here? You want cold blood? You're on the road now, Truby! Come and say it out here in the corridor. Taken out of context, it sounds like I'm some right sort of Johnny Rotten, but I must have been provoked.

If Southern was there as a replacement for William Burroughs, he was still himself a kind of countercultural rock star at the time, having helped Stanley Kubrick write the screenplay for *Dr. Strangelove*, and having been immortalized on the cover of the Beatles' *Sgt. Pepper's Lonely Hearts Club Band* album, among other things. But by the time he appears in Frank's footage, he does look a bit like a replacement player. About a cameo that Southern would later prefer to forget, his biographer, Lee Hill, writes, "Southern looks remarkably disheveled in jeans, matching jacket, and turtleneck. His beard is scruffy and his glasses look like the kind of cheap frames that need to be taped. It is a jarring contrast to the cool, elegant hipster in sunglasses staring from the cover of *Sgt. Pepper*. Joking backstage, Southern is filmed snorting cocaine and then saying, 'If you had a million dollars a week to spend on coke, you could probably develop a habit.'"

At any rate, Southern and Peter became fast friends on the tour, as Hill notes, in part because "Beard's combination of nihilism and gung-ho preppiness intrigued Southern." The two guys even began collaborating on a screenplay adaptation of Peter's *The End of the Game*, a project they would kick around for much of the rest of Southern's life. Mostly, the writer and photographer used the writing of the script—or, rather, the getting together and not writing of the script—as Hill notes in his biography of Southern, "as an excuse for Beard and Southern to riff off each other for a few hours and then go partying," which could work as a description of many of Peter's male friendships. Despite their process, such as it was, the script that emerged, Hill writes, was at least unique. He describes it as *Dr. Strangelove* meets *Walkabout*, with an *Argo*-style framing device—studio execs in Hollywood trying to make an action film of *The Man-Eaters of Tsavo* on the back lot.

But that was later. On the tour and the chaotic plane, Southern said, he and Peter started bonding over San Quentin.

When we first started talking, we were flying to San Francisco and there was this terrible storm. It was so severe that we had to make a wide approach to San Francisco airport, so we flew right over the Golden Gate Bridge. When we crowded around the window to look down at the bridge, we saw these buildings. . . . Truman Capote said, "Well, that's probably the most horrible prison there is. That's San Quentin." Keith said, "What a gas it would be to play a gig there." And Capote, who was ultragay, replied, "Well, they would love it, and they would certainly love you and MICK! They would just devour Mick." So Keith spoke to Mick about it and Mick asked Truman and me to go check it out. So we did that. The prison was a horrific situation . . . talk about stress and density [Peter's favorite term for the pressures on a population and its resources that led to all the problems of the world]—they had a record number of stabbings . . . in the end, basically the warden said yes, but the security people said it was [too difficult to arrange]. And there wasn't enough insurance to stage the gig.

The visit to San Quentin created other, personal repercussions, for Peter particularly. He and Capote had the idea that they would do a story about the prison, interviewing and photographing the Manson family affiliate Bobby Beausoleil, who was imprisoned there for murder. Capote was going to do it for *Life* magazine, but then, again, never delivered. Peter's photographs of the visit, on the other hand, of Beausoleil and Capote, did find a way out and remain quite special: especially the portrait of Capote, standing in a quarter profile, perfectly in center of frame but cut off at the knees, making him seem both terribly significant and hobbled somewhat, overly shortened, interrupted—in the middle of a cement corridor, along which runs a series of cells. He is centered in a kind of phalanx of men, flanked in wonderful symmetry to camera right by Beausoleil, who is tuning up an acoustic guitar, absurdly, and to camera left by a stern man in dungarees (a prisoner? just walking about?), plus, well back, a guard perhaps, or a warden. Above and behind Capote, the high, barred windows let in great glowing spears of California sunlight, spears that seem terribly intent on making their way to the impenetrable cells across the corridor where the unseen prisoners must be waiting, desperate for some of that light, light that looks like some sort of salvation out of an illuminated Bible. Capote, though, has caught and basks in a great shower of that brilliant light, that biblical light, pulling him almost out of the frame, as if it were a religious icon, and still he manages to look aloof, smug, indifferent, but somehow demanding.

Whatever hijinks they were getting up to and whatever art they were making together, it seems that Lee became a bit envious of the time her lover and her best friend were spending together. Perhaps she felt that Truman was trying to lure Peter away from her (and perhaps Peter thought Truman, if left to his druthers, would poison Lee against *him*). And so Lee threw down a sort of gauntlet.

"She was eager to return home and she expected Peter to return to New York with her. She ought to have known by now that Peter would do whatever Peter wanted to do." And things only escalated from there. "It was Lee and Peter's first argument, and she went back to New York alone."

Peter carried on with the tour, continued taking pictures. And knowing what we do about all of the mayhem behind the scenes, about the power plays, the debauchery, the preening, we might expect some of that to show up in Peter's photographs. But what Peter saw, perhaps what he was looking for, and what his pictures celebrate—particularly those of Mick, mid-performance, topless against a jet-black backdrop, isolated within infinity, but drenched in sweat and adrenaline and emotion, high like we can only imagine, feeling the power of tens of thousands of people pouring their energy into him—is not at all about a delicately managed celebrity, not at all about artifice. Naked, crazed, balletic, afraid, enraged, enthused—in Peter's pictures from the tour, Mick is an animal, a human animal and even a rock god, but base, powerful, vulnerable, wild, alive.

They may not be altogether perfect, or even among the better pictures taken of a rock tour. But it is remarkable what Peter saw, even within this context, and they fit squarely with pictures he has taken of people on other, different frontiers of experience. In all of his work, it seems, he was looking for what was alive and wild and maybe even possibly, given the right conditions, free, inside of his subjects and, obviously, within himself. These pictures are the only things I ever heard Peter brag about. He told me that he had simply the best pictures of Mick and the tour—that he had billions of them, as if by their sheer numerosity they promise to contain some gems—if only he could be bothered to go back through them all.

Many have suggested that Peter was always falling a bit short of his potential without a great editor who could have seen within his mess the diamonds, and who might have led him to see more and further, as he created his work, who might have coaxed him forward toward revelation instead of repetition.

"Every artist needs an editor," his third wife and widow, Nejma, would say, claiming to have filled the spot by necessity. "What he needs is someone who can prod and browbeat him further into the midnight of his mind's eye," Owen Edwards wrote. "Beard is better than he knows. . . . He is assembling a rolling landscape of life and death that is never mawkish, and in the process he is dredging up out of himself (and those of his pictures' viewers who don't turn away too glibly) primeval stirrings that fundamentally alter what we see."

EVENTUALLY, WHEN PETER AND TERRY SOUTHERN RETURNED to New York at the end of the tour, they were greeted at JFK by Lee Radziwill. "I had a car parked in the long-term lot at JFK. It was a blue '65 Mustang convertible," said Southern. "We got to the airport and Lee Radziwill met us."

Back in the city, Peter too was accustomed to staying with friends, as he didn't have a place of his own—indeed, throughout the 1970s Peter was the Kelly Slater of couch surfing. As his brother Anson notes, Peter was sleeping on his brother Sam's couch so frequently that their mother had gotten involved, disapprovingly making offers of real estate to Sam and his wife if they would teach their brother Peter a lesson and give him the boot.

The photographer Bruce Weber, who would eventually become Peter's neighbor in Montauk, but was then a film student at NYU, would run into Peter at Lexington Labs, where they both had their developing done at the time, and he remembers asking Peter where he was living.

"'Out in the car,' Beard replied, 'in front of the lab.' He'd sleep there at night before going to a friend's apartment to shower and brush his teeth."

It was at this time, too, that Peter developed the reputation for wearing only his Peshawari-style chappal sandals, whether in the bush or in Manhattan, in summer or snow, to parties at Halston's place or 54. Peter bought his sandals in Nairobi, where British colonials and Indian labor had brought the style in the late nineteenth century, from Pitamber Khoda, a shop on Moi Avenue (once called Garment Avenue), and wore them almost exclusively his entire life—even, on an impulsive health kick in the 1990s, going jogging in them.

One has to wonder about a man who goes about in nothing more than a pair of beat-up Afghan sandals, no matter the weather. Like the seemingly thick-skinned and harebrained college kids who wear basketball shorts in the snow to the internet's great merriment, the callousness seems to be the point—an announced immunity to social mores like dress codes, and a performative insensitivity. One wonders if gallivanting about the syringe- and soot-speckled streets of Manhattan in the closest thing to bare feet is the act of a man numbed by his own entitlement trying desperately to feel something, anything, or that of a determined Peter Pan willing the wonderland of his fantasy life into reality.

BUT THE NEVERLAND THAT PETER WAS THEN IMAGINING FOR himself, he felt, was due to include some recognition for the artwork he'd been making, and so he determined to at least get on the ladder of recognition with a gallery show. For this purpose, Peter retained the services of his former schoolmate at Yale, Bobby Zarem, soon to become an infamous publicist in the power circles of Hollywood. Zarem found his way to Joseph Helman, an entrepreneurial young gallerist, recently returned from a sabbatical of sorts in Rome—a former real estate developer who had begun his collecting with Jasper Johns and gone on to give Richard Serra his first show, as well as brokering career-making bids for the likes of Ellsworth Kelly, Frank Stella, and the other high holies of American modern art. Not exactly the type of scene in which you were likely to find Peter or Peter's work. Nevertheless.

Helman was opening a gallery in New York with Irving Blum, the gallerist who'd given Andy his first show, in Los Angeles, and so there was a good deal of interest for their new venture when Zarem called. Helman wasn't all that interested in Peter's photographs. "But they were very persuasive," Helman says. He had lunch with Zarem and Zarem's associate Peggy Siegal, who would go on to create her own rather notorious firm and later represent Jeffrey Epstein. They tried to sell Helman on the event, the glamour and glitter of the opening party. But, Helman says, "I looked at Peter's things and I loved his diaries. I thought the diaries were terrific. I said, 'Yeah, I'll show the diaries.'" And that's what they did. Peter being Peter, he asked his friend Joe Eula, who was then the creative director for Halston (and perhaps the second most famous illustrator in fashion behind Andy Warhol) to help him arrange and install the work in the gallery. "They installed the show and Peter and I became pals," Helman says, "He lived with me for quite a while." Peter's friend Lauren Hutton hosted the party at the gallery on opening night.

"What singles Beard out from the mechanized army that clicks across Africa is the same thing that singled out Ahab from the average sea captain—a kind of madness," Owen Edwards wrote in the *Village Voice* at the time. "For the past several years his intensely personal viewpoint has made me anticipate the emergence of a compelling and unique visionary. In fact, all that has stood in the way of this emergence is Peter Beard himself."

Edwards thought the Hutton and Halston and Warhol crowd confused viewers about the show, and even about Peter, forcing them not to take him and his work seriously. "Whether as a thoroughly novelistic character, a stranger in a whole geography of strange lands, or as a photographer, Beard does not sit lightly to be examined," Edwards wrote.

Edwards, however, took the time to consider the work and took it very seriously indeed. He continued to write about and work with Peter for years and thought that "attention ought to be paid to pictures that contain the kind of portents some raving prophet might bring back from his purgatory under the desert sun." But he felt the society trappings, the celebrity and the champagne were a terrible distraction. "There is a temptation to see Beard, with his manic energy and charged conversation, as the Ancient Mariner, trying with a sort of helpless anguish to ride out all the famous kisses and hugs and get the wedding guests to listen."

But how did the show *do?*

"I'll put it to you this way," Helman told me. "The only Beard I ever sold was to Dick Avedon who wanted to join the gallery also."

FROM THAT FIRST SUMMER OF 1972 WHEN LEE RENTED THE main house of Warhol's Eothen in Montauk, Peter had returned to the little fishing village out past the beaches and country clubs where he'd spent his summers growing up, feeling quite at home there, as free and wild as he had when playing on the beaches there as a boy. And Montauk seemed to be a preserve of the kind of peace and purity he was drawn to, this little hamlet out on the end of the island, at the end of the world. But, he said, "No one could find a house better than Andy's."

What Peter found, though, may have been better even than he could've imagined. In 1972, for $135,000, he bought the last six acres of residential land at the eastern tip of the island. A commanding cliff-top property, bordered by the forested state park, Camp Hero, to the east, to the west by the imposing estate soon to be purchased by Richard Avedon, but to the south, only by the sea, the horizon, infinity. The next year, in 1973, Peter found an old windmill across town, which he picked up and put on a flatbed, trucking it the eight and a half miles to his plot of land, where he gave it pride of place among the scattered clapboard cottages, and thus installed himself as the eccentric resident of the easternmost property on Long Island.

His commitment to spend about half his time in Kenya continued, though, and so in 1974 Peter turned the mill over to his friend, the fashion designer Halston, in exchange for Halston redecorating it. What Halston and his entourage did was get very very high there for a few summers and end up painting the rocks red.

When Peter finally put his touch on the place, he made it a bit like Hog Ranch West, with prints and negatives sitting everywhere collecting sand and sea salt, with tusks and trophies from his African jaunts standing here and there, next to Warhols and Rauschenbergs and Wyeths and Bacons. When Mick and Keith used to visit, there were parties all night—and rumors even made it out that there was a snake pit in the windmill.

"The snake pit was very real," photographer Larry Fink tells me.

In July of 1977, Fink traveled out to Montauk to photograph Peter, and made some of the most incredible images of the artist at the time—partying and carrying on in and around his home—despite the fact that the two didn't exactly get along. "He was such a spoiled mess of a guy, and he wasn't for me a personable guy," Fink tells me. "I of course bumped into him at fashion shows or what have you, but it was only ever a bump into because he was actively out courting another skinny blonde. But as far as work is concerned, I actually liked it. I am a political guy; I come from the Left, low middle class energy. My mother and father were communists. And Peter and his work represented such an upper-class experience, that, back then, it had no appeal to me. Now, looking back, he was an artist; he told *his* story."

In 1977 Fink had just received a Guggenheim grant, to photograph two poles of the economic spectrum. "One was the upper class . . . debutante balls and masquerade parties, and finally I found out about Peter and his soirees and it led me out to him." So if Fink came out to photograph Peter as representative of the upper class, Peter certainly played to a stereotype of a rich prick. "He was enthralled with me because I'd just gotten the Guggenheim and that was big stuff." Fink says. "He wanted to know how I got it and he said, 'How much is it?' At the time, it was twelve grand, which was a lot of money for me; it was taking care of the whole year. And he said, 'Oh, I just spent that on a helicopter ride to bring these beautiful women out here.'"

Peter had indeed flown three women out for the occasion. The guys were smoking weed. Fink says there was cocaine. And then, to show off, or to make a scene, to provoke those in attendance, Peter went out on the diving board he had installed on the edge of the cliff. "If you went off it you would die," Fink says now with some astonishment. "He went out on it, backwards, with one of these women in his arms, and started to bounce on the board," trying to get Fink to take pictures of it, Fink says. "And I said, 'Hey man, what's up with you? Get back here. I'm not going to take a picture of that.' And he refused because he was this adventurer. But to me he was extremely vulgar."

Caroline Cushing Graham, who was for a while Peter's sister-in-law (when he was married to Minnie and she was married to Minnie's brother Harold), with whom Peter lived for a time when he got out of Payne Whitney, says that the very first time she met Peter, she watched him dive off this diving board—and break his back.

One of the images Fink did take from this time in Montauk is of Peter and a young topless woman having a picnic out at the cliff edge of the property. (Fink told me he thought that the woman—presumably one of those who'd ridden out on the $12,000 helicopter ride—was Delfina Rattazzi, whom Joyce Maynard had profiled in the *Times* earlier that year in an article titled "Heiress, Working Girl." At the time, Rattazzi was Jackie O's assistant at Viking; she was a part of the Agnelli family [who own Fiat], and a consultant with the Dia Foundation, working at the time on Walter de Maria's *Lightning Field* in New Mexico and helping to acquire the dormant volcano in Arizona where James Turrell is still working on his *Roden Crater* installation. She was, according to the *Times*, the It Girl of the day, friends with Diana Vreeland and Babe Paley. But when I asked Rattazzi if it was her in this picture, she told me that, no, in fact, she was not in the habit then or ever of going around topless to be photographed with infamous rakes.)

This image, which is now in the permanent collection at MoMA and ICP, captures perfectly the lifestyle Peter had constructed for himself at the time. Grand as the natural landscape over which he presided like a kikoi-wearing Pan. As free as the wind sweeping in off the Atlantic, carrying the four corners of the Earth in its gusts. Effortlessly sexy, as chic sophisticates along the Côte d'Azur might've been in the jet-set age, topless, promiscuous, louche. Supremely elegant.

God, Fink would hate that description. "My aspiration with the upper class was to understand them," he says. "I thought they were going to disappear! Such was my belief in the revolution."

IN 1977 PETER GOT WHAT WAS TO THAT POINT THE BIGGEST break in his career, a massive one-man show dedicated to his elephant images at the International Center of Photography in Manhattan. A show that would put him in the pantheon of fine artist photographers, alongside the other crossovers from fashion, like Avedon.

For years he had been documenting the unfolding of an event he had long forecast, the massive die-off of elephants in Tsavo National Park—and for the occasion he went back to complete the story.

He found thirty-five thousand elephants that, having reproduced to a number well beyond what the resources of their fenced-in Eden could sustain, were dying en masse from starvation and dehydration. Over the span of two weeks, in a borrowed Cessna plane, crisscrossing thousands of acres of Tsavo wasteland, where there had once been dense forest, heavily wooded by baobabs even, but which was now a desert, torn to shreds by the elephants, Peter (illegally) took thousands upon thousands of frames.

From this bird's-eye perspective, as opposed to the shoulder-high POV with which we are familiar, a vanishing point or horizon giving us scale, depth, and a sense of our place in the world, these images are at first a bit disorienting. Almost claustrophobic as they squash us up against the gory subject and the ground immediately beneath them; everything is foreground; they force our confrontation of the images in an almost scientific way—resembling matter on a slide seen through a microscope. The pits in which the elephants lie like dark cells, their wreck and ruin evidence for a kind of plague, a rottenness in the core of our life, a pandemic that we cannot soon cure, if even we had any interest in doing so.

Sometimes the shadow of Peter's small plane enters the frame, passing over the divots in the dirt, the literal pits of despair, dug by their dying, writhing inhabitants, and the scale of the plane triggers another human association, something now buried in our DNA, of images of bomber planes in the wars of the twentieth century, planes dropping bombs that leave craters just like these we see, and create death on the same sort of industrial scale, another echo of the massive destruction of which we and nature itself are exclusively capable.

These are the images that so enchanted the painter Francis Bacon that he planned to create sculptures inspired by them, by the massive scaffolding of bleached-out bones of the elephants, and their thick hides, sagging over the bones like terrible circus tents.

Back home with these harrowing images of doom and destruction, Peter set about creating a new edition of *The End of the Game*, adding an extended coda of his incredibly bleak, graphic images of the Tsavo elephants, which he called *Neither Hope nor Dread Attend*. While he was assembling the proofs for the new book, kneeling over a mosaic of prints scattered across the floor of a friend's studio in Manhattan, on the night of July 27, Peter received a strange phone call. It was the caretaker of his home in Montauk. The mill house, as well as all of the works by Warhol, by Robert Rauschenberg, Andrew Wyeth, and Francis Bacon, not to mention his own daily diaries going back decades, and souvenirs, gifts from Jackie, from Lee, from Karen Blixen, and objects he had collected throughout his life, had gone up in a massive fire. Everything was gone. Ash.

Peter absorbed this news in silence and hung up the phone. He returned to work.

"I had so much pressure on me," he said later, looking back on this moment, "I didn't have time to think of any negatives. And for a moment I felt a tear coming up on my tragic and sentimental eyeball . . ." Then, catching himself, as if he'd gone off message, and suddenly remembered the spin he had settled on, the version of the story that suited the image he was trying to project, to hew to—or, perhaps, just suddenly remembering the epiphany—he added a second reason, subtly canceling out the first. "Whoa, I thought, now here is a choice: you can either feel sorry for yourself, worry, and do all of the negative things, or you just forget it and go on. It seemed clear to me that a lot of people's problem is self-pitying and worrying and it's not necessary."

A bit of a tricky thing to say when one has the good fortune to own an excess of works by Andy Warhol that one can afford to lose. On the other hand, this was at the core of Peter's ethos. This is truly who he wanted to be in the world, and how he tried to conduct himself, whether he had to do it with knuckles gone white from the exertion or it was merely in keeping with his natural inclination.

When, moments later, Ruth Ansel, who was designing the new book with Peter, asked him about the phone call, Peter just muttered something about everything being lost and carried on working through the night, much to Ansel's astonishment. Perhaps as some form of grieving, or as a way to avoid being confronted with the evidence of his loss, Peter didn't even go out to the mill site in Montauk until more than five months later, in late November, when even the ash had blown away. And if he refused to view even that catastrophe as a personal tragedy, he was hard-pressed to view what came next as anything other than a farce.

In the hopes of outdoing even Avedon, perhaps, who had famously printed his photographs for the 1975 show at the Marlborough Gallery in New York on a scale suited to the side of a barn, Peter printed up a few massive images of his elephants for his show, prints with which he wrapped the entire façade of the ICP building at 1130 Fifth Avenue the day before his opening—like something on par with the work Jean-Claude and Christo were doing at the time, wrapping an entire building, but with elephants the size of a city block.

That night, with fate sufficiently tempted, the elements kicked up again, this time wind that shredded the prints and scattered the bits all down Fifth Avenue. Pictures from that day show Peter, alone, chasing the ribbon-scroll remains of his images across the street to Central Park, his face set in a kind of determined scowl. But if his idea to wrap the building was sort of brilliant, what he did with the torn prints was even better—reassembling them inside the townhouse, in a curtain of strips, so that, upon ascending to the second floor, viewers would be walking through and among the massive, almost life-size creatures. As with everything Peter did at the time, it caused a stir, as did the sunken pit of pictures below, giving the attendees the feeling of looking down on the elephants in their self-dug graves.

The show was a hit. Afterward, Peter and his friends—all the stars in heaven, it seems, from the Stones to Jackie O and Lauren Hutton and Capote and Warhol and the rest—went to the recently opened Studio 54 to celebrate.

CHAPTER 7

Beyond Gauguin

Until recently," Gore Vidal once wrote, "I assumed that most people were like myself." It was Vidal's experience, he said, that the Walter Mitty–ish fantasies of youth—imagining oneself to be as dashing as James Bond, say, as adventurous as Robinson Crusoe—*that* sort of "daydreaming ceases when the real world becomes interesting and reasonably manageable."

After a close consideration of the enduring appeal of Edgar Rice Burroughs, though, especially the Tarzan books, Vidal had to say, "Now I am not so certain. Pondering the life and success of Burroughs leads one to believe that a good many people find their lives so unsatisfactory that they go right on year after year telling themselves stories in which they are able to dominate their environment in a way that is not possible in this overorganized society."

When everything gets too crazy, too confusing, too overwhelming, it is our natural tendency to dream about unwinding it all, about a life we might live free from all the concerns that we deal with today in our superconnected, hyperdigital lives. In his idealized man of the jungle, swinging vine to vine, speaking to the birds and the beasts, and summoning all of the strength and wisdom of nature, Burroughs gives us a kind of un-superhero, an elemental masculine avatar we can imagine ourselves to be if only we were not so entangled by the matrix of modernity. Tarzan is who we might be if we weren't so addicted to social media, tethered to our cubicle desks, working pointless jobs to pay off insurmountable debt. He is man unsullied by civilization, pure, prelapsarian Adam, perfectly at home in the real world—as opposed to the paved, plasticky, preprogrammed, air-conditioned world many of us now inhabit. Tarzan's jungle is, like the Eden of Genesis, a kind of romanticized national park—sometimes a bit scary and even supernatural, but ultimately as lush and lovely and benign as Kew Gardens in the springtime.

This sort of fetishizing of a semi-mythological, prehistoric nature (and natural man)—the ultimate in "the good old days" imaginings—is what Peter called *primitiva*, and he both loved it and smirkingly scoffed at it. Of course, we all participate in a little low-grade *primitiva*-pining these days, from our scenic screensavers of pristine (i.e., untouched by man) landscapes, to the calm, Corona-commercial coastlines of our holiday moodboards. From there, if we were to punch up the aesthetic involvement and personal stakes of our personal Eden imaginings, past the lifestyle influencers draping themselves about the caverns in Petra, say, past even Henri Rousseau, who fetishized the forests of the South Seas and the indigenous peoples of the Americas though he never left his home in France, all the way to the very end of the *primitiva* spectrum, we would get to Gauguin.

In Gauguin's Northern, Western Gaze aesthetics, purity and artistic truth become synonymous with primitivity. In his Tahitian pastoral pictures, we see and feel, vividly, that idea of equatorial abundance—this is a land of purity and plenty, we sense, left by a benevolent creator, before the fall, where the forests of fruit trees by balmy shores lay down their sweet treats to beautiful Adams and Eves without their ever having to lift a finger to find them.

It is tempting, even natural to place Peter within this tradition, and of course he even courted this idea, titling one of his pieces *Beyond Gauguin*, as if to suggest he'd gone even further afield, farther South, deeper into the DNA of man than the stockbroker-turned-painter had, for a more raw and vivid experience of reality, the better to communicate it back to the rest of us through his own art. Peter probably thrilled at the similarities between himself and Gauguin. As a punchy synopsis of Somerset Maugham's *The Moon and Sixpence*, which was based on the life of Gauguin, puts it, there is plenty of room for comparison, even if much more would need to be said about awfulness: "The story of Charles Strickland, a middle-aged stockbroker who abandons his middle-class life, his family, and his duties to start painting, as he has always wanted to do. He is from then on an awful human being, wholly devoted to his ideal: beauty."

In life, Peter did quite closely follow the Gauguin/Strickland model, moving to the exotic southern climes, adopting a lifestyle (or at least a simulacrum of it) free from the trappings of the more "civilized" world. And he did indeed dedicate himself to beauty, to his pursuit of its many forms—in people, places, and wildlife. Maybe as an escape from a life that would have required lace-up shoes and scratchy slacks. Maybe because he didn't ever want to grow up, didn't want to age out of the stories of Burroughs and Haggard. And maybe he was an entitled decadent who ran away from the world of worries because he could, ran after women because he wanted to, and decorated his life and work just so because he liked it that way. But maybe—and if we consider the substance of his work and philosophy, this checks out—maybe Peter's entire project, the sum of his life and work, was an effort to rewild himself, the way a gardener might seek to bring a plot of land back to its original and most harmonious state, an effort to bring himself back to a place before the fall of man, before stock markets, before wool slacks, before even Tarzan and Jane.

Imagine if you could unlearn the programming of modern

society, not just table manners and the etiquette, but the compulsions, values, aspirations, trappings . . . , if you could remove yourself from the expectations of the Joneses, could divorce your aesthetic values from the marketplace and fashion magazines. What if you could return your body and brain to a sort of Tarzanian, prelapsarian state, could unlearn all that you had been taught that you feel is against your nature and could return again to a purer state of the human animal, free in the world. What if you could be totally wild? Might you then, there, be closer to the natural rhythms of our species, your real appetites and desires, real forms of fulfilment—and further from the anxiety and worry that consume you now?

That was Peter's mission as I see it, to bring himself back to the purer expression of the species, to become animal, or at least be more comfortable with his nature than the rest of us are. He desired to return to his more natural state of being, to become more a part of the "wild-deer-ness," as he liked to call it, in order to be free from the phoniness he abhorred, to see in a way that was truer to himself, to the fullest expression of man, outside of his own particular time and the duties and moralities ascribed to him.

"I would like to make images which reflect all kinds of things that I feel instinctively about my own species," he wrote in the diaries (on March 31, 1986, thirty-four years to the day before he went missing), "and I would like, in my arbitrary way, to bring one nearer to the actual human being. Now this is a very difficult thing. I get nearer by going farther away."

Part of the way Peter hoped to achieve this rewilding of himself was in study and imitation of cultures he felt retained a bit more of the purer stuff, closer to the raw, primitive source, closer indeed to the wildlife and the soil, less sullied by civilization's slacks and shoes, if you will. Not precisely a "fake it 'til you make it" scenario, and perhaps not even what we might now call cultural appropriation, though he did indeed revere the wisdom, lifestyle, legacies, and beauty of the tribal men and women in East Africa and elsewhere and sought to celebrate them and come closer to them by nearing their ways of life and dress, etc. But he was not exactly on a journey to become one of them, to assimilate with the Maasai or Waliangulu. He hoped to absorb their stories, collect some of their teachings (and talismans), in order to give him a fuller, richer understanding of the world—the better to flavor his own stories when he returned to couch surfing around Manhattan.

Coming of age alongside the beatniks and the jet-set eccentrics as he did, artists or remittance men of the imperial nations who'd shucked off their families, or vice versa, moving to somewhere exotic and permissive was quite ordinary in Peter's day. The aesthetes with their pet toucans and heroin habits in Tangier were of course well known by then, as were the be-turbaned rock stars from Liverpool on the hippie trail in Goa, yogi poets in the East Village, and Italian heiresses in kaftans and rubies. Collecting clothing, styles, artifacts, and insights from others' cultures might be the way your eccentricity manifested, but it was also a way to demonstrate cultural openness, worldliness, perhaps decadence, but certainly a kind of cultivated wisdom about the world and its peoples. It might have been superficial, but those with the privilege to appropriate the customs and fashions of other cultures, the better to costume themselves and behave in ways that amused them, would have thought of it as progressivism, sensitivity, even solidarity—indulging in the freedom to identify as whomever they pleased as a way of biting their thumbs at society's judgments (of them, and of the "other" with whom they were identified through talismans, clothing, affectations), all with the primary goal of better inhabiting some more pure version of themselves—but justified, surely, as being a bridge-building operation to a more open world, a kind of polyglot utopianism, where all were one and recognized the oneness in one another.

Of course, what they were actually doing was a kind of tokenism, taking a piece of a culture, removing it from its context, its heritage, and even its intended meaning, to place it within their own narrative, as part of their own image, to signal something else entirely. This is what I mean when I suggest that Gauguin, for example, as well as Rousseau and Peter, were working with something we might call the Northern Gaze. Peter knew very well how the folks back home would read the tribal markings and jewelry and Maasai *shukas* and spears *because he read them that way*. Not that he really troubled himself about it too much, but I suspect that he understood that, if an audience existed for his work, his audience was indeed the folks back home. People who had the same referents, the same general viewpoint on the world, et cetera. In reality, in his mind, he was probably his only audience—his elaborate, compulsive, obsessive, visionary work on his diaries, in most cases, never even received an audience other than himself. He did it only to please his eye, to arrange the world that he could control just so, to his aesthetic liking, and to keep his dangerous mind occupied with anything other than introspection.

When trained on the subjects in his pictures from Turkana, for example, Peter's Northern Gaze necessarily *others* its point of study, making a fetish object of the person, the tool, the necklace, the thatched-roof home. Even if Peter might have said he was merely reporting in the early days, or working closer to religious iconography later—Beat-ifying the subject, so to speak—the gaze cannot help but cast upon the person, the landscape, and their legacy a kind of hysterical projection. The gaze is capable of assigning only the meaning and morals that are particular to the artist and his home school of thought—because it is a tool of a cultural type of colonialism. And like the other, original sort of colonialism, the gaze bags up the bits and pieces that it can plunder and pillage, to bring them back into the marketplace in the North, leaving little in the way of benefit for its subjects. But its effect on the imagination and understanding of the audience, the citizenry of the North, is the same. The Northern Gaze is a central tool of (neo)colonialism. It creates a necessarily reductive image for a purpose: To scare and create fear and loathing, in some cases. Or to titillate, stimulate, and endear—if the propaganda is aimed at bringing in, say, tourism. And even if we are to always grant him the benefit of the doubt, read in his efforts the best intentions, there always creeps around the edges of Peter's pictures a bit of this fetish for *exoticisme*, a kind of fantastical othering of Kenya, the magical kingdom of Maasai and lions into something that might scan in a pavilion at Epcot Center: a land of great big beasts, broad horizons, and Stone Age tribesmen just barely if at all raising a fig leaf to cover themselves.

This remains probably the stickiest bit of Peter's work to unpack. Of course, he would have screamed and moaned that he was the most uncivilized man of all and if anything he was celebrating the nobility of his subjects and anyway all of that is phony nonsense. The fact is that when he does center non-white Kenyans in his writings, it is to ascribe to them superhuman attributes of physical strength or acumen. Particularly gifted hunters and trackers are assigned mystic intuition, possessed of arcane ability. The Turkana tracker Larsili, "who could read the plain like an open book," for example, is described in *The End of the Game* as having *Dr. Doolittle* levels of animal insight and being able to run for eleven miles (at five thousand feet altitude) just to deliver a message, "confident about everything and nothing."

Galo-Galo, in much of Peter's writings, is cast as a kind of Man Friday (with Peter, of course, the ultimate Robinson Crusoe) except for when he is brought under the Gaze for elevation into the order of the sublime. Here he is rendered as man at his best. A symbol. An avatar. Not a specific being with a personality and weird humors, but an emblem, an idea.

It is interesting, within this context, to consider Peter's book from 1975, *Longing for Darkness*, in which he lends his space and cachet—his platform, as we'd say now—to his friend, chef, and figure from Karen Blixen's *Out of Africa*, Kamante, to tell his own story. Or, well, sort of compelled him to tell it, in the way that Peter the charismatic cajoler was wont to do. I imagine that what Peter was thinking was that he might create a kind of parallax view on Old Africa, complementing his own favorite work of literature in the way that, say, *The Meursault Investigation* retells Camus's *The Stranger* from the point of view of an Algerian character who is affected by the narrative, to retell a classic story of colonialism from the perspective of a Kikoi man who as a boy was taken in by Blixen and worked in her employ until she pulled up stakes and left for Denmark. In the creation of the book, Peter of course did a lot of the leg work, recording and having translated the memories and myths remembered by Kamante, and then packaging and art directing it all just so—Peter's specialty. In fact, the project lingered for some time until Jacqueline Onassis took up the cause and agreed to write an afterword, which was all the publisher needed to put it to press. (This was the same year that Jackie began her work as an editor at Viking.) If it is perhaps not on the literary level of, say, Paul Bowles translating the poems of Mohammed Mrabet, that is to say nothing of the caliber of Kamante's stories and the folktales he brings into it. The book is still a bit of a marvel and certainly was astoundingly unique at the time. It is an almost direct-to-Westerners communication from a lifelong subject of English colonialism—a rarity then as it would be now, and we can imagine the pride and congratulatory glow Peter must have felt in its creation.

With hindsight, though, the book is unsuccessful precisely because of its Peter-ness. What in some of his other mediums comes off as playful and humorous, in this context reads as somewhat infantilizing of its subject, diminishing the context and experience. The book itself suffers from the flattening gaze. Folktales and huts and spears are depicted in line drawings, made by Kamante himself but with the opposite effect of the embellishments made by Peter's constant collaborators of the time, Mwengui and Kivoi, whose work on Peter's great big prints of his photos makes for a wild and explosive juxtaposition. Here Peter's *primitiva* feels a bit icky, as if he is equating oral traditions and folktales with something childish.

Ultimately, the book fails because it does not appropriately attempt to create a clear portrait of Kamante, with the kind of interiority we expect in Northern, Western writing; instead it gives up, settling only on the *other* Kamante and his Kikuyu tales and experiences, painting them as a sort of quaint, folkloric picaresque. Which raises the question, who benefited from the work? The literal, financial question caused a great deal of trouble, for Peter and for Kamante and then for Kamante's family, who claimed they should be granted ownership of a part of Hog Ranch as compensation. Kamante has said that he never received a single dollar for the book and was only ever paid a small sum, around $50 a month, for his work on the ranch. Peter, for his part, maintained that the $75,000 he received as an advance from the publisher was quickly spent, as well as some more of his own money, in producing the book. But more abstractly, who came away from this project in better shape? The readership who took away perspective-enhancing insights from Kamante's experience, delighting in the exotic tales and imagery? Kamante, whose story is now perhaps fuller than first rendered as a character in Blixen's book? Peter, who celebrated the release with a lavish party at the Carlyle with all the press and feting available, whose art and self-image project (and perhaps rely on the strength of his claim to) a kind of intimate fluency with Africa and Africans?

If the latter, then is Kamante's story, in Peter's grand oeuvre, very much different from the giraffes leaning into the frame in his self-portraits, from the spears and skulls and safari tents with which he decorated his life and work? Is it anything other than a prop? This question would be made of his work with increasing regularity into the 1980s, as he began to bring together the fashion shoots of home with the Africana of Kenya, draping models on rocks and cheetahs or vice versa. What is the prop and what is the message, and with Peter, how much did it matter?

PETER THE JESTER, PETER THE PROVOCATEUR, PETER THE publicity stuntman liked to play with these elements—and hoped to capitalize on them when in 1975 he met the young daughter of a former Somali diplomat studying in Nairobi. "I'll start off with how Iman got out of Africa," he said later, when he was going to set the record straight, untangling fact and fiction, "because we invented a more glamorous story for our mutual interests."

At birth, Iman Abdulmajid was called Zahra, meaning luminous, something miraculous, but was renamed the Arabic equivalent of Faith by her grandfather as being more pious and masculine. The daughter of a Somali diplomat and Arabic teacher, she was born in Mogadishu in 1955, five years before Somalian independence from Italy. Raised in Ethiopia and in Somalia, at boarding schools in Saudi Arabia and Cairo, a straight-A student, Iman with her family fled the revolution and chaos in her home country. She had recently been a resident of Kenya and was a little bit obsessed with American popular culture when she first met Peter Beard in the New Stanley Hotel. "This was March of 1975," he said later. "Kamante and I were just going to have lunch . . . in the usual stress and density of Nairobbery, the most clogged up, ex-colonial nightmare of all time. This amazing Somali girl was striding down the street, and I just said, 'Kamante, look at that amazing sight, in the middle of Nairobbery.'" As they were sitting down to lunch, who should appear in the hotel but Iman, the "sight" he had just pointed out. "I just went up to her and said,

'I hope you're not going to let all those aesthetics go to waste. Don't you think we should just record some of it on film. Get you into the world of visual communication?' Of course, like every African, she was desperate to get out of Africa. So we had a nice conversation."

And the rest of us shall applaud Iman's forbearance in not pouring Peter's probable bullshot all over his head and walking away. For her part, Iman credits the Kenyan photographer Mirella Ricciardi with first seeing her and inviting her to Hog Ranch to shoot pictures with her and Peter. However it came about, Iman did sit for portraits by Peter and Ricciardi at Hog Ranch—with cameos by Kamante and Peter's pet eland. But she denies any part of the mythmaking Peter began spinning about her from that moment. In his version, when he called up his friend, the model-turned-agent Wilhelmina Cooper, who had recently begun her own agency, he said, "This is a great African, with great poise and wildness and beauty. She could add so much to the New York scene." Which was apparently not only an acceptable appraisal but enough to secure Wilhelmina's approval and plane tickets.

Of course, Peter called a press conference to greet his "discovery."

"At the press conference," Peter later said, "what we said was that we'd run into each other in Kenya's Northern Frontier District"—this the bleak wilderness around Lake Rudolf where he had recently done his study of Nile crocodiles with Alastair Graham. "Big fucking deal," he says of the fabrication. "Who wants to say I ran into someone on Standard Street in Nairobi? Probably hooking."

Well, in very short order, the journalists who were not taken in by this very obvious chicanery gave Iman a very hard time. As if she were to blame for Peter's publicity stunt. Eventually even the Black Panthers issued a statement, wondering why the fashion industry needed to import beautiful Black women from Africa when there was plenty of homegrown beauty about. Chaos ensued. And still Peter managed to go on about believing in *authenticity*. "We wanted authenticity," he said. "Iman came with her amazing neck and her poise and her elegance and her authenticity."

He went on to say, "This was before Black models," before correcting himself to acknowledge that Beverly Johnson had previously covered a Condé Nast title, but still putting Iman forth as a pioneer. "I think Iman made work for models."

Then he proceeded to launch into what reads today as a completely unhinged rant about the state of Black America, presuming both to speak on behalf of Iman, of Black Americans, and of the body politic in whose interest other, different representations of Blackness he was then recommending. At one point, he even veers into a strange justification for inviting Richard Avedon and not Gordon Parks to move into the house next door to him. It is objectification and racist rationalization down the line. "Forget black," he said. "Because Iman is elegance," which he seems to suggest is somehow in contrast with Blackness. "Black America is having a very hard time achieving elegance," he said. "They're going into ugliness and rap culture aggressiveness and loudness." The "they" there is repellent enough, but still he goes on. "Iman is elegant, that's a big difference. . . . And that's what blacks need, and nobody wants to hear that. . . . Iman brought an enormous elevation of pecking order possibility for the blacks. She was a work of art. She was a living sculpture," he says, and then perhaps tells on himself as he never had before, making plain that in his way of thinking Black is distinct and separate from art, while art and elegance exist elsewhere, within the world of whiteness, we can presume. "That's what I'm into now. A marriage of opposites," he says, "the most primitive and the most poised. Sophisticated and primitive. Strong and very sensitive. Beautiful and tough. Sense of humor and very serious. Very much for the black cause, very far from the black cause."

SOMETIME AFTER THE FIRE DESTROYED NEARLY EVERYTHING of the mill in Montauk in July 1977, Peter was able to salvage a few charred, smoke-blackened diaries from the ruin. Of course he absolutely adored these, loved the bites the fire had made to the edges of the pages, how the heat had fattened the leather bindings, melted the glue, and cast across the pages a kind of magical treasure map patina. He immediately began photographing the diaries themselves, artifacts of his creation and ruin and evidence of the vitality and inferno of nature. Some of the most famous images from this time feature the model Donyale Luna, who would later be called the first Black supermodel, sprawled out, nearly nude, in a catlike arch atop the charred diaries on the very edge of the clifftop in Montauk.

They are extraordinary pictures, among the most recognizably *Peter* in all of his work. I think they suggest that it is all props all the way down in his art: nudity, nature, and decoration. The blindingly beautiful Luna is slim and sexually suggestive as she straddles the leather masculine diaries embellished in ornate style like illuminated religious texts, the wisdom and labor of all of mankind, bound, preserved, and then burned to a crisp by forces that will always render our efforts here futile, petty, and insignificant. These forces are palpable everywhere in frame, from the harrowing descent of the cliffs behind Luna and the diaries to the violent winds we can feel, ready to pull us all over the edge. And it is all so breathtakingly beautiful! Maybe that is the point of all of Peter's work, that this terror and titillation, the vastness and danger, the futility and lust and depravity and fear and brutality and violence, is all so, so beautiful, if looked at in the right light and, of course, arranged just so.

Peter's girlfriend at the time, the German model Magritte Rammé, was featured in two similar sittings the year before— nude, lying between two elephant tusks on the basement floor of the British Museum, and nude sitting astride a single giant tusk at the edge of Peter's property in Montauk, the ivory almost incandescent white in an enormous phallic curve from her thighs up to the heavens. Various prints, with unique embellishments, were made of both of these rather striking images. If we are to see Peter striving for symbol and suggested meaning anywhere in his work, it is right here, in the images of Luna and Rammé. But apart from the sort of totemic significance the things themselves bring with them, and the almost adolescent arrangement of the ivory phallus, I think we have to accept that, in fact, there is no there there, no deeper symbolic meaning to these or any of Peter's works. See, for example, the diaries.

The endlessly intricate pages of Peter's diaries, made with religious if not compulsive consistency every day, in some cases all day, from his youth until well into his old age, were his closest companion throughout his life. So if we are to find meaning, thought, insight, planning, we would find them here. And yet . . .

"Is this a passion, an inertia, or a sickness," Peter's friend, the poet, filmmaker, and historian Jonas Mekas wondered about Peter's diaries in his own notebooks of the era, "this effort to retain, to preserve the past? Is it a sentimental preoccupation, a child's box of colorful mementos, scraps, miniatures, pebbles? Or is this a laugh into the face of the present, this pompous rooster which, as soon as it's gone, ends up in Peter's book, on one of the pages, and it takes glue to hold it together—that much and nothing more. History, past, all its emotions and its bustle, its dreams, fetishes, all the objects, they are all gone except what's left in Peter's books, displayed there for everybody to see, time metaphors," well, those that survived the fire. "It's Peter's gallows humor," Mekas concludes, "a joke on reality, history, civilization. . . . I don't think he keeps it in order to remember it. I don't think he's doing it for any reason, purpose, or goal. He just does it, like some insects or worms do. Collecting crumbs of civilization into huge anthills of books and diaries."

This line of thought leads Mekas to consider himself in the process, to wonder, "Isn't a cinema verité, a diarist filmmaker motivated by the same urges? Peter . . . or myself—we all end up in the same personal fantasy world, expressing not the outside but the inside, the verité of our minds. How else could it be? Isn't our inside made up of bits and strokes of the outside? And vice versa?"

But then surely there would be some trace of portraiture within Peter's diaries. Until, considering still further, Mekas comes to the same conclusion I have. "By seeing and reseeing, during the last ten years, Peter's diary books," he writes, "the uncountable number of 'real' details and bits of civilization glued and penciled and splashed upon the pages—every page almost a sutra—signs, signatures, representations, I have often wondered if, in truth, any of these details really mean anything in themselves. If there is any meaning in them or to them, it's the design itself, the book itself, the effort, the act of doing it—which is both bigger and more simple than any individual meaning of any individual page or detail."

There is, in this image Mekas gives us, of Peter compulsively collecting the entirety of pop culture and regurgitating it, rearranging it, annotating it, embellishing it, editing it, and presenting it just so, something of a character out of Borges. Keeping so detailed and thorough a record of his life and times that he is in fact re-creating a to-scale scrapbook of existence as it happens, or as he experiences it. Peter is making an entirely new pop culture out of the one in which he lives. Cut-and-paste: by collage and annotation, he is making the material of the real world his own. And, in a way, that is a lot like what one does on the internet every day today—picking, curating, capturing, and collecting the detritus of culture to cobble together something like memory, something like identity, something like a way of life and even in some cases a career.

"Time," Mekas wrote, "turns everything to dust—paintings, stones, pyramids. Films fade, frescoes fall off the walls, polluted rains eat up the architecture." And diaries go up in flames. "What survives, survives only through a mysterious act of grace, and even so only temporarily."

It cannot then be that art matters because it endures, because it prevails against chance, by mercy or miracle. What matters, surely for creators like Mekas and Beard, is the miracle of creation itself. Their play, then, is the thing.

That seems expressly the point of the diaries for Peter: the doing—and not only as an act of construction, but also, and maybe especially, in its opportunity cost. For what they afforded him an escape from, in that they helped him to avoid thinking, planning, and entering into the realm of introspection, analysis, and higher consciousness entirely. The process of gluing and inking, and often bleeding on these pages, in trancelike fixation, focused, occupied, obsessed, for hours or days on end, was Peter's form of meditation. This work kept him grounded to a very specific tactile point in the universe, kept him at work, problem solving—where to put this cutting, how to stretch this curlicue on a letter, blotting, dotting, crossing tees. It is here that he was able to retain his "Zen mind, beginner's mind," to borrow a phrase from the midcentury (and D. T. Suzuki's treatise that had been a hit, particularly among the Beats) that he would've understood. He was at play, childlike, creating, sure, but also, and this may have been the most important point, *not thinking*, not second-guessing, not planning or regretting, or feeling guilty or walking the dangerous ladder of thoughts that had previously led him to the bottle of sleeping pills and a private room at Payne Whitney.

"It is kind of fun to go through them," he told me, after he'd made another fifty or so, after the fire. "Not for any proud reason—it's just infantile, that's what it is."

"But they're a documentary of your existence," I said, trying to lead the witness, if you will. When he didn't bite, I told him that I keep a diary. "I'm sort of obsessive about it—less so than I was when I was younger—but a lot of it is my trying to describe what I'm feeling or figure out who I am."

"Well, that's a real diary," he said.

"But I won't go back to it. I'm scared of who I was."

"I got around that," Peter said. "Being so pathetic, I don't read. I just . . . do things—writing out interviews you can't read, on pictures of footprints and things like that. I kind of like the idea of nailing the thing down and not really showing too much about it. There's just so much you can take for collage nowadays."

And even with all of that available to him, in thousands and thousands upon pages of diaries, collaged in beautiful, vibrant color, layered in newspaper clippings and magazine tears, inky and bloody splotches, as well as Peter's own indelible, incredible handwritten script, there is absolutely nothing about what he was thinking, no trace of an interior monologue, of reflection, critical analysis, self-examination—not a whit. No tremors, even, from some deep subconscious cavern to suggest he was particularly occupied with . . . anything. No pattern whatever. Just decoration, purely and utterly superficial. And I wonder if that makes them even somehow more remarkable. For all of their potential to communicate—with all of the various media and all of the latent messages within—they say absolutely nothing. Well, nothing other than the score of the Giants game, the number of the hotel where Mick Jagger was staying when he called, and the address of some letter that just arrived. They are like shopping lists that manage not only to hide the recipe around which they were constructed, but also suggest that their author had no appetite whatsoever.

As we know, after the accident on Shingle Island in Lake Rudolf, during the production of what would become *Eyelids of Morning*, when Peter's colleague Wildman so carefully preserved the pages of his diary, Peter had a kind of aesthetic revelation. He now saw the layering of media and collaging as a method of making even more beautiful the images he'd been taking. The diaries became a kind of workshop for that process. Not that he made studies the way we think of some artists as doing, building up to scale from smaller renderings, trial sketches, and the rest. Every single time Peter began a page of his diaries or a new collage, the end result was utterly unique, possessed of its own purpose, reason, and goal, its own thing, one of one. He never made one piece in service of developing another. But the smaller-scale diary pages were lighter lifts than some of the grand-scale collages, and it was through the repetition of the work he had done in those various volumes, day after day, year after year, that he had established his sort of artistic signature. Which is not to lessen them. They are, each of them, astonishing in their own right, on the same level with all of his work. To his mind they were certainly all of a piece, part of the same project. It is just a bit more difficult to sell a diary page than a collage at Christie's.

They are, as Owen Edwards said of Beard, better even than he knew. They are more extraordinary, in fact, than we have given them credit for being, in part because of the way they recorded their times, and in part for the absolutely visionary state in which they were made, like outsider art made out of mass media. The diaries are remarkable for what they might tell us, and future generations, about what it felt like to be alive in the twentieth century. They seem to be the greatest transcription of a modern life, boring, beautiful, banal, and sublime, with a brain saturated in popular culture—a life lived with a fascination for and proximity to the beautiful and damned of his time.

Although the diary pages are themselves not exactly meta-reflections on a primary subject, they *are* pure stream-of-consciousness transcriptions of the rhythms and the visual and temperamental interests of a unique figure in pop culture. As such, they are among the best renderings I know of the workings of our mind today—of our distracted reality, our provisional and superficial readings of headlines, our interest in images flitting past, calling to mind some half-learned passage from philosophy in our adolescence, or the weird strings of phone numbers and sports scores we can call up like crazed cabalists, the incidental, the accidental memory, the weird juxtapositions that have settled in our brains, the arcana we can spout at a cocktail party, the private witticisms with which we comfort ourselves. This vast stew that is our brain these days, what parts of our brain that have not been outsourced to regions of the cloud or the computer, the brain as it is invaded by consumerism, colonized by culture and ads and media, fragmented by images, phrases, opinions, ideas. Like the internet, these pages are hyper-present-tense, but they're assembled in geological strata of crushed-together bits of history, containing images of disturbing violence and decay and death that we cannot look away from. Peter's pages—like his collages, which grow out of his style of image making—do not contain intertextual commentary: his annotations, in looping sinuous script, like thorny grapevines laid flat to dry on the page, do not always amplify or even correlate to the pictures and pieces of culture with which we find them, but they lead us instead to a land of his enchantment, the mindset of his fixations and obsessions, the figures that populated his pantheon, a land not of good and evil, but a place glowing with the frenzy of vision, a Blakean place made of Kellogg's boxes, tabloid covers, fashion tear sheets, and assembled with an UHU glue stick.

In a letter to the Getty Museum Group in 1986, perhaps as an encouragement to invest in them for future protection and display—as well as drumming up some money for perpetually cash-strapped Peter—Francis Bacon wrote, "Having for many years seen the remarkable Diaries and photographs that Peter Beard has made to record a unique and remarkable life, I believe this form of documentation has enormous value and interest to a wide range of people, especially to Artists, as a compost from which they could draw vast types of inspiration."

Peter would never have claimed as much himself—even if he may have agreed with that assessment. "If you're into collage, you're an escapist," he told me on a chilly spring afternoon in Montauk, looking through some of the old diaries he'd salvaged after the fire. "I did old master drawing. I pulled off a couple, but it's very difficult to do. If it wasn't doable, I didn't do it. I only ever did things that were easy. This is a lazy man's thing. It's an escapist thing because it doesn't tell you anything, does it? But I kind of like it when the years pass by."

PETER BEARD DIDN'T DANCE, EVER, AS A RULE. WHICH DOES rather contradict his image of the freewheeling, uninhibited wild man in touch with his ancient, primal self. Or perhaps it corroborates another still more deeply held trait, by showing the white-knuckle control of vanity—or insecurity, which is of course the same thing by a different name.

What Peter did do was party.

He was on the scene. And while his late-night ranting about the fate of the rhinos in East Africa was riveting to some, a whole lot of people did not take him terribly seriously at the time. "This wasn't a serious group of people," Fran Lebowitz told me, speaking of Peter and his pals, "you have to understand that. This wasn't a bunch of philosophers. This was basically a party crowd."

Part of the crowd, of course, was Andy Warhol, and Peter pops up with almost hilarious regularity in Andy's diaries from the era, always out and about, at the opening of Nell's downtown, at a who's-who dinner uptown, and always at 54. (I wonder if Andy's suspicion of Peter, his sort of low-grade distaste for him, had to do with the fact that he was just a brash and extroverted version of Andy himself.) A short while after the fire at the mill in June 1977, which burned up his diaries along with several Warhols, Bacons, Wyeths, and others, Peter ran into Warhol at the bar at 54— always at the bar, of course, which was pickup central, and never on the dance floor. "And for the first time I saw him so drunk that his words were slurring," Andy wrote in his diary. "He told me he was glad after the Montauk fire burned his mill-house down that he wouldn't be doing his diaries anymore, that he was actually relieved they'd all been destroyed. I told him *not* to be relieved, that he *had* to do more."

This description of a morose Peter, maybe asking for reassurance (from another known diary keeper), showing a glimmer of his own self-pity, if only ironically, as a way to mock himself and ask for encouragement, does nothing to change Peter's own descriptions of his feelings at the time. But it does rather enrich his claims of having forced himself to turn away from regret or guilt over all that was lost in the fire, to go only forward, determinedly forward, marching his mind militarily ahead lest it tarry in the regions of introspection that had proved so dangerous for him before. And I wonder if that wasn't the last, great, final test of Peter's yen for introspection, for self-consideration, and in turning his mind so mercilessly away from the past, he did something to obliterate the last vestiges he might have had of that muscle—the muscle that, if overdeveloped, leads to anxiety and second-guessing.

Not that Peter was normally spending his time crying into his beer. His friend, and the first gallerist to show his work, Joseph Helman, describes a more typical night with Peter in 1977. At the time, Peter was dating Carole Bouquet, who will be very well remembered by any James Bond fans as the dreamgirl and scuba diver in the 1981 Bond film *For Your Eyes Only*. She was also, in the '80s, the face of Chanel No. 5.

"I was dating the most gorgeous girl in the world here in New York," Helman says. "Her name slips me at the moment. But at any rate, Peter wanted us to go to the wrestling matches, Carole, and my date and Peter and I. We're watching Dusty Rhodes and Andre the Giant in a tag team match," at Madison Square Garden. Afterward, as Helman remembers, Peter turns to his party, indicating the wrestlers they've just watched, and says, "'Those guys want to join us.'"

The foursome meet the wrestlers at the exit, where a flock of autograph hounds descend on Andre the Giant, sending them running to the garage and into the stretch limo Peter had hired for the occasion. "We get to the top of the drive to go out and the car bottoms out," Helman remembers. "It's stuck up there. So Andre says, 'I'll fix this.' He gets out, he lifts the back of the car up. We go to Studio 54 and it's closed for a private party. The private party is because the Rockettes were on strike and they thought they were over with. So this was the parting party for the Rockettes. There's fifty young girls and us. Andre and I spent the whole night chatting at the bar and all these girls were just flying all over the place. . . . That was an evening Peter set up."

Like most evenings Peter set up in Manhattan since the club had opened in 1977, it centered at 54. In November of that year, Peter had the after-party for his ICP opening there. And in January of '78, he had his fortieth birthday party there. Imagine being such a party monster that your fortieth birthday party is at Studio 54. Not that he could top Bianca Jagger's party the year before, for which Peter's pal Halston had arranged a white horse to escort the lady of honor around the club. But Peter did have a rather elaborately designed cake, in the shape of an elephant, which, Andy Warhol notes in his diary, descended from the ceiling, in front of the famous "moon and spoon" wall sculpture, as the crowd of beautiful and damned, from Truman Capote to Halston and the Rolling Stones, looked on.

It was in 1978 too that Peter met Cheryl Tiegs—maybe at the famous bar in 54, though they were both vague unto the point of evasion when describing their meeting. At the time, Cheryl was America's sweetheart. She was the girl next door and a bombshell siren on the (record-setting two) covers of *Sports Illustrated* swimsuit issues. In an era before reality TV, before the internet, when movie stars and moguls were the talk of the town and the tabloids, Cheryl became one of the most famous women in America—and the first supermodel, though the metric by which we judge that remains a bit obscure.

She was, at the time, also married, to Stan Dragoti, a director who would soon make a string of successful movies, including the Michael Keaton comedy *Mr. Mom*. But that didn't stop Cheryl and Peter from dating, even rather publicly, throughout 1978 and into '79, when she and Dragoti were finally divorced. In September 1978, Andy even *tsk*s in his diary that Dragoti is "really unhappy about Cheryl Tiegs running off to Africa with Peter Beard," on the trip that would really cement the two as a couple, in both their minds and in the imaginations of the public.

Up until that point, Cheryl's image was very clean, proper. Having grown up in Alhambra, outside of Los Angeles (though she'd been born in Minnesota), she was regularly described as having the California look. She had a somewhat surfy aesthetic and was thought, even by many of Peter's friends, to be on the square side—at least in comparison to Peter and the 54 crowd.

It was in March of that year, 1978, that Cheryl appeared on the cover of *Time* magazine, under the cover line, "All-American Model." In the story, she is given the kind of canonization these sorts of profiles provide:

> Top Models are not elected or anointed, but every couple of years the ball of flaming gas that is the U.S. communications industry indicates that a new One is at hand. By assuming office she becomes the nation's muse, our new moon. In earlier manifestations, the Top Model was

Lisa Fonssagrives, Suzy Parker, Jean Shrimpton, Lauren Hutton. Now, lambent in the pages of Harper's Bazaar and SPORTS ILLUSTRATED, ineffable on a talk show, utterly right at the right disco, a splendid beacon in the mind of every wistful teen-age buyer of eye enlarger and cheekbone sharpener, a poster pinned across Farrah's, a secret smile on the face of a dozing commuter, her name is Cheryl Tiegs.

Cheryl was thirty. Approaching the very height of her fame, her marketability, as we'd say now—about to release a book on natural beauty—she was a megastar. And as she says now, she fell madly, instantly in love with Peter, who was, she says, the love of her life.

"She's a toughie," Andy wrote in his diary in February 1979, after having lunch with the couple. "So she'll probably make Peter marry her. I've decided Peter is just a playboy, though. He's really looking great, he never ages (lunch $100, tip $30). Cheryl said she wants to be in movies, so I told her she'd have to lower her voice, like Betty Bacall did—talk from the lungs, not from the nose. She said that people like her the way she is, though. They'd let their limousine go, so they walked home."

Less than a year later, when Andy ran into the couple again, at Le Club, Cheryl was wearing a cast. "She'd fallen down in Montauk," Andy wrote, "and I bet Peter pushed her." Which seems to come as quite a shock, if not to Andy. Nowhere else in the diaries does he describe Peter being physically violent in front of him. Nowhere does he give any reasoning for his suspicion that Peter pushed Cheryl or caused her injury. And then he just leaves it, never to speak of it again. "I had a fight with Peter in the car," he goes on, "we were talking and he said that 'everything was coming down.' And I said that Cheryl should look more glamorous and beautiful when she goes out if she's going to be the number-one top beauty in the world. She looked good but plain. She wears the worst, funny clothes."

In fact, Cheryl did make a few television appearances at the time, mostly as herself, including in *Playboy's Roller Disco and Pajama Party* special. In 1981, she and Peter worked on a few episodes about wildlife and conservation for ABC's long-running show, *American Sportsman*. Filmed in Africa with Cheryl narrating, one of them won an Emmy. And whether she made him or not, the couple were indeed married, in 1981, at the house in Montauk, under some chaotic weather—one moment rain showers, and the next, sunshine.

Paparazzo Ron Galella was on hand to take pictures. As was Peter's friend and Montauk neighbor, the great sports photographer Walter Iooss, who reminisces with a wry smile as he thinks about the smallish party of maybe several dozen people spilling out into the semi-sodden grass and tents after the ceremony, of the bottles of Dom Perignon and other more illicit party concessions consumed in great abundance.

It's funny—maybe the two of them telling stories about their life together after the fact have colored the way those wedding-day pictures look, but as drop-dead beautiful as they both were at the time, and especially on that day, neither of them looks particularly happy. Cheryl, looking somewhat hassled by the rice someone has thrown in her face, Peter grimacing more than glowing, both of them smiling as if they are gritting through something rather than gleefully running into a place of joy and wonder.

And in fact, as they would both regularly characterize their marriage—this despite the nondisclosure agreement both had signed during the divorce—it was not a happy one. "I think he liked the beauty of women and he liked to spin the web, and then he would walk away once he ensnared you," Cheryl said, grasping for explanations of his all-or-nothing interest. "For four days he'd be an angel," she said. "We would lie in bed, watch movies, hug, snuggle, but then he'd be off and running. That's not a marriage."

They went to a counselor who, having heard Cheryl describe these vacillations in mood, wondered aloud whether Beard had ever perhaps heard of something called bipolar disorder, Cheryl told *Vanity Fair.* "Peter's personality is so bizarre," she told them. "I don't know if you could ever carve out all of the things that made Peter who he was. He was incredibly mean and incredibly intoxicating and interesting. . . . I loved him deeply but I didn't know . . . He hurt me so much, so deeply," she said, shortly after he passed away. "He was abusive, physically abusive. . . . The disappearing. It was emotionally abusive. It just got to be intolerable."

Cheryl says the couple tried repeatedly to conceive, and lost pregnancies through miscarriage, even intimating that Peter's brutality and physical violence could have been the cause of the miscarriages. "Was Beard's violence the cause of any of [the miscarriages]?" *Vanity Fair* asked. "Tiegs pauses before she quietly replies, 'Possibly.'"

When I ask Cheryl about the event, she tells me that she and Peter were in the car when they began arguing. She was driving, she says, and "he hit me very strongly in the stomach. . . . It took an hour then to get into Manhattan, and when I got out of the car, I was just doubled over in pain. So who knows? There's no way to tell why anyone has a miscarriage. Those are the events that happened. He hit me on the stomach, and three, four days later I had a miscarriage. That's just the facts."

She seems sure that Peter's intent was not to cause her to miscarry, though. "No," she says, "he was desperate for a child. Desperate for a child."

Peter spoke, sometimes vaguely, about the ills of marriage itself, as if the institution were cursed and not his specific iteration. "The institution of marriage should be re-examined because of its overwhelming claustrophobia," he said. "The odds are stacked against spontaneity and effervescence. It's an institution that was brought about for the sake of family and children, but biologically, it's very unnatural. It's masochism and torture the way it's been organized." He regularly, rather nakedly, made mention of how seldom they had sex.

And what is it that the books say? Money, sex, and disagreements about children are the three main causes of divorce? Add Peter's use of cocaine, his mental instability, and abuse, and you have the couple's drift pretty well mapped.

"I GOT A CALL FROM MOHAMED AL-FAYED AND [HIS SON] DODI Fayed," Peter Riva tells me. For many years, Riva worked as de facto manager and agent for Peter. "'Can you meet at the Waldorf Towers to have a conversation?' They want to meet with me to talk about my clients because they have an idea for redoing one of the hotels they've just bought, which is the Hotel Ritz in Paris."

"So we go," Riva says, "and we're having a conversation about it and Cheryl is bored to tears because it is just not her thing. And I wanted to get out of there. And Dodi says, 'No, stay. I have some coke coming up.' Well, the door opens and this guy arrives with *a kilo of cocaine.* And Beard goes, 'Great, we're staying.'"

Riva and Cheryl left and Peter stayed. Two weeks later, Riva says, he finds out that Peter and Dodi Fayed have "concocted this idea that Peter can do artwork all through the hallways of the Ritz and the Hemingway Bar, and make it all Hemingway-esque." The idea was for Peter to redo the famous bar and surrounding hallways and entries in much the same way as he had covered the walls of the ICP during his 1977 show there, with large-scale prints and immersive, installation-style work. To iron out the details, Fayed invited Peter, Cheryl, and Peter Riva to Paris.

"So we all go to Paris," Riva said. "And they've got a room for me at the Ritz in the back in the servants' quarters, you know, and they put Peter and Cheryl in the Presidential Suite. And they ask us to put a credit card down for extras so I put my credit card down and Cheryl does the same for their room—which is fine, you know, everybody figures that *they own the hotel*, they can pay for it."

They stayed for five days and got the deal done. Peter would get a $75,000 down payment to begin the work. All systems go, apparently. But when they get home, Riva says, "My American Express bill arrives at $10,000 and Cheryl gets hers for $35,000. They'd charged us for every meal at the hotel, every part of the trip, including flying to London, driving down to Sussex, to have a private lunch with Al-Fayed and momma Fayed and Dodi and the wives, chauffeured limousines to meet them, and everything else, was included in the bill, every dime. They'd reneged on the whole deal. *Because*, during our lunch in Sussex, Al-Fayed says to Peter, 'I can make this deal better for you. I'll give you a million dollars. You divorce Cheryl and Dodi can marry Cheryl; she's good for him.'

"And Beard says, 'Are you out of your fucking mind?'

"Al-Fayed says, 'I'm serious. This is serious. You just trade wives. And it's worth a million dollars. I'll give you a million dollars now.'

"And Beard had the good sense to say, 'Uh, no.' And, of course, when they go back to New York the bill for $35,000 was kind of the kick in the teeth. Cheryl was furious, and that kind of led to the final moments of distaste for her. God bless her. I saw her five or six years after that. She said, 'You were always a better friend to him than he deserved.' She says, 'But, boy, thank God you got me out of there.'"

When I am able to check this story with Cheryl, she seems a bit baffled:

It has zero to do with me. I never heard of it. It may have happened and it may not have happened. I've never had a man pay for anything, especially a man I don't know, Dodi's father. We only met one day, and he showed us the presidential suite and that was it. There was no laying out of blueprints, no talking, and I never expected the bill to be paid. I paid for everything in our marriage. I paid for the tickets. Peter and I, we went to the Ritz-Carlton, had a beautiful room, and at the end I paid the bill. That's as far as I know. . . . If he did offer a million dollars, which is ridiculous, they would've had to have done it in private, and I was just always with Peter while we were at the Ritz. So I don't know. I just think it's a silly, fantastical story.

A representative for Al-Fayed says he has no recollection of any dealings with Peter whatsoever.

IN DECEMBER 1982, ANDY WARHOL NOTES IN HIS DIARY THAT Peter came by the studio hoping to cash a check Cheryl had written, "because he wanted to go around the corner to Paragon and buy some sports equipment," Andy writes. "So I guess he's being kept by Cheryl. She's really got the bucks, she's got the Sears contract."

By then, the couple's contract seems to have already fallen apart. They were divorced a few months later.

"We went to marriage counseling," Cheryl tells me, "and he is certifiably manic-depressive, bipolar. He was diagnosed and given medication, which of course he tossed in the basket." Not in lieu of any other drugs, either. She says, "There weren't a lot of drugs around. We didn't even drink that much." But at some point, quite early on, she says, "I think he pushed the manic button and didn't stop. I think he got onto this roller coaster of being manic, and he just kept going, and he became a monster, really. I can't imagine being attracted to him when he was manic, because what I loved about him was when he was depressed and we would just lie in bed, and hold each other, and watch movies, and take long walks, and all of that."

With all of that seemingly gone for good, they agreed to divorce, but they lived together another three days, she says, while she was packing things up. During this time, when she went in search of him to talk about some matter or ask where something was, she says she carried around a can of mace. "Now, who carries around a can of mace?" she says. "And I thought, 'What am I doing?' But I didn't want to confront him or see him because I didn't know what he would do."

When the papers were signed and Cheryl was safely out of the house, she says she never spoke with Peter again. "I had no desire to continue a friendship with this nut. We just cut off communication. He wrote letters to me after we got divorced and everything, and I just tossed him in the basket. You'll reach that point where the last period is on the last sentence."

And still, she says she doesn't regret their time together. "It was 50-50," she says. "As horrible as some scenes are in our relationship, it was also magical. Because he . . . brought me to Africa. I wanted to learn and grow, and I did that with Peter. I loved him deeply, passionately. A lot of people have never had that. They ask me, 'What is it like to be passionately, deeply in love?' They don't know. They've never had it. So I'm fortunate to have had it," she says. "I did get something out of it."

CHAPTER 8

The End of the World

n 1984, at the bar of the New Stanley Hotel, Peter met Nejma Khanum, through some friends. Stern in cadence and carriage, aquiline in appearance and temperament (eagle-eyed, you might say, as in, with her eye on the prize), the Kenyan-born daughter of an Afghani judge, Nejma was everything Peter was not. Sober, straight, even strict (the name Khanum is the feminine of Khan, as in the military Mongol rulers, an honorific for women of high standing in Afghanistan). And she was immediately enamored with this man twenty years her senior.

"He was outlandish," she said, "everything to him is a green light—but so incredibly refreshing. He has a sort of magic to him that when he concentrates his attention on you, it's like the sun suddenly coming out." And of his digs at Hog Ranch, she said, "It has the elegance of simplicity and, to use one of Peter's favorite words, authenticity. You sleep in tents that are wide open to the animals and the elements, and you wake in the morning to birdsong."

As he had with Cheryl, and with Minnie in some ways, Peter ran headlong into a romance with someone who immediately set about taming him, corralling him. "I knew she was the only person I could be married to," he said of Nejma later. "And the African connection was absolutely essential." Which, for someone as careful and grandiloquent with language as Peter, who was forever striving for perfect and profound poetry when expressing the state of wildlife or the nature of man, is not exactly a sonnet.

For their part, Nejma's conservative parents were quite poetic in their clarity on the matter: they didn't want their daughter anywhere near this rapscallion, and so they organized a kind of emergency exfiltration, sending her to Germany. "They smuggled me out of the country," Nejma said later, sort of amused by the whole thing. "I only had with me something like $200 and I gave it all to [a friend] if he would post a letter for me. And, all of a sudden there is Peter, in this tweed suit he had borrowed from someone. He just walked into the room and went down on his knee. He spent four days crying. . . . What woman could resist this man crying for four days?"

"He swore to me that he was a one-woman man," she says, playing it for a joke that she knows we're all in on, and then ladling on a little pathos, to remind you who you're meant to be rooting for. "He swore that he would never leave me. . . . And I believed him."

"He grew up in a very organized family," Nejma went on to say. "And he's never going to be anything but what he is." But there is a chilling sort of imperiousness in her tone when she adds, "You can always be a rebel, but how much can you rebel, and then finally you go back to what you came from."

Back in New York, Peter and Nejma bought an apartment in the famous Osborne building on Fifty-Seventh Street in Manhattan. Their fellow Osbornian Fran Lebowitz wrote their reference letter to the board. And in 1986, just as Nejma had suggested, the couple were indeed married, at the house in Montauk, and went about building the kind of nuclear family Peter had always railed against and rejected, swearing oaths before a god he didn't believe in to an institution, marriage, he had very recently likened to torture, and promising lifelong fidelity, which he thought was patently absurd.

People are hypocritical, saying one thing and then doing another, even meaning to steer their lives one way and, as Nejma suggested, falling into the same cycles, patterns, and even traumas and hang-ups with which we are familiar—the devil we know, perhaps. But, generally, Peter thought himself above that sort of inconsistency. He was if anything a fanatic, devoted to his beliefs and way of life to the extent that he regularly risked everything in their pursuit. And in all cases but this—marriage and attempts to build a family life—he never once gave a whit about social customs, mores, or even laws if they infringed on his pursuit of immediate gratification. He would have happily rotted in a prison rather than compromise an inch on something utterly meaningless, so why was it that he regularly went completely against his own preachings in this arena? And why did he marry women who seemingly wanted to enforce some of those barriers he so flippantly disregarded?

Existentialism might have been the closest thing to a philosophy or religion that Peter had, and its idea that people are what they do, to be judged by their actions only, is a great *political* reading of events, but it does nothing to suss out the psychological underpinnings of those actions. It ignores them just as Peter did, preferring as he did to live on the topsoil of life exclusively, hiding his head above the surface, either afraid of or uninterested in any discussion or consideration of his memories, his feelings, or his subconscious. For Peter, everything was on the outside, outward, on the surface, superficial, and he shrugged off any concern for interiority. Except that, when looked at with any kind of perspective, the contours of his life are heavily grooved by repeated behavior, hinting at powerful patterns below.

Throughout his life, Peter protested vehemently against psychoanalysis, but it would have made light work of his marriages. A quick scan of his rants about his mother and his wives would have made it quite clear to a Freudian that, for Peter, marriage belonged to the world of rules, his mother's world, the world of plans. And

Peter hated plans. He couldn't stop talking about how he never made plans. How life was so much better without them. That it was in fact accidents along the way of life that brought about all of the good, in art, or otherwise, that life had available. And what is a relationship but making plans with another person? A plan to have a date. A plan to go on vacation. Plans for dinner, for which friends to send holiday cards to. Plans to raise children together.

Plans are what Peter's mother harangued him with. "Every night at dinner she would ask, 'What are your plans?'" he said. "And I realized that that is just the worst imposition." I wonder if he felt this aversion in part because a plan comes with implicit accountability: Did you follow through on your plan or not? How well did you execute the plan? Was the plan a disaster from the start? And obviously Peter wanted no part of that, wanted to have no responsibility, to himself or others, no accountability. He didn't go in for guilt or regret, so what is the point looking back on something that might give you a negative feeling for having failed to plan, or having made a bad plan, or having executed the plan poorly? Everything was in the now, riling up the wild animals around you to provoke a reaction, sticking pins in the world to see what it would do next.

And Peter couldn't really stand criticism either, couldn't stand to be seen to fail or to be called out . . . for anything. So he ran as fast as he could to occupy the most self-effacing position possible. Anticipating that he might face criticism for his inability to make or keep to a plan, he bragged about never making them. Thinking someone else might critique him for his lifestyle, his habits, his poor custodianship of himself, Peter went ahead and labeled himself "a bum." He called himself "the most irresponsible man alive" and said, "Everything I do is chaotic," making himself sound a bit like the Joker in *Batman*—an agent of chaos—and certainly not someone you could count on, judge like other civilians, or hold to any sort of standard of conduct.

He did any- and everything to subvert any criticism he might've fielded for his lifestyle; he owned it, we might say today, but in a way that seems to undercut his claims. If he were such a liberated free spirit, wandering the Earth, doing as he pleased in sync with the pure rhythms of his artistic yen, why would he need to judge himself according to our square rules? Why would he need to throw himself down in a kind of judo move to the lowest point so that society could not attack him where he stood?

Just the idea of putting that question to Peter makes me laugh— at how evasive, defensive, and antsy it would've made him. What he did in those situations, in response to anything that pressed him too closely, was to run, to flee. Because if home, and civilization, security, money, and rules were his mother's world and thus to be detested, nature always seemed to suggest itself to Peter's imaginings as a place of childlike freedom and carnality, a prelapsarian freedom from morality and tailored clothes. It was in nature—specifically, in Africa—where he could be totally free, where he could totally escape, he said, "with no one looking over your shoulder." We don't need to guess who that someone was that he was imagining.

The natural world, for Peter, was the domain of art, of spontaneity, of an escape from guilt and regret, a perfect party for the senses—the opposite of what he had said marriage was. You had a wife/mother at home, in Peter's worldview, but on the savannah you went on the prowl for sex, art, excitement, authenticity, real *life*. At home he was a servant to societal norms, but in the metaphorical bush, then, Peter came alive as the great seducer. Out there, he could once again be properly wild.

Peter himself seemed to make this connection between sex and safari in a subtle way when he used to say, as he frequently did, that "the only thing left in nature is the beauty of women." It's interesting that, even as Peter spent his life catastrophizing about our destruction of the natural world, a friend of his for well over forty years says that Peter did his part in damaging what he himself had called the best part: beautiful women. *"Le destructeur,"* the friend called him, suggesting that Peter's long-lasting psychological and emotional damage to his ex-wives caused them alcohol and substance abuse problems, and to his long-term romances, irreparable trauma.

Cheryl Tiegs famously described Peter as a kind of conqueror of women, a man who seemed interested only in ensnaring them in his web but, when he had captured them, lost all interest. Peter's obsession with trophies also sounds like someone bragging about his conquests. He made sure to note that the tusks with which he posed nude supermodels—as if with giant, white, gleaming phalluses—were the biggest of all time, "world record" tusks, the longest, the best, the heaviest.

The fashion consultant and editor Anne-Laure Lyon said that Peter "has a certain reputation, either as a playboy or an artist. . . . He's a very extreme person. He's a fanatic . . . he is such a trauma trigger with women. He loves to trigger women because that's how he feels great about himself. . . . Peter has a lot to do with seduction, whether it is through his work or his charisma or his eccentricity," she said. And she should know. "Man Ray was my godfather, so I am very accustomed for people with that kind of temperament, and in a sense they are very difficult people to live around, but in another instance they're great."

"He's an artist," Iman said of Peter. "He does not live in society; he doesn't play by their rules. He's like a wild animal. He doesn't own a pair of socks; in winter he's wearing sandals and sloshing around in the snow. He would rather have grand disasters than just have a mediocre life." Which is precisely how Peter would have liked to be thought of, and judged, but still he carried that superego within him, the set of standards and judgments imparted to him by his mother, like software he couldn't delete.

As though obeying some rule of gravity, it seems that every time he would run away from responsibility, he'd come running back in search of a mother figure. And each time he did so, in a long relationship or marriage, he followed a pattern of deferring to the woman all the responsibility, including oversight of the finances and maternal care (for him, the child), the better to free him to play. It's a chicken-and-egg question whether his arrested development and inability or unwillingness to manage money, or even himself, brought forth enablers and the conservator-style relationship he seemed to crave, or vice versa. What is quite clear is that he was looking for replacement Roseanne Beards even after all the wreck and ruin he attributed to his mother.

WELL AFTER HIS MARRIAGE-COUNSELING SESSIONS WITH Cheryl, in 2013, Peter was officially diagnosed as bipolar. It is a little amusing to think of seventy-five-year-old Peter checking out what all these crazy kids at the American Psychiatric Association have to say, except that it is difficult to imagine him going in for something like that of his own volition, even if he was in real pain, and looking for a solution. Which seems to suggest an alternative reason, that Peter was sent to the doctor, compelled to go. It would be easy to speculate that the diagnosis was for someone else's purposes, a way to name his behavior and perhaps to shame him for it, or to diminish him—to remove him from authorship of his actions. He was a patient now, suffering from a specific disease, which on some job applications is listed as a disability. Still in compos mentis, you might say, but with an asterisk.

Peter, of course, would've hated it. "He hated to be pigeon-holed," his cousin Christopher Schroll told me. He hated labels of any sort—even that of "photographer" or "diarist." He insistently defied categorization, did not want to be lumped into a group, and regularly railed against our obsession with health care. One wonders what treatment he was prescribed and with what rigor he absolutely disregarded it.

Psychiatry categorizes; that is what it does. So we can well understand the doctor who received Peter and, having to place him somewhere within the *Diagnostic and Statistical Manual of Mental Disorders*, settled on bipolar. He would have been hard-pressed to express Peter's actions any other way within that limited language. How else to categorize his excesses, his highs, his lows, his regular flight from restrictions, from society, running away to the woods, running after wild animals, and then returning home? His endless, fastidious, obsessive doodling and diddling with his diaries? His regular binges—"He was an enormous binger," his friend Gillies Turle, a resident at Hog Ranch, told me—lasting days, or longer, consuming any- and everything in sight, every*one* around him? He left nothing in the tank, nothing in the bank for what comes next—as Schroll put it, "Never giving a thought for how he'd pay for tomorrow."

Then came his days of wallow, as we say of a hippo, who sinks itself into the mud, to hide, to heal, to restore itself for another charge. Cheryl Tiegs said that during their marriage, after he'd run off without a word for days, he would come crashing back home and curl up on the couch, mute and childlike, and remain there unmoving for days on end. Peter's girlfriend in France in the late 2000s describes him as a baby, needing to be cared for, bathed, dried with a hair dryer because the towels were too abrasive, and held in her arms for days.

So, another kind of chicken-and-egg question. Did Peter feel the wounds of the world so intensely that his passions and subsequent crashes were distended? Was he pulled out of balance by the gravity of the world around him? Or did he see the world with visionary gloom and doom because he was wired the way he was? Did his own interior experience of cataclysmic terror, fatalism, fear, and a longing for solace, lead him to, or help him to more clearly see the world as a paradise lost–become–hellscape?

"The Old Africa," Peter said, "as a metaphor of the biggest

thing in our lives: Nature. And we're basically the destroyers of Nature. And we're gonna destroy ourselves in the bargain. That's how smart we are. We've done it here in Starvo [Peter's punny name for Tsavo, where he witnessed the elephant die off], we're gonna do it in China, we're gonna do it in the Mid East and Japan and just about everywhere because we haven't learned how to be civilized yet."

This rant, this harangue, went on largely unbroken for all of his adult life, with little variation, little room for anyone else to agree, to even hem or haw, for fifty years. It was a colorful apocalypse he described—indeed, he searched for the purple language as if he were writing a new Revelations, and the end times he described were no less gruesome. And this ruin, this coming apocalypse was the obsession of his life. Obsession, literally, in that any conversation with Peter from about the 1970s until he could no longer speak would spiral quite quickly into a rant of his nightmare imaginings for the world to come: "A lot of robbery," he said, "cheating, stealing, murdering, torturing to death, army takeovers. Fascism. Totalitarianism. Black, dark, horrifying *black* totalitarianism," he said, emphasizing the word to make it especially suggestive of what he meant, I guess.

"We always have an argument about what Africa really is," Iman said, in a 1996 interview. "Is it the animals and the landscape, or is it the people? Peter loves the myth of Africa more than I do. . . . He has no respect for Africans, but it's their continent—not his. For him, there are no people involved; they get in the way of his myth."

In Peter's myth, Africa had been a literal Garden of Eden as recently as the 1910s, when Karen Blixen arrived there, during and after the First World War, a place where age-old civilizations lived in harmony with nature as represented by the region's megafauna, which flourished still. And then we moved in, crowded everything out, starved the land and one another for resources, and caused all the stress and density that would lead us inevitably to annihilation.

"It took about three million years starting in Kenya for human beings to reach a population of one billion in the middle of the nineteenth century," Peter told Charlie Rose in an interview on his show in 1993. "Now we add a billion people every decade. That's a hopeless graph. There is no way of dealing with it unless one of the leaders of the world decides that population is an issue. We are completely blind. We're incredibly un-evolved, and we're not educating ourselves to survive and we probably won't [survive], as a result of [our] ability to adapt to the damage we cause. We're adapting every minute."

I cite the Rose interview here because it is actually the mildest of Peter's prophetic performances, among the more concise, coherent. In later videos, Peter revs all over the place, glitchy and coked up, or else he seems intent on perversity, trying to provoke his interlocutor. In these latter versions, Peter would go on at length about culling the herd, our herd, humanity, "but nobody wants to talk about that," he'd say. And then he'd suggest that epidemics like AIDS were nature's gift, helping us to thin out our numbers, that pandemics ought to be allowed to kill at will. "The only solution at the moment, because of the immense populations on every bit of land, would be some kind of catastrophe. We need agents of mortality. We're billions overpopulated. Nobody wants to hear that because nobody liked Hitler that much and we're getting very righteous now about slaughter and death. But we've never killed more people in the whole history of humanity than in the last century. So our concern is highly suspect."

As he was playing with his rosary of talking points around overpopulation, getting himself worked up into a proper sermon, Peter liked to mention our extraction of resources from the planet, the external source of so many of our problems, in connection with our overspending, as he saw it, internally, on keeping everyone alive and well, causing overpopulation, which then compounded all the problems caused by extraction, in fact increased them exponentially.

"Well, 'Is it too late?'" Peter asked Charlie Rose rhetorically, and then continued. "It's never too late," he said, sounding more hopeful than he ever had or would again. "While there's life, there's hope. All the clichés are true. Just consider that demographic curve. Three million years to achieve a billion people and then a billion every decade . . ."

A moment later, in answering a question about Karen Blixen, Peter pivoted in just a line or two into full rant. "We have forgotten nature," he said. "We are not interested in being related to animals, nature or anything. We call it Mother Nature. What do we know about Mother Nature? We know nothing. It's a very cruel, scary world, the natural world. We [think we] don't need it. We're into cutting down trees. . . . We are destructive. We're like bacteria on a slide. We are moving like an army of locusts."

This, chiefly, was Peter's diagnosis of humanity's psychological blind spot and the root of our ongoing problem. We are in denial, Peter said, because we want to feel that we are set apart from nature, above it, not of it, not an animal, behaving in much the same way as, say, the elephants of Tsavo, who reproduced to unsupportable numbers, destroying their habitat by depleting its resources to support those numbers, running themselves to all manner of destruction, from heart disease to stress-related disease due to the level of competition they were facing, and then dying off in a desert of their own creation. This happened to them and may happen to us because we deny our wildness, our connectedness to the natural world.

The elephants as a metaphor for life as a whole, the microcosm of our world coming to the brink within a few square miles of Kenya—he says this is what made the place inescapable to him up to that point. "The end of Africa," he said. "The end of wildlife—a Francis Bacon theme—is the end of us. That's what I'm here to say," he said to Rose. "Until we figure out the principles of art and nature, two subjects that we dismiss in kindergarten, we're doomed."

He said Nairobi and Kenya had already crossed the tipping point, and he had no interest in returning anymore. "What's the point?" he asked, wearing all of his biases quite clearly on his sleeve, "of going to Bedford-Stuyvesant eight thousand miles away from here?"

Not that Peter necessarily thought the actual robbers and bandits in Nairobi were the real bad guys here (to him they were more like a karmic force). Nor even the industrialists, the corporations draining the world of its resources and compiling pharaonic levels of wealth. He preferred to aim his ire at environmentalist organizations, which he said were not only ineffective but actually helping to exacerbate the problem. "The do-gooders," he called them. "Preposterous organizations that are basically into money raising. That's their industry."

He particularly had it in for the adopt-an-animal organizations—"Buy an elephant a drink," he joked—organizations he imagined with enormous stores of capital and, sadly, influence within Kenya, prescribing methods of care and control that only led to overpopulation and would hasten another massive catastrophe. He saw clearly the hypocrisy and contradictions of bans on poaching—a politicized term for the taking of game, whether for food or clothes or ivory, by individuals not licensed by the recognized powers that be—for the racist practice and the industrialized care and slaughter that they were, throwing populations out of balance. While Galo-Galo was prohibited from stalking and killing an elephant that might help to thin a herd in an overpopulated area, rich guys from Texas could pin a lion into a cage and shoot it for a Facebook picture.

Galo-Galo was, of course, a god in Peter's pantheon. And he

wasn't railing against Exxon-Mobil or whoever in his rants. It was the misguided protectors of paradise, you'll notice, squaring the circle of Peter's psychology, who were in his estimation the real devils. It was not the native Gardeners of Eden who had lived in perfect harmony before we showed up; no, it was those who came in to "mother" the Africans for whom he reserved his vilest venom.

BY 1996 PETER WAS ALMOST COMPLETELY ESTRANGED FROM Nejma, and seeing Zara only very rarely, if at all. Divorce papers were drawn up, awaiting signatures. Among other things, Nejma claimed in the filing that Peter had molested Zara. He denied anything of the sort, and ranted and raved about this "divorce tactic" of Nejma's, and what she was putting him through.

"It's so awful that he would put it in the public arena," Nejma said, when *Vanity Fair* contacted her about the claims she'd made against Peter. "This was only meant to be a family issue," she said. "But Peter has seen fit to talk about it in every restaurant, every nightclub, with a bunch of hangers-on and sycophants and third-rate human beings." Crying on the phone with the writer from *Vanity Fair*, Nejma proceeded to say, "I don't want to say anything terrible about Peter, because he's Zara's father. But this is something that's very, very serious. I literally begged him to go and get help, but he didn't want to. I was completely crazy about Peter; I would have done anything to save our marriage. I did my best to help Peter out of this, but when he refused to deal with the situation that existed in our family, I had to leave."

Peter's agent, manager, and close companion, Peter Riva, with whom Peter and Nejma were staying when Zara was born, says the claims are false. "And Peter allowed this profile in *Vanity Fair* because he thinks Graydon Carter's his great friend," Riva says. Carter was at the time the editor of *Vanity Fair*. "He tells all his friends to talk to them." Riva claims to have sent Carter a copy of the Suffolk County police report that, he says, stated that they'd investigated and found the claims to be "so far without merit they were going to *destroy the file.*" (Carter did not answer emails inviting him to comment for this book.) In Riva's estimation, "Nejma made it all up, thinking, you know, that she could get his $60,000 a year from his trust fund as a payment on her end."

"I'm just not that sort of person at all!" Nejma said, when it was suggested she'd made it all up to sweeten the potential divorce settlement in her favor.

> I've gained nothing with this! My daughter's lost a father; I've lost a husband. I have absolutely nothing! Peter's problem always has been too many drugs. Anything that's out there, anything that anyone gives him, he'll do. I think it does erode a lot of your morals; you have no boundaries, and when I felt my child was in danger, I had to do something about it. I have not turned against him; even today, if he were to go for help with her, I'd be all for it. But I think Peter has started believing his own hype. Once you become a public person, you create a persona as sort of a mask, and you can't get out of it. I love him very, very deeply, but he's hurt us so much.
>
> It's going to be between him and his daughter one day, and I would not like to be in his shoes. There's too much darkness there. But he has no remorse about anything.

Zara, crucially, has finally gone on the record about her mother's claims. In an article in *Vanity Fair*, Zara is quoted as saying, "It is absolutely untrue. It's disgusting. It absolutely destroyed him. He doesn't deserve his name attached to that story."

According to this article, written after Peter's passing, "Zara explains that there is a story around the false charge that she cannot discuss, emphasizing that her mother is not to blame. At the time of the molestation allegation, Nejma and Zara moved into the Greenwich, Connecticut, home of Beard's brother Anson M. Beard Jr., according to his son, Anson H. Beard. 'Zara was evaluated at Yale New Haven Hospital and there was no evidence that she had been molested,' he says."

Riva is still pretty riled up about the episode. "I mean, he loved Zara," he says of Peter.

You know, they were living at my house when Nejma had Zara, at Mount Sinai, near us. We walked her over to the hospital and there was a wonderful moment where Peter and I and my wife and my son, Matthew, we were visiting after the baby's born. Nejma was quite ill. She had a pulmonary embolism. And you do that thing of looking through the window at all the babies, you know? And my son said, "Which one is yours, Peter?" And Peter was furious. He said, "The only one that's beautiful. That one! Can't you tell that's my child?" It's that father thing: that's my child. It was really palpable. It was quite lovely to see that. And even through all the trauma with Nejma, I'd be driving back up to the country with him and we'd always stop at a pay phone so that he could talk to his daughter before she goes to bed. I think he was determined to be a better father than either of his parents had ever been to him.

And that's why it was always weird to me that he allowed Nejma back in. But then my wife said to me, "Well, he's not stupid. He's got to let her back in or else he won't have access to his daughter."

CHAPTER 9

Chasing Lightning

For the young, ambitious, beautiful, and really, really rich in the early days of 1987, New York City was a party. On Wall Street, greed was good. Hair and shoulder pads were high, and so was everyone in town. To this already heady hedonism of cocaine, clubbing, and sex, the fashion industry added luxury and glamour—and with it an extended sense of permissiveness: *If this is the life that magazines and advertisements are telling us we all want and desire, then surely it must be good, no?* Then it put that fantasy on jet planes, took it global.

Maureen Gallagher was a beautiful twenty-two-year-old model in 1987. She was up for an adventure and down to party. So one night in dreary February, at Heartbreak club in Manhattan, when her friend Grace Jones introduced her to the dashing forty-nine-year-old photographer Peter Beard, she did not exactly turn and run screaming for her coat. "Daarrling," Grace said, "you have to meet Peter. You're bananas from the same bunch!"

Gallagher had to admit, this rakish-looking guy was actually pretty charming. And interesting: he had all sorts of fascinating, urgent opinions about art, about animals and far-off places. But when Peter invited her to join him the following day in Kenya for a photoshoot, Gallagher basically rolled her eyes and said sure, yeah, whatever, "and disappeared into the bathroom," she says.

Growing up in New York, Gallagher had heard a line or two in her time; she was a wily veteran by then of the shit men will talk, especially in clubs and under the aegis of fashion. But, the next morning, when she checked in with her agency, Elite, she found that a Peter-bought plane ticket to Nairobi was awaiting her.

"I would be replacing Iman, of all people, in a TV movie he was shooting for ABC called *Last Word from Paradise*," she wrote, in a remembrance published in *Vogue* magazine. "As I was handed the ticket, I was given the obligatory speech about how Elite girls should behave, along with instructions to be 'very careful of very adult situations.' In those days, it was par for the course to show up at a shoot and find a pile of blow on a table in the dressing room. My motto was 'Take it easy—but take it.' Peter's approach, I would soon learn, was 'All is for the best in the best of all possible worlds.'"

This favorite saying of Peter's is borrowed from Voltaire's *Candide*, the whole point of which was to satirize this optimistic worldview as espoused by Candide's philosopher mentor, Professor Pangloss. And yet Peter used it in precisely the opposite way, without irony, whether because he misunderstood or was looking to provoke a reaction that never came. He meant by it something akin to "It is what it is."

"I didn't understand that until I got older," Gallagher says. All that she needed to know then, she says, was that "it was winter in New York, and I was going to Kenya to see things most people only read about.

"On my first night, as we walked around Hog Ranch, I thought wild animals would pop out and surprise me. Peter had to hold my hand, and things were electric from the first touch; we spent hours kissing in the tub tent that night. We had the most chemical and physical attraction: end of story. I listened to his tales about life, love, and the way we were losing all of Earth's most beautiful treasures, about how many creatures would be extinct in my lifetime. He told me about Karen Blixen and *The End of the Game*, the book he wrote in 1965, the year I was born. We talked about his past marriage, and how sex had eluded him. He was amazed at how easy it was with me. We had long hours alone and were, frankly, addicted to each other."

When I first speak to Gallagher, shortly after Peter's death, she is simultaneously grieving the loss of her mother, and the pandemic has turned her Staten Island neighborhood, populated largely by first responders and their families, into a place of constant mourning and stress.

She tells me that on the night she met Peter she was fleeing her apartment and her then-boyfriend, "who was abusive." She ran to the apartment of a friend who happened to live above the Heartbreak club, and the friend, hoping to cheer her up, suggested a night out. The friend gave Gallagher a pair of sunglasses to wear to hide her black eye—bruises that, in Africa, the producers of the ABC documentary gave an extra four days to go down before filming.

Talking about these sorts of things is complicated at the best of times. In the darkest patch of the pandemic, shortly after losing both Peter and her mother, it was enormously painful. But what isn't complicated, what does not come alloyed with pain, is Gallagher's love for Peter. She always found him sexy, she says, well into his sixties. And maybe I'm being an uptight Gen-Xer worrying about things like their age difference or the power balance between a famous photographer on his home turf and a young model whisked away to a kind of wonderland. "Everybody went to bed with their photographer," Gallagher tells me, with nothing at all like remorse attached to her words. If anything, she sounds a bit wistful for the innocent days of pre-AIDS eighties life, when, she says, friends would sleep with friends, or their friends' partners. It was no big deal, and anyone could be gay on the right pill. Not that Gallagher was just anyone.

"I was a sexual superhero," Gallagher says. And, well, the nudes that Peter took of her at the time do nothing to raise doubts there.

Of Peter as a lover, Gallagher marvels at his tenderness, his thoughtfulness. "He was always such a gentleman," she says, "so considerate, which is sort of surprising." Another time she tells me, "He treated me like a piece of gold," before immediately changing tack to say, well, "He lied and cheated and stole and disappeared," but, "he lived with me. I was the love of his life. I have the letters to prove it."

Just when I start to do the math in my head and place this trip a matter of months after Peter's wedding to Nejma, Gallagher says, "No one told me he was married," this time with some vinegar in her voice. "And we didn't have, like, Google to find that out."

What they did have on that first encounter was an epic love adventure, culminating in, one evening, Peter and Gallagher climbing the slopes of Mt. Kilimanjaro on LSD, and a short while later, an unexpected pregnancy.

Gallagher has never spoken of this before, she says, but on that first visit to Hog Ranch, she got pregnant with Peter's child, a child she would later miscarry just as she was learning of Peter's deceit—or at least his omissions: failing to mention that he was married, to begin with. The pain of the loss coupled with the shock of these revelations was terrible for Gallagher.

When Peter returned to New York, Gallagher continued to answer his calls, and they enthusiastically carried on their affair—as they would for another twenty-seven years, some of which they spent ardently trying to conceive another child.

ON THE LAST NIGHT OF GALLAGHER'S FIRST VISIT, AT AROUND two in the morning, Peter and Maureen made one of the best-known of Peter's nude-in-the-wilderness photos, titled *Maureen Gallagher and the Late Night Feeder.*

In stark black and white, the ghostly black background giving faint evidence of Hog Ranch but hinting at the immensity of the forest beyond, "a frontier that leads right back to the Stone Age," as Peter would say, Maureen stands in full body profile, nude under the power of a blast of flash, her body as unbelievably formed and dynamic as something sculpted by Bernini, offering up a platter of food to a giant, brilliantly bright Rothschild giraffe who nods down toward the offering but in so doing seems to be appropriately bowing to the goddess before him. "She has a kind of living sculpture/Olympic gymnast body," Peter said of Maureen. "Who is to say when those rippling muscles . . . might give you winged victory or something miraculous?"

There is a kind of graphic subtlety to the piece that makes it appear to our eye now out of another time entirely—Daguerreotype-ish in its antiquity—as if this tableau took place not in the late 1980s but in a time before time, some Homeric era of mythic gods coming into contact with mortals and the animals whose form they sometimes adopted as their own. The midnight mystery of the image may in fact be what makes it so enduring, why it continues to command such enormous sums at auction houses around the world.

Not that Maureen has ever seen a penny from one of these sales. "I never even owned a print of it," she says, "none of our pictures together." Nor, of course, did she profit from their towering asking prices in the resale market. Several times, she says, Peter had made special editions of these images for her, embellished with his blood, personalized with messages to her, but when she'd arrive to collect them, "they'd be gone."

But to return to the image for a moment—as Peter was constantly returning to it, reproducing it like he did so many of his images, to re-imagine it anew, with new marginalia, new illustrations and embellishments, just as he would re-create similar moments in an attempt to re-create a similar sort of magic. Can we isolate what makes this particular image so special, even among Peter's other giraffe photos, among his other nudes? The repetition of the *use* of an image (even with the slight differences from various addenda to the prints) is textbook Warhol—reproducing again and again the same pictures so as to reinforce them in the brains of the audience, to make of them something beyond recognizable, something like an icon, a logo. However, the re-creation of the mise-en-scène within the photo is different. I may be cynically ascribing to Peter the intent to *brand* his images, to make them famous by familiarity. After all, if Hollywood and celebrity branding today are anything to go by, the reuse of existing intellectual property with which the audience is already familiar is commercially successful. But maybe that isn't the case at all. Maybe he had the negatives for only a chosen few images throughout his life and so continued to reprint those for his diaries, collages, illuminated prints. Maybe he just liked only those.

Re-creating the staging of the photos was not accidental. "I never did anything that I didn't think could lead to an accident that would be the greatest thing that ever happened to me," he said, trying to explain this habit, but also terribly foreshadowing much else in the rest of his life to come. The photography he was practicing was a little bit like chasing lightning. If he got all the right pieces in place and pushed and pulled and shimmied through the motions, maybe, just maybe, the thinking went, the lightning would strike, and he would have a picture like *Late Night Feeder*.

The risk of this, of course, is that if the magic doesn't happen, or doesn't happen often enough (or does, diluting the magic of other photos that also captured it), you are stuck doing shtick. A lot of photographers have tricks and tropes to which they return, stages they build looking for something electric to come crackling off the model or the natural elements, whatever their subject matter. This is a bit like conversational patter (of which Peter was also a great user); when you are building yourself up for a full flow-ing conversation, repeating bits and barbs with which you can get yourself in the mood, wait to get in the zone, go full flood. But until the lightning arrives (and, as I say, even sometimes when it does), you are sort of just an old rocker, playing the hits of your youth a few times too many, with less and less feeling, to a steadily diminishing response.

A couple of years prior to this shoot, for the January 1986 issue of *Playboy* magazine, Peter had run the same shtick when he photographed Iman in Kenya. It was hailed by the magazine as her return home, unbelievably, and instead of counter-steering away from the fiasco of his press conference and his racist, insulting claims about how and where he first met her, he took the shoot the whole hog, dressing her up as some sort of Somali Jane of the Jungle, taming wild beasts on the one hand and running wild as a banshee on the other.

There are, in fact, a few incredibly striking images from this series—mild magic, but it strikes! One of them features Iman, in a red and white wrap, standing in the foreground, while a giraffe wraps its long neck over and around her to eat from her hands. In clean, crisp color, Iman looks utterly enchanted, and her infectious delight, along with the giraffe's obvious playfulness, makes for a really sweet portrait.

The most famous image from the set, perhaps—only ever seen in a diary-style collage, with Peter's written ramblings, another photo, and a news clipping attached to it—is an almost tintype black-and-white image of Iman, down on all fours, in a cheetah-print swim cap and cheetah-print bathing suit, climbing a mount toward an actual cheetah. At the moment of the image, something off to camera right has drawn the attention of both Iman and the cheetah, and they both look up and off with that frisson of animal attentiveness Peter so adored, the moment of fight-or-flight adrenaline on glorious display. But is there something a bit icky in his arranging Iman in this bestial, catlike pose, wrapped in synthetic hides, dressed up as a simulacrum of the "Iman" he had invented for the fashion press?

Of the other images in the spread, there is no doubt that they are clumsy, offensive, or at best silly. Maybe the worst of these, which has recently resurfaced and received its fair share of excoriation online, finds Iman beneath an acacia tree, in only her sexy Eve skins, with the great vastness of Kenya behind her. But then, impossibly, just in front of her (maybe composited in?) a pair of antelope stand in a mounted coupling, mating. The whole thing is so crude, so base, it has almost gone all the way around and become parody (if only it were, alas).

Although Peter was then playing his old hits, slightly out of key for a younger audience, he was, like so many aging artists in their shtick years, probably at the height of his commerciality as a fashion photographer. Of course, he would say, "I don't think of it as fashion," putting supermodels in the bush, or standing Maasai and Turkana tribespeople in Alaïa couture. "I think of it . . . as opening up a new area of perspective—*vivre la différence*—a new understanding."

He even refused to be called a professional photographer at all, let alone a fashion one. "No, most photographers are boring," he said, "because they deny the importance of subject matter." He felt he was damned either way. "People think if you are photographing wildlife you are in the right, you are suffering in the woods. And if you are involved with a fashion magazine you are a spoiled rotten lazy Park Avenue drip."

And really, Peter Beard was not a fashion photographer—at least not in the mold of his contemporary Avedon, the fantasist Norman Parkinson, the fetishist Helmut Newton, or conceptualists like Jean-Paul Goude. From this period in the late 1980s through the 1990s and well into the 2000s, when stylists and creative directors displaced them at the top, fashion photographers occupied a very rare place in the industry and the culture. With little or no feedback from the audience in the way we have now with the internet, fashion photographers were given mountains of cash with which to project their fantasies on the public, feeding us a language of images that told us how to feel, what to want, who to be.

It wasn't that Peter had no interest in working with that material, but he was never going to run a full platoon of assistants and employees as, say, Bruce Weber did when he was getting paid $1 million in a weekend to shoot Abercrombie & Fitch campaigns. He wasn't going to observe the protocol and whatever else Mario Testino had to go through when he was photographing the queen and the royal family. Peter wasn't building the same sort of contained cinematic fantasies as the Tim Walkers and Peter Lindberghs, either. Maybe because he wasn't interested in the schedule or whatever politics he would've had to play, I cannot imagine Peter shooting ten covers and ten campaigns a year as the photo stars were capable of doing at the time. I can hardly even imagine him executing a shoot from an editor or creative director's brief; more to the point, I can't imagine him ever receiving something like that. Think about it from a brand or magazine's perspective at the time. If you were going to hire Peter Beard, you wouldn't want Peter in the studio shooting something ten other people could do; you'd want the full Peter Beard experience—blood on the print, lions, cheetahs, and rhinos, oh my.

Because he had just that one fantasy, that one gear, his work became increasingly difficult to justify, financially and otherwise, especially when the aesthetics of the industry began to shift very heavily toward the pristine, the pop, and the celebrity. This is the time in photography when Terry Richardson's star was in ascent, and his project of making people look like shiny, plastic products, shellacked and shrink-wrapped in the glaze of his flash, like something you'd find on a supermarket shelf, was in high demand. It's the time when cuddly celebrities in Gap chinos and crewnecks were at the apogee of fashion's advertising creativity, not a time in which Peter's *primitiva* was of increasing relevance.

The opportunities in fashion photography ahead of Peter were shrinking, but the landscape he'd already staked out as his own was not altogether safe from intrusion. In the 1990s, Goude and Arthur Elgort were taking supermodels on safari, and Weber was writing all over collages of his images in *L'Uomo Vogue* and *W.* Not that Peter was overly protective of his shtick, either. He continually downplayed his work, his grasp of the craft, and especially of the technical side of photography, telling me, "I did whatever I was attracted to. I could always get anybody to do good pictures. Photography is really subject matter. So if you can just somehow set the scene . . . ," shrugging it off, to say, *that's what's important.*

Even if you could set the scene, he seemed to believe, it was worth completely pulling the rug out from under everything before you got started just to spice up the day. Fashion editor Anne-Laure Lyon says she once arrived in Kenya for a shoot she was doing with Peter only to be greeted by Peter when she got off the plane, asking her where the cameras were. He'd broken all of his, seemingly just to upset the whole apple cart of the shoot, she thought, and Lyon had to scramble around Nairobi, ultimately tracking down an English photographer willing to loan his cameras to Peter to save the day. You can imagine Peter just beaming about the mayhem and stress he'd caused.

"I've manipulated events, I've manipulated crowds, I've manipulated people," he said—and, indeed, video and stories of Peter on set reveal him to be somewhat less than a hundred percent zen, getting at times a bit shouty, short-tempered, and cranky, as you might expect from a demanding narcissist with a vision and a massive budget burning down with the last of the natural light. "But you don't want the manipulation to be seen."

Build the stage for the lightning, he was saying, do the lightning dance, get all the best lightning conductors you can assemble in one place and then . . . maybe. "That's unique, I think," pointing to a very bloody print he'd made of a photo that got all the lightning in one little frame. "It's not easy to make that."

And unique really is the thing. For all the other artists and photographers who worked in a similar vein, if you'll excuse me, none of them made work that looked anything like his prints and collages and diaries. And that is something I have come back to again and again while thinking about his images—they are so satisfyingly Peter-y. The mess, the mulch of feathers and sticks and dirt and beer-can labels, the blood and ink and ephemera, arranged with his drippy, droopy, absolutely brilliant sense for design, is like nothing else in the world of art, and yet it is comfortingly familiar. Even the gore and yuck of it all feels very soothing and sort of profoundly right, on an organic level, as if he has somehow projected that protozoic pattern of spots and smears and spirals that we see behind our eyelids onto the entire world. The sense of recognition with something fundamentally human is deep and pronounced, throughout his work.

Just graphically—and whether he began to embellish the pictures because he was insecure about the images standing on their own, because he was just a busybody looking for surfaces to scuff up in his downtime, or what—his work will never be touched, will never age in quite the same way that the work of his contemporaries will, because he was able to transcribe, in all of his mess, something we all knew we knew but hadn't quite discovered a language for, a system of imagery, or style of art, something utterly human, enchanting. I joked with him that Francis Bacon sort of owns organs and gore in painting, and anyone encroaching on that will be seen to be copying him. Peter owns the human fingerprint (and footprint and everything else besides). All of his painting and doodling and, yes, stepping on and putting handprints on his prints, are, all of them and each of them, a kind of seismographic reading of the shape of human movement, a direct-to-medium tracing of the pace and contour and rhythm of our thoughts and reflexes, of our instincts and sense of harmony—the nautilus swirl or Fibonacci spiral of human-ness, splattered on a photo in butcher's blood.

THE DOCUMENTARY ABC WAS SHOOTING ABOUT PETER, which Gallagher had come out to appear in, was described, and marketed in some places as a profile of the artist. Elsewhere, it was characterized as "a dramatic photographic essay intended, in part, to depict the plight of wildlife in a changing Africa for a U.S. audience." In loglines and references to this now vanished artifact, the two premises seem almost interchangeable, as if Peter's life and the state and fate of wildlife in Africa, to an American audience, were inextricably intwined, or one just naturally went with the other.

To facilitate the filming of wildlife in the bush, the film's director, Robert Nixon—who had previously worked with Peter on the episodes of *American Sportsman* in which he was featured, in 1979—brought on board the veteran guide Terry Mathews. Up to 1977, when Kenya banned hunting, Mathews had been a prolific hunter himself, but in the decade since, leading up to his work on the film with Peter, he had segued to guide work, as well as sculpting wildlife. In fact, he was quite well known for a rhinoceros he had welded out of metal to celebrate Richard Leakey's theatrical bonfire of several tons of confiscated ivory. He and Peter set out straight away spotting and stalking rhinos, while Nixon and his crew filmed them from a hundred yards back. On these occasions, the two men were accompanied by a park ranger, Duncan Ogutu, who carried with him a rifle, "for security purposes," and they were trailed by two more of Ogutu's colleagues.

On February 17, Peter and Mathews spotted a rhino cow, a mother, whom Peter described as "windy" and unpredictable. She was probably a bit twitchy, what with these biped creatures coming into such proximity while she was watching over her calf. Of course Peter probably thought her anxiety would make for good images, so, after approaching the rhino in a crouch with Mathews and Ogutu to about forty yards distance, Peter stood bolt upright and began walking toward the rhino alone, filming her with "an inordinately loud" 16 mm camera. Which she did not exactly appreciate.

Up to this point, both men had been as careful as you'd expect from wildlife veterans, remaining downwind from the animals, approaching slowly, quietly. But what they didn't know is that, during their approach, tourists saw the rhino themselves and had stopped their vehicle to take in the view. Ogutu had diverted from Peter and Mathews to quiet the tourists, leaving the men alone.

In footage later presented to courts in Kenya and Manhattan, Peter is seen approaching the rhino, filming with his camera until the point where she takes a bit of umbrage.

The rhinoceros cow, apparently having become aware of Beard's presence, turned and moved slowly toward him, paused momentarily, then charged. Beard retreated immediately, leading the animal's charge toward Mathews and the film crew. Mathews initially stood his ground, reflexively shouting "bugger off" in an attempt to impede the rhino's advance. The rhino hesitated but was ultimately undeterred. As the rhino continued its charge, Mathews began to retreat but tripped and fell in the underbrush. The rhino cow continued its charge toward Mathews, goring and seriously wounding him.

In an affidavit submitted during the subsequent suit that Mathews filed against Peter, ABC, Nixon, and the production companies, he stated that he used the term *bugger off* because it has a lot of *grrr* to it; it sounds like a growl.

In the melee that followed the goring, while Mathews lay bleeding in the tall grass, no one could quite decide what to do. Mathews was the field man, the general of this outing, the one to whom they had all deferred during such operations; with him down, there was a vacuum in leadership. When he finally did make it to the hospital in Nairobi, eight hours later, he was in serious condition.

He sued the aforementioned parties, and very much especially Peter, for negligence. Not only had Peter recklessly and needlessly provoked the rhino, who they already knew to be a bit skittish, he had led this raging beast right at Mathews. In the affidavit made public, Peter and his co-defendants were filing for a dismissal of the suit, claiming that as a wily veteran of the bush, as a guide and former hunter, Mathews knowingly took on the risks of stalking a rhino at close enough proximity to film it. Citing Peter's behavior on the day, the court threw the filing for dismissal out the door, finding probative the argument that "Beard . . . in wanton disregard for the safety of others, including plaintiff, failed to heed the warning that he advance no closer to the rhinoceros and her calf." The court goes on to lecture Peter for all of his missteps in no uncertain terms. "Defendant BEARD panicked," they wrote, "and fled in the direction of the plaintiff and the accompanying crew thereupon placing plaintiff in imminent danger by drawing the animal's charge towards plaintiff and the said camera crew."

During the depositions, Nixon is quoted as saying that when he had previously worked with Peter, he pulled the same shit. "Nixon also testified that, in connection with a prior film, *End of the Game*, he had told Beard 'again and again, that it wasn't necessary . . . to get so close to wildlife,' yet 'it seemed to go in one ear and out the other.' Beard's reaction to this advice, according to Nixon, was to call Nixon and his camera crew 'chicken' and 'cowardly.'"

Ultimately, the court concluded, "This footage, in connection with the evidence discussed above, raises a triable issue of fact concerning whether Beard's conduct recklessly provoked the rhinoceros to charge and whether Beard's conduct was the proximate cause of Mathews' injuries," and suggested the suit move forward. But Terry, hemorrhaging money on lawyer's fees, broken physically, in and out of the hospital, acceded to his wife's entreaties that he give up the case. He bowed out.

"Peter called me on the phone, called me a chicken," Mathews told me. "He wanted to take the thing to trial. He wanted the publicity."

ABC did in fact cover Mathews's hospital bills for a couple of years. "And then they just pulled out. Stopped shut." Mathews remains significantly incapacitated from the event. His sight is now also fading, and he moves about his property near Nairobi with the help of ropes which he has strung up like railings. He still sculpts every day. And holds very little in the way of a grudge, though I gather that his wife and family are nowhere near as forgiving as he is.

After a halt in production, ABC hired a new director, and the show went on, all the way to completion. With very little fanfare and almost no publicity, *Last Word from Paradise* aired on ABC on April 22, 1988, and almost immediately disappeared. It is now nowhere to be found on YouTube or streaming services. A representative from Disney, now the parent company of ABC, recently claimed that they have no record of the title in their archive.

PETER, TOO, WAS LOOKING AT SOME SIGNIFICANT LEGAL fees, as well as his general lack of cash. Lack of it, that is, once he'd spent it all as fast as he'd gotten it, whether that be his roughly $60,000 in annual trust fund payments, or his editorial and commercial commissions (neither of which amounted to much), or his book and print sales, which weren't bringing in anything in the late 1980s and early '90s. He needed money and went about looking to raise it. Anyway, that is how he later spun the story.

At the time, Marlene Dietrich's grandson, Peter Riva, who had been working as a literary agent, asked Peter why he didn't have an agent. "He said, 'No, no, no. I don't have an agent; agents are useless.' And then I got this phone call from Peter Schub," Riva says. "Now, I didn't know Peter Schub from Adam, but I quickly found out who he was and it turns out Peter Schub was very, very well connected. Andy Warhol was one of his clients for commercial work." As were Gordon Parks and Lord Snowdon. "And Peter Schub called me up one morning, and he said, 'You're welcome to this asshole. I never want to talk to him again.' He'd upset Peter Schub in a conversation or something because Peter [Beard] was, quite frankly, homophobic. And Peter Schub was homosexual, and it got to the point where he said, 'You've got him, he's your client. Now I'm taking everything that he left at my house. I'm putting it in the dumpster.' And I went there at five o'clock in the morning to see what he was talking about. And, sure enough, in the dumpster was all Beard vintage prints and everything else, which I took out of the dumpster. All the early Stones stuff and San Quentin and with Truman Capote . . ."

There is a thread of this sort of behavior running right through Peter's life. As Riva remembers, "You'd see Peter in Africa with Mwengui or Kivoi [who worked with him on his prints at Hog Ranch], and he was [acting] superior to them, but he didn't think that he was a better human being than they were. But his position was 'I'm the overseer.' I hate to use the word overseer, but I mean it like that. They did what he told them to do or else." There are some videos of Peter at Hog Ranch that bear this out. In them, the tented campsite appears like a sort of al fresco artist studio and Peter a cartoonishly bombastic director barking orders, then taunting, teasing, cajoling, threatening playfully, and generally acting the way a megalomaniac studio artist would be portrayed in a *Law & Order* b-plot.

But, as Riva suggests, Peter was an equal-opportunity asshole. He was terrible to people from all walks of life. He was racist, sexist, anti-Semitic, *and* homophobic. There is, of course, the well-documented occasion, during a dinner party in the early 2000s, when Peter was seated next to Tom Ford. At some point during dinner, Peter turned to him and said, according to Riva, "Thank god you're not a fag like all the other designers." In a *New York* magazine article that touched on this episode, Peter was quoted, speaking about Tom Ford, as saying, "But he looks absolutely normal. I sat right next to him and I studied him and I thought, Whoa! A fashion exception. I'm not homophobic, but the odds are getting a little heavy, aren't they?" And then, Peter added, of homosexuality:

Let me assure you, this is a societal illness. . . . I went on the Stones tour with Truman Capote. He was one of my best friends, and he was kind of like Napoleon of the gays. We went to the clubs. For once, I have to stand up for the old pope. This is a societal illness of every single species in nature. I went to the Darwinian centennial, and some very high-up professor told me it was already well known in scientific circles that the separation-of-the-sexes phenomenon is in large part due to the chemicals in our food and drinking water. This is the first effect of exceeding carrying capacity. AIDS, cancer, heart disease—they're all sent by nature.

And still went right on thinking he'd said nothing out of place. "Which is so much like Trump," Riva says. "Beard can only accept his own reality," despite help or guidance enlightening him to the contrary.

Still, despite calling Peter "difficult to work with," in what one imagines to be one of the bigger understatements of the century, Riva helped Peter get magazine work, among other things. In the wake of the ABC shoot, with fond memories of the money he'd gotten in working with *Playboy* on his shoot with Iman in 1986, Peter and Riva wrangled another commission from Hugh Hefner's outfit.

Janice Dickinson was at the time thirty-two, a bit fed up with the modeling industry in New York, spending some time in Milan and, as she would for some time, struggling with alcohol and drugs. Peter and she had met in 1981, when Peter was still married to Cheryl Tiegs. Dickinson had wanted to show Peter some pictures she had taken, maybe get a little creative feedback, advice. Peter told her that, until Cheryl moved in, he'd had a giant, seven-foot-tall poster of Dickinson in his apartment, a photo taken by her ex-boyfriend, the fashion photographer Mike Reinhardt. "You know," Peter said to Dickinson, as she recalls, "when Cheryl saw that poster, she ran her fingernails down the length of your entire body, like a cat, and said, 'Peter, you take Janice off the wall or I walk.'"

It's a typical Peter story: told to titillate, and certainly to flatter the listener, appealing to her vanity, perhaps, making her feel honored, having had pride of place, but also displaced, called upon to regain her status, drumming up notions of "catty" drama between competing women eager to hold exclusive real estate on the walls of his imagination, underscoring his notions of a pecking order, even as he will likely go on to say how nonsensical the whole industry and apparatus of power is.

"I loved that story," Dickinson wrote in her autobiography, *No Lifeguard on Duty.*

Peter loved Dickinson's photos, which she had taken in China; he made a big fuss over them, flattering her once again. Maybe he made a few calls around town, or perhaps he knew that the

Bloomingdale's store on Lex was looking for just that sort of thing, but he helped arrange for Dickinson to exhibit her photos in the store, to her eternal gratitude. Also, very typical of Peter.

So, seven years later, Dickinson says, she gets a message from Peter, who was in Rome at the time, and she calls him back.

He says, she wrote, "'Janice, you bitch. Where the hell have you been?'

"'Hiding.'

"'Nobody can find you.'

"'That's sort of the point,' I said.

"You look fantastic," Peter told her, having seen recent images of her in Italian ads. "You're everywhere—all over Europe. You look delectable. You look like a little boy."

"Tell me something," she says she asked him. "Do all heterosexual men hunger for little boys?"

"Peter laughed so hard he almost choked," Dickinson wrote.

"'Are you all right?' I asked.

"'Tell me you'll go to Kenya with me and I'll be all right,' he said.

"'What's in Kenya?'

"'An assignment for American *Playboy*. It's perfect for you. And the money is very good indeed.'

"'Is it slutty?' I ask him.

"'Janice, darling—you couldn't be slutty if you tried.'

"That was the right thing to say. The following week I was on my way to Kenya."

Peter picked her up at the airport, and, upon arriving at the hotel, she was received by "two dowdy women from *Playboy*'s Chicago office" who presented her with duffel bags of the tackiest, sluttiest clothing imaginable: "Fuck-me pants. Undies with zippers. Cowboy hats. See-through bras—as if I needed a bra. And I said, 'Ladies, this cheap shit doesn't work for me.'

"And one of them said, 'I'm sorry. This is what you're going to wear, sweetheart.'

"'Yeah? We'll see about that, *sweetheart.*'

"So I went to see Peter, to whine about the outfits, and he agreed that the outfits were tacky in the extreme. And the two of us spent the rest of the morning in the local markets, buying incredibly beautiful African wraps. . . . And that's what he shot me in."

But if he was championing Dickinson here, supporting her voice and taste and opinion, and going out of his way to get her the materials that made her feel comfortable for the shoot, the way he cajoled her into some of the dicier situations on set is a little less than exemplary.

"In the morning, Peter grabbed his equipment and we drove to a nearby village that was popular with the tourists," she says. "They had a collection of crocodiles there that were goddamn prehistoric. Some of them were up to sixteen feet long. Real monsters. Peter had the croc wranglers anesthetize six of the biggest ones and tie their snouts together with transparent fishing line, then asked the men to pile the beasts on top of one another.

"'What the hell are you doing?' I asked," she says.

"'I want you on top of that pile,' [Peter] said.

"'Oh no,' I said, 'No fucking way. You're crazy.'

"'Here, Janice. Have a beer.' Seemed like a good idea."

You will remember that at the time Dickinson was trying to contend with her alcohol abuse.

"I fortified myself with beer," she says.

"Finally, it was the moment of truth. Peter helped me out of my wrap and the men in the crowd ooohhed and aaahhed with delight. I was wearing the skimpiest little thong, and a tiny little top that barely covered my tiny little nontits. And I was a little drunk, to be honest. I don't see how I could've done it sober.

"'Come on,' Peter bellowed," she says. "'Hurry, before they wake.'

"I began to climb. I could hear them purring like cats, asleep but not asleep enough for me. I could feel their low, guttural grunting; I could hear their wheezy breath.

"But I was on top now. I'd made it. My bare feet hurt against their hard, leathery skin, but I didn't care. The crowd was cheering; Peter was snapping away. And there I was, vamping and posing and kicking my legs like a crazy, drunken ballerina."

Fashion.

But it seems working with Peter was never just one thing, and seldom even just two. There was the tireless flattery, indeed, the emotional support and encouragement, the ally-ship, ensuring that Dickinson had what she needed to feel beautiful and empowered. But then there was the taskmaster, bellowing at you to climb a pyramid of crocodiles, to do anything necessary to get the shots he wants. And then of course there is the third thing, that which is always present, for any and everyone who met Peter: the grand gesture, sweeping Dickinson and everyone else off their feet.

"He asked me if I minded extending the shoot," Dickinson says. "He had a ranch right at the base of Mount Kenya . . . and he wanted me to see it. So we flew out in one of those lumbering prop planes and landed on this dirt strip, where a Jeep was waiting for us. Peter hopped behind the wheel—very macho—and we drove on the rutted dirt roads to [t]his ranch. It was pure, unspoiled wilderness. The place consisted of nothing but three tents in the middle of nowhere. The trees were so graceful they made me feel like weeping.

"'It's nice, isn't it,' Peter asked me," she says.

"'Nice? Nice? Are you out of your fucking mind? It's paradise.'

"There were servants everywhere and they cooked us dinner out in this big open pit. Venison, I think it was. We ate and drank champagne and watched the sun set, and I felt like Meryl

Streep. . . . We finished our champagne and turned in—me in one tent, Peter in another. And in the middle of the night I woke to hear the most frightful growling and I screamed at the top of my voice: 'Peter! Peter, goddamnit! Get in here!'

"A few moments later, I hear him coming. And I heard that sound again and I leapt into his arms, terrified. And he began to laugh. 'What are you afraid of? It's just a couple of big cats, fucking,' he said. And I said I didn't care. I wanted him to stay with me, in my tent. And he slipped into my cot and held me. And it felt nice."

Nothing sexual happened then or ever between them though, Dickinson said later, because he was always so filthy. "He was gorgeous and so charming," she said, "but I'm a germaphobe."

DURING THIS PERIOD THERE WAS A RAID ON PETER'S PROP-erty at Hog Ranch. Officials found *bang*—marijuana—growing on the property and trumped up some charges that might've led to jail time or even eviction for Peter. Riva thought it was a setup, plain and simple. "Basically someone wanted his land," Riva said, and those people knew enough corrupt government officials to free it up for them. "What would've come next," if Peter fought the charges, and didn't cede the land, "is they would've killed him. I mean this is Africa," Riva said. And Peter did not then have a great many friends, whether in government or anywhere in Kenya, who might've come to his rescue.

By the late 1980s, and early '90s, Peter's reputation within Kenya was . . . well, right about where it had always been. His great friend from the early days, the first warden of Tsavo National Park, David Sheldrick, fell out with him over disagreements about how to handle the crisis in Tsavo. Second-generation safari guide Glen Cottar, who'd given Peter some of his earliest work in Kenya, had, of course, cut him off for his recklessness in the field when working with wildlife. "He didn't do it the right way" was generally the line. And he was a bit of a nuisance, always making a spectacle of himself, flying in with great fanfare and some supermodels and a camera crew in tow. His was not the right attention for Kenya.

Others, like Alastair Graham, with whom he had made the study of Nile crocodiles in Lake Turkana that formed the basis of their book *Eyelids of Morning*, and Ian Parker, the writer and enormously important voice in wildlife affairs, with whom Peter had crossed paths in the Aberdares in the late 1960s, remained cordial enough with him. At least until 1992, when, to their minds, Peter crossed a line. Now neither man will even speak of him.

What happened in 1992 was that Peter, along with the sort of de facto manager of Hog Ranch, Gillies Turle—an Englishman who'd worked as an antiques dealer for years before moving to Hog Ranch—published a book, *The Art of the Maasai*, in which they claimed to have discovered an ancient tradition of something like shamanism within Maasai culture, and with it, artifacts dating back to great antiquity.

Among the pieces, which Turle said he got through a secret source, a man who turned up at his shop one day with news that he had something Turle might be interested in, were staffs made of rhino horn, as well as "horn and bone pipes, arm bands, amulets, the carved splints young Maasai warriors used to pry open a lion's jaws in the ceremonial hunts that were their initiation to manhood," as the writer Susan Zakin described them, in an article sympathetic to Turle's cause.

According to Turle, a middleman approached him, saying that he had these sacred items, which were once in the employ of holy men, *laibons*, but which they now no longer needed. He was unloading these pieces, sometimes one at a time, and for which Turle estimates he spent around $150 a pop. It didn't matter how much he got them for to Peter, though, who was incredibly fond of claiming that the craftsmanship of the pieces themselves, the artistry "went well beyond Brancusi and right up to Picasso."

But the book Peter and Turle produced hit with a bit of a thud. The guys had been hoping for invitations from museums to house their collection, perhaps, or maybe a very steep offer from Christie's. What they got instead was the silent treatment, and maybe some titters from people embarrassed by their credulity, or their conspiracy—as it was hard to discern then, as it remains so now, who was fooling whom, if indeed fooling went on.

"The chief *laibon* up here has never heard of such a thing," Glen Cottar's son Calvin says of the guys' precious discoveries—which of course they had claimed were specially made for and used by the *laibon*. Calvin, who has lived on the edge of Maasai country and worked with many dozens of Maasai men and women throughout his life, has no doubt that the objects are not what Peter and Turle presented them to be. But as to how it all came to pass, he scratches his head.

Could've been some hustler, hawking wares he thought Turle might like, spinning a story about their provenance to wheedle a bit more money out of the exchange. Then Peter, perhaps a bit optimistic in his reading of the situation, hoping to find a way for Turle and himself to make a few quid, really did believe they were on to a discovery bigger than King Tut's tomb. There seems to be no other way to describe the zeal and energy with which he took up the cause, selling the idea to anyone he spoke to, taking photographs of the objects (along with Mark Greenberg) for a book they published, hoping to drum up real academic and commercial support.

Turle, for his part, when I visited him near his home in the village of Shela on Lamu Island, off the coast of Kenya, is absolutely adamant that the pieces he assembled are of a profound historical significance and testify to a secret practice of shamanism within the Maasai culture that has hitherto remained undiscovered—and is now at risk of being lost forever. In making their case, Peter and Turle's greatest champion had been the American anthropologist (and later, antiques dealer and real estate consultant in Kinderhook, New York) Roderic Blackburn. During his time as a research associate in the Department of Anthropology at the Museum of Natural History in Manhattan, and in the Institute of Anthropology, Gender, and African Studies at the University of Nairobi in the early 1990s, Blackburn visited Peter and Turle at Hog Ranch. He heard their story of the objects, felt their fervor, and was himself mesmerized by the pieces. According to a recent piece by Susan Zakin, "He expected the visit to be purely social. Instead, Beard and his friend Gillies Turle showed him a vast array of objects—pipes, amulets, staffs—carved from bone and horn. Acting in Rod's words 'like eager schoolboys' they told him about Maasai diviners called *laibons*. . . . *Laibons* could foretell the future, smite enemies, or heal wounds suffered by a *moran*, a young Maasai warrior, when he participated in the ritual killing of a lion. . . . Their stories, if true, were astonishing. None of the literature on the Maasai, one of the most studied ethnic groups in the world, mentioned this mystical tradition."

But did none mention it because it was utter hogwash, or because tribal leaders, having suffered generations of torture and persecution at the hands of the colonists for "practicing witchcraft," weren't about to share their stories with white anthropologists? If the latter, then what would be a monumental discovery, bringing insight into traditional culture—as well as the interconnectedness of various tribes who worked together, it was suggested, to produce the objects in question—would very soon disappear. As Maasai and other tribes were slowly but surely pulled away from their heritage and practices, interest in, use of, and knowledge about this craft would soon go extinct forever. At any rate, that was Peter and Turle's story.

At this point in their pleading, Peter and Turle asked Blackburn to take up the research of these objects, and of the practices behind them, to validate their discovery in academe. According to Turle, Blackburn agreed, set about applying for permission to conduct the research with the National Museum of Kenya, and arranged for a meeting with its director, Richard Leakey.

Richard Leakey had no doubts on the matter of the objects and no qualms about alleging who and what were behind the spurious claims, and he was supported by just about everyone, including Professor Donna Klumpp Pido, who described the book as "littered with inaccuracies regarding Maasai life," and the artifacts themselves as recently made, intended for the art market. Of course, Leakey might have had just a teensy-weensy bit of a bias in the matter. He and Peter had loathed each other since 1969, when Peter punched a poacher and then tied him to a tree on his property and went off to have lunch. Leakey spearheaded Peter's subsequent prosecution. And ever since Leakey put on his frightful bit of conservationist theater, publicly burning twelve tons of confiscated ivory—a wild publicity stunt aimed at raising foreign capital (which it did, to the tune of some $140 million from the World Bank)—Peter thought Leakey the worst sort of showman, corrupting the conservation of wildlife by inviting in the sanctimonious White Saviors with their idiotic ideas and misunderstandings of the landscape.

This latter event, the burning of the ivory, took place in 1989, shortly after Leakey took charge of Kenya's Wildlife Conservation and Management Department (which has since evolved into the Kenya Wildlife Service), making him, effectively, the Eliot Ness of the government's crackdown on the illegal ivory trade—historically a very iffy, very corrupt aspect of the Kenyan government. One might describe those in charge of policing the illegal capture and trade of ivory since the ban on elephant hunting in 1973 (the sale of ivory at the time still remained legal, as it always had, to those with the right permits) as gangsters with immunity and a free hand, stealing from the thieves and making a fortune while doing it. With his new millions in the bank and a shoot-to-kill order for poachers in Kenya issued directly by the president himself, Daniel Arap Moi, Leakey turned his Wildlife Department into a kind of "paramilitary force," in Zakin's words, shooting one poacher every four days in Leakey's first year at the helm.

I am not suggesting that Leakey was himself corrupt. But when seventeen of the eighteen boxes of artifacts he'd assembled, many of them made from rhino-horn ivory, were confiscated after a raid at Hog Ranch ordered by Leakey, the thought did cross Turle's mind. "I don't know where they all are now," he says of the contents of those boxes, "sold to the highest bidder, I imagine."

When he met with Blackburn, and later, with Turle directly, Leakey implied that Peter and Turle were smugglers, dressing up their catch in historical nonsense to ferry it outside the country, where they could sell it as what it really was, plain old ivory. More, he accused the men of conspiring with poachers to kill rhinos for their ivory, which they had shaped into these delicate objects, to which they then added a patina of age with smoke. An outrageous claim, Turle feels, but he remains hopeful that some recent and forthcoming articles sympathetic to his view will not only clear this slander against him, but also fully validate his great discovery.

It is Turle's life's work, the assemblage of these pieces, for which he estimates he has spent over the years something like $200,000, and for which he says he was put in prison, after the second raid of Hog Ranch in 1999 (though all charges against him were suddenly and unceremoniously dropped a year later with no explanation). But the fire and brimstone with which Leakey came down on him was always, fundamentally, really aimed at Peter. In fact, Leakey later said that he only regretted that he was out of town when Turle was arrested, because had he been there, he surely would have "broken" him and gotten out of him actionable intelligence on Peter. Either way, Leakey's tactics did get rid of his problem. Peter fled the country after the '99 raid and stayed away for years.

BUT WAS PETER HIMSELF A CON MAN? WAS HE A QUIXOTIC fool, duped into seeing something magical in what was ultimately mundane? Or was this some sort of game to him?

We know the man could lie like the best of them, publicly, on the record, in front of the whole world. The charade around Iman's introduction to the fashion media, *performed at a press conference* with an absolutely straight face, tells us everything we need to know on that score. And no one can maintain myriad overlapping romantic relationships without the occasional fib, about where he is and with whom and why, as well as lies by omission and general deceit.

Whether he decided to never indulge in guilt, as he said after the mill fire in 1977, or whether he was constitutionally incapable of it, he never troubled himself too terribly much about what others thought of him, how his actions affected the lives and feelings and well-being of others—even if they were longtime bosom buddies or romantic companions. "He lied, cheated, stole, and disappeared," Gallagher had said. And he was mercilessly cold about it.

When, in 2004, he and Gallagher saw each other for the last time, they spent the weekend at the Bowery Hotel in Manhattan, camped away in their room, as she described it, watching the Sochi Olympics.

> We had bullshots and room service. Peter was still great-looking—I loved his jawline, the shape of his face. He was always sexy to me, handsome and romantic. There was never going to be a love like ours again. I didn't know it would be the last time we'd see each other. There was a lot of commotion about a lawsuit, and lawyers coming to

the hotel. I had to act like I wasn't there with him. I met him down in the lobby, and the last time I heard his voice he pointed to me and said to someone standing next to him, "That's Maureen, the girl in the giraffe photo."

Twenty-seven years of love and friendship: "the girl in the giraffe photo."

Relationships, marriage, and any other social norms were not of much consideration to Peter. He felt himself to be completely outside of our moral scales of right and wrong, good and bad; he simply did not recognize them. He wasn't always even consciously in rebellion against them. He just felt himself to be outside of the box and never considered whether or not to do something, only whether he wanted to (and perhaps, whether he would get in trouble for it).

His cavalier disregard of close contacts was not exclusive to his romantic relationships. I think that Peter saw people in two categories, essentially: those whom he needed to seduce to get something he wanted, and those who were superfluous. Heaven and all of the stars in the cosmos could shine down upon you if you happened to fall into the former category. No one on Earth did the song and dance better, could be more charming, more attentive and charismatic, a better host, dinner party guest, friend, lover, what have you. But heaven help you if you fell into the latter category.

Even if you were on his good side, he would risk your safety at the drop of a hat if he happened upon an impulse breezing by that called him to action, summoning him to slake some desire, for experience, for a picture, to get closer to a rhino cow, for example, and never think for a second he was in the wrong. Never would he even consider that he was at fault, for Mathews's injury, for anything that might've happened to Dickinson, even for his own calamities.

"He used to say, 'I'm never going to apologize. I'm never going to explain. I'll never say thank you,'" Peter's friend, longtime agent, and manager Peter Riva told me. "His mother said that he had adopted that [way of thinking] from the age of eighteen or nineteen. I felt it was a weakness on his part. As if, if he said, 'Thank you,' he was showing weakness. Or if he apologized, it was showing he was less than strong. It was sad."

He could even be playful, puckish, too—but there, I think, we cross a line into something else, something a bit more like controlling, as with practical jokes very often made at another's expense for the joker's own amusement. "Impish," is the word Gallagher used to describe him. "He wanted his way, and he wanted his way."

I think that Peter liked to watch people feel things that he made happen to them. And perhaps he laughed in their face afterward, charming them into nervous laughter themselves, making them feel as though they were in on the joke. He laughed at points while he was talking, but seemingly all out of rhythm with whatever humor lay in the content of his speech, rather as an effort to defuse something he'd said, or as an act to conjure a response, but not to reflect a feeling of fun he felt.

It seems to me, in watching footage of him, playing back our own conversations, and reading things he's said, that he altogether lacked the register of compassion required for humor. He couldn't, even if he was performing jokiness, really hear laughter or silence—or really care which he did hear, which is probably more to the point. And perhaps what is even more telling is that there is no self-awareness, no knowingness, no wink, no irony, no humor whatsoever in his work. Reams and reams of work. Cleverness, yes. And what camp there is, is unfortunately unintentional. But no humor.

So I wonder how this flattening of his experience might've affected his life and work. Did it trap him in his stentorian key with his adolescent idée fixe, the elephants and apocalypse, about which he was only ever as serious as a soapbox screed? Did it lead him to settle on that cause, that mission, because he found in looming mass extinction a kind of flattening of everything else to meet him on his own level? If the world is ending, nothing else really matters, not even humor. And if you devote your life to documenting the evidence of our decline, making it beautiful and sensational so that people will pay attention, will heed your message, and they do not, is there any other way to behave than in total hedonistic frenzy, disappointedly lecturing all who will listen about the sky coming down with a crash?

CHAPTER 10

Stress and Density

I n Maa, the Maasai language, the word *mara* means "spotted," as in the Maasai Mara, the great, 580-square-mile game reserve in southwestern Kenya, the backdrop to many millions of your favorite wildlife photos. And viewed with any sort of perspective, from height while in flight or through the long telephoto lens of wildlife photographers, you see why: the umbrella-topped acacia tree, famous from every travel brochure image of Africa, speckles the grassy plains here like so many spots on a big tawny cat.

Up close, of course, the acacia is an oddly elegant tree, gnarly limbs tapering the wrong way around, down from its thorny canopy to the earth below, its long lean trunks twisty and angular, like thin wizards bent together in conspiracy. From a distance, though, from one gentle golden grassy slope to another, these icons look like flattened stick figures, like the trees a child might draw. And there, the lone elephant, standing in a clearing between solitary acacias, too, looks just the way a child might sketch it with a crayon. The scale of the vistas here, in both their immensity and then the sudden proximity of the nearby slopes with their acacias and elephants, can be a bit startling—not in a way that feels strange or uncomfortable, but rather immediately and eerily familiar.

I seem to know this landscape before having ever arrived. Of course I have, throughout my life, seen it in various media, in Disney movies, and probably in dreams, but still that doesn't quite explain it. "It is because you are at home here," Calvin Cottar says. "We all are. This is the place we became human."

Calvin owns and operates the luxury safari outfit and its 1920s-style camp at the edge of the Mara, near the Tanzanian border, called Cottar's Kenya, which was established by his grandfather, Chas, more than a hundred years ago. Chas came to Kenya from Oklahoma, looking perhaps for even bigger skies, a greater outdoors in the only place on earth that might have them. He stuck around, starting, alongside the Bror Blixens and Finch Hattons, the Kers and Downeys, one of the first safari guiding outfits. After Chas passed (in a field near here, where he'd been hit by a rhino while photographing it), his son Glen Cottar took up the reins. One of Glen's innovations was to arrange fly camps— a nimbler camping setup to allow clients greater movement to cover the vastness of Kenya by plane, raising the possibility for sightings enormously. In the 1960s, Glen hired Peter and Galo-Galo to build some of the hides (blinds) for these camps—the safe spots where the tourists could see the game but still feel protected— and Glen and Peter worked together for decades after that. You'll remember that Peter shot many of his most majestic elephant shots in Tsavo, and he had his run-in with the lion while building these hides for Glen. So Calvin, Glen's son, now in his mid-fifties, with adult children of his own who may take up the mantle eventually, knew Peter from the time he was a child, and remembers the way Peter would blow into their lives for brief stints, like a merrymaking tornado, before soon enough blowing right out again, leaving the Cottars to laugh and tell stories, marveling about this "force of nature" they'd encountered.

In 1988, after Terry Mathews was gored by the rhino while working on the ABC special about Peter, Glen had finally had enough of Peter's dangerous antics. He had always thought Peter's behavior around big game, pushing the envelope at every chance, pushing, pushing, pushing, and pushing some more, was going to get him—or someone else—hurt or killed, and all for a photograph, just like Glen's own father. Although he believed both Peter and Terry Mathews bore responsibility for the accident, the goring proved Glen right. He wanted nothing more to do with Peter and told him so, cutting him off forever.

After Glen passed away in 1996, Peter got in contact with Calvin. He wanted to bring some people out to the recently established Cottar's Camp near the Tanzanian border, where the Mara gives onto the massive Serengeti, for a safari. And Calvin thought, *Sure, why not? Let's let bygones be bygones.* He invited Peter out, and Peter brought along a photographer who was making a film about him. If the hairs on your neck just stood up because this setup sounds a bit familiar, you're not wrong. The circumstances were so strikingly reminiscent of those leading up to the 1988 accident that left Terry Mathews in the hospital that, if Peter's senses weren't tingling, something was a bit wrong. Here again someone was making a film about the legendary wild man Peter Beard, who, with the cameras rolling, may again be compelled to do something spectacular, something to make great content, something to put himself and everyone around him at risk.

The long grasses rolling away in every direction for as far as we can see look like waves of combed cashmere, a kind of downy cream color, turning gold, pink, and mauve in the spring sunshine. There are a series of controlled fires burning on the Tanzanian border now. As Calvin is talking, we come to a stop about twenty yards from a lone elephant—seemingly alone, that is. "You see," he says, "she is happy to turn her back if she is outside of the flight path." The range of an arrow or spear, he means.

Over millennia we evolved together, the human and the megafauna here, to the point that they recognize our range of danger instinctively. Finding themselves beyond the reach of human propelled projectiles, an elephant, a lion, a leopard will happily just turn tail and jog off, content to be away from bothersome men. But! If we should surprise one of these creatures on its own, somewhere within the range of our airborne missiles, Calvin says, "They have no choice but to charge." Instinct has wired it into their programming that if they find themselves that close to that grave a threat—within reach of an arrow or spear from this biped hunter with killer intent—they must attack it first. "Which is why there are so few megafauna elsewhere. They hadn't evolved alongside us," Calvin says, so they didn't know our tricks, weren't appropriately suspicious of us wily humans.

When we did return to these parts, only a few thousand years ago, the megafauna here were still plentiful enough that we haven't yet had time to stomp them all into extinction. Or not quite yet anyway. This is one of the reasons Peter felt most at home and most alive in this part of the world.

He loved to cross over the threshold into the arrow-flight range of experience—into the zone where instincts kicked in, where every animal from elephants to humans was operating on something purely primal, beyond reason, closer to something like genetic programming. That is where Peter wanted to live, where he found the pictures that most interested him. But in following Peter's footsteps across three continents, talking to his friends and intimates, wondering aloud with them and writing here in solitude about Peter's continual flouting of the boundary between safety and its opposite—his flouting of all boundaries—I have come to doubt that we have the proper language to describe his behavior. We fall into trite-isms only, but seem to wave away the workings of whatever machinery propelled him into the pathways of lions and elephants. We collapse in our imaginings this behavior into a lump, equating it with his need for attention and for beautiful romantic company. At times we describe him, as Bob Colacello did, as *liking* danger, and so explain away his courting it whenever he could. Maybe we say that he thrived on adrenaline, as his friend Mick Jagger must, but without the same sort of stage to provide it for him. We can agree that he was compelled to bite his thumb at forms of control, even his own feelings of safety that relied on them. But the need, the continual compulsion to cross that line . . . even Peter couldn't properly describe it. Was it about going a step further than anyone else had the will to do in order to provoke a better photograph? Or to hit a greater payload of his favorite adrenaline rush? Or was it indeed to feel that real, final boundary, the boundary between life and death, and to thrum it just as he had every other line in his life, the better to hear its music.

To ask analogous questions in another but perhaps related arena of his life, was his vanity ever properly slaked by the adulation and conquest he chased alongside a parade of beautiful women his entire life? Are appetites like those, like the one he had for danger, ever really satisfied, or are they in fact more like addictions than a healthy hunger?

One possibility—and before I begin to sound too terribly puritanical in reading the runes of Peter's life, I should say that the following is the reading that I and all of his intimates on whom I tried it favor, namely that Peter's constant crossing of the line, like his constant chasing of women, was simply something to do. Something to which he had become habituated, sure, and which suited his temperaments, his aesthetic interests, his era, and his metabolism, but merely one possible response to the cold indifference of the universe. I would suggest that Peter behaved the way he did, around elephants and supermodels both, as a response to and a desperate rebellion against his own overwhelming fatalism. In his heartbreak over the destruction of the natural world—and, thus, along with it, all other worlds there might be—Peter resigned himself to a belief that in truth there is nothing to be done to save us, that all is doomed and nothing really even matters.

"I have no idea what the point is," he said. "And I think we are, as [Francis] Bacon suggested . . . living a meaningless existence from birth to death. No one knows the answer. . . . We don't know what consciousness is. We don't know what reality is. We don't know what time is. We are just ants on an anthill."

Lost in a void, in nature. And there is no morality that matters in nature. The cruel, the corrupt, and the accidentally lucky win, momentarily, until all is rendered unto rot and ruin forever. Nothing man-made will last, all will pass save the desecration we have wrought. Finding that the world he saw to be as close to paradise as can be hoped for was being destroyed by our own hand, knowingly, with only short-term comfort and minuscule capitalist gains to be had at the cost of everything, of Eden, he gave up all hope that he had. Peter understood that God was dead, you might say, so he figured, we might as well party. Might as well enjoy the world that remains, find beauty, which he regularly said was the only thing left that mattered in the cosmos. And so he did. He fucked and flailed like someone desperate to soothe himself, someone who is desperately crying out, for attention, definitely, in pain, maybe, and definitely in disappointment. But he carried on, as he had to do, because that's just the way we are programmed.

In a digression on human evolution in his book *The Songlines*, Bruce Chatwin records meeting the South African paleontologist Elisabeth Vrba, who mentioned to him, he wrote, that "antelopes are stimulated to migrate by lightning. 'So,' I said, 'are Kalahari Bushmen,'" Chatwin wrote. "'They also "follow" the lightning. For where the lightning has been, there will be water, greenery, and game.'" And I cannot think of a better way to describe Peter's energies, in his work, with wildlife, indeed, even around people, with whom he was always trying to create electricity, if not thunderstorms: running toward the dramatic, the dangerous, the electrifying. Maybe there was some evolutionary strand in Peter's DNA that led him as it did the wildebeest and antelope and human hunters, to run toward the lightning.

PETER RIVA TOLD ME THAT HE BELIEVED PETER TO BE SOME-
thing of a savant in the bush. Instinctive in that arena, with a special talent. Skilled in a way with animals that even those with great familiarity and long experience are not. As if, in his constant strumming of that tripwire between safety and danger, between an animal's bluster and belligerent rage, he had acquired some deeper knowledge of game. Or was he like some great sport stars, born with an innate brilliance in the field, a gift for anticipation, for reading mood, sounds, smells, animals' intentions, and levels of maliciousness? Maybe he had some sort of special gift. More in touch with his instincts than the rest of us?

"Well," Calvin says, "he was no Galo-Galo, I can tell you that."

In every sport, every walk of life, there seems to be a Michael Jordan, against whom all others will be gauged, and in the world of wildlife, there is Galo-Galo, possibly the greatest hunter of all time, who once filled an entire lorry truck with elephant ivory on a single hunt. "He was like a god to us," says Moses (through a translation), a Giriami hunter and guide who has worked with the Cottar clan for decades. And then he mimes the feelings of absolute awe, reverence.

Calvin is now speaking in a sort of bush slang with Wilson Mpatiany, a Cottar's guide who is driving the Land Rover. It is clear that Calvin is giving directions, but not by any means I recognize. This fig tree, that rock, the old road (that has been gone for maybe a decade). "No problem," Wilson later tells me. "In Nairobi if you tell me go here, there, I have no idea. In bush speak, I know right away. This road, that tree, you see, we arrive here right away."

We pass an enormous fig tree, biblical in its proportions, hundreds of years old, and then double back above it, toward a granite rock the size of a suburban mansion, and park beneath an acacia. "Right where we were parked on the day," Calvin says.

We have come to this site in particular, and even parked the Land Rover just as it had been parked on the day in September 1996 when Calvin and Peter, with a couple of intern guides and the filmmaker Guillaume Bonn, came to this spot to pursue a group of elephants they'd seen nearby.

We park the car and Calvin marvels a bit to himself that he hasn't walked this field, re-created that day in all the time since. When he drifts off, the wind in the tall grass is the only sound.

Calvin is prowling now, and I have to hustle to keep up with him, to hear him narrating the events, beat by beat, as they took place on the day. He is determined to re-create it just so, and he's clearly affected by the emotion of reimagining it for the first time.

We are now about to enter a bit of an open space with no coverage. The group of elephants would have been quite close. Uphill slightly and maybe thirty yards away. At this spot, on the day in 1996, Calvin told the others to hang back, and went ahead with only Peter. Right now, he points over to a thicket of bushes, noting, quite casually, that there is a "big black beast in there. It'd be a shame to recreate the day all the way."

And then we set out, Calvin and I, just as it had been Calvin and Peter.

"They are fading away from us slightly now," he says, describing the movement of the elephants in '96, "walking parallel but angled a bit away . . . posture upright, alert . . ."

He is hunched over a bit, walking carefully. He puts his right index finger over his lips. "We know to be quiet, quiet . . . It is just Peter and me now . . . He's not photographing . . . just walking, looking . . . just spending time with the eles . . ."

It is a kind of interspecies communion. A get-to-know-you session. Meet and greet.

"What we didn't know then," Calvin says, "couldn't've known, is that the mother ele, a young girl herself, had just dropped a calf, maybe as recently as the day before." He puts a flat hand, palm facing earthward, down around his shin. "So small we wouldn't've seen it in the grass." As for the mother, "You might think of a teenage girl. Like a sixteen-, seventeen-year-old girl, maybe. Tusks only about the thickness of a quarter, you know? And this was probably her first contact, first fake charge, first charge."

That is how it happened. Drifting a bit down from the group, the new mother eyed the two men a bit contentiously just as they had entered clear field. She screamed, snorted, scuffed her feet on the ground and began to barrel toward them five steps, ten. And then pulled up.

This fake charge is meant to scare off anyone or anything and it scared the men plenty. They bolted. But the elephant, still a bit unsure, committed herself to a real charge. Maybe following the momentum or just really really wanting to attack—Calvin will tell me later that when an elephant crosses over a particular line, it goes a bit berserk, like humans when we see red. "They develop a blood lust," he said, "and need to kill or destroy completely."

By now, Calvin and Peter are running, still together, at full sprint, or as full a sprint as the erratic footing on the gentle slope slightly tilted to their right will allow. And then they split, Peter to the left, Calvin to the right, in the general direction of the truck, though it is some three hundred yards off. But their split gives the momma ele no pause, no moment of indecision. She is after Peter, no question, no hesitation, and she will be on him in a moment.

As he passes a massive termite mound, about ten feet high and thirty in diameter, Peter darts hard to his left trying to hide, but the ele is already on him, knocking him down and pinning him with her feet.

At first contact, she headbutts him, smashing his body between her tonnage and the dry earth, shattering his pelvis. And then she is at him again, and again. A tusk pierces Peter's left thigh. And with bones broken all through him, pinned variously by her feet, trunk, and head, Peter is having to dance and dodge her feints and attacks as she grows madder and madder.

Drawn in defense and intoxicated by the fury of the mother ele, the entire troupe of elephants has now joined in, surrounding Peter and his attacker, screaming, streaming in a circle around the carnage, cheering, crazed. Calvin's colleague, the guide at the truck, is frozen in shock, his hand on the horn, blaring away impotently. Calvin finally reaches the truck and pushes him aside, hops in and drives at full speed to the now writhing, undulating ele festival that is taking place, honking and screaming as loudly as possible. By the time he can urge them off, away enough to get to Peter, Peter had a full *four to five minutes* beneath the elephant, with his broken pelvis, gashed leg, and internal hemorrhaging but still somehow continued to draw breath.

"We absolutely thought he was a goner," Calvin says now. We are standing atop the termite mound looking down on the very spot. "Right here in the field, surely, if not later in the hospital. Just amazing that he was somehow still alive."

As Calvin reached down to cradle Peter up and into the truck, Peter said, "Well, my screwing days are over."

Calvin shakes his head, now, in total disbelief. But also in a way that communicates, *that was Peter.* "And in between bellowing in pain, you know, like a buffalo—*brrrrrruuuuhhvvv, burrrrrr uuuuvvvhhhh*—he would just keep making jokes the whole way to the hospital. At one point he said, 'Well, now I finally have something in common with Daphne Sheldrick,'" a sort of faux nemesis of his who had also been attacked by an elephant and was then the doyenne of elephant conservation in Kenya.

"And Calvin Cottar began the drive of his life," Peter said later, "and mine. I could feel the slurping blood lapping against the walls of my body cavity as we bounced along, radioing and drivingly wildly around obstacles. You can't write about these things," he said, "because pains of this nature aren't describable."

As they rattled along the dirt tracks, sometimes no more than a couple of lines of trampled grass, toward the airstrip, at least an hour away (my trip along this same route took about two), Peter's lost his vision entirely. One of his lungs collapsed. Calvin was able to radio ahead to have a plane awaiting them to fly Peter to Nairobi, where an ambulance met him to ferry him to the hospital.

"It took four hours to get to Nairobi hospital," Peter said. "It was a sensory overload at the very edge of survival. As the airport AMRET ambulance pulled into [the emergency bay], I bled out into the driveway and was wheeled into emergency on the dead list."

His pulse had stopped, and by the time he went under the knife, he'd been officially declared dead.

And, because Peter's story is a sort of black comedy, the doctor who was able to bring him back was the same one who had worked on Terry Mathews after the rhino goring, and he is reported to have said, "What goes around."

AFTER AN INITIAL SURGERY, TO SET BROKEN BONES AND stanch the bleeding, while doctors waited to see if another surgery would be needed to deal with internal bleeding, Peter did a little press. As ever, he remained on message, defending his attackers. "Elephants are like humans, very individualistic, idiosyncratic," he told the *New York Times*. The goring, the crushing, the flatlining was nothing in comparison with the run-ins he'd had with club doormen, "in the middle of a real jungle—New York City," he said. "A really tight squeeze with an elephant is very preferable."

Plans were made to transport him home to New York City, where he took up residence, in effect, at St. Vincent's Hospital in

Manhattan. In between bouts of surgery there, Peter set about decorating his new digs, turning his non-visiting hours into a kind of invite-only after-hours party. "Like Studio 54," says his friend and first gallerist, Joseph Helman.

> We go down there and now the room is hung with his photographs and his fabric, candles and all this shit. My wife and I were there and we're having a great visit with Peter. Pretty soon, there's a knock at the door and a girl comes in. She was Japanese. She had a body like Jessica Rabbit. She must've had ribs removed or something. She had this dress on which was about a foot and a half above the knees. Peter's on the bed, he's got a bar overhead. He grabs the bar. He hoists himself up, moves his self over a few inches, slams the bed and says, "Up here, babe." She gets on the bed. Now the four of us are in the room and we're chatting. Pretty soon, there's another knock at the door. . . . He had Nobu cater a dinner for us.

Peter's manager, agent, and friend at the time, Peter Riva, estimated that some 320 people came to visit Peter while he was in the hospital in Nairobi. Even with the Nobu concessions, it seems the guest list at St. Vincent's was slightly more controlled—in part because of Nejma's return to the fold.

Of the court politics around Peter in the aftermath of the elephant accident, Peter Riva says now:

> You know, it's funny. A year before he got mauled, Peter and I sat down with Lucien Clergue to watch a documentary on Picasso that Lucien had participated in. Of course, Lucien was a kind of Picasso protégé [and it was through him that Peter met and photographed Picasso, and even accompanied him to a bullfight in Arles]. And in the film

Picasso only ever referred to Jacqueline [his then wife, who functioned as the gatekeeper for the artist during their life together in Cannes at La Californie] as "*la gouvernante*," his governess. He never referred to her as his wife, ever. And Beard said, "Well, that's a perfect arrangement." And I saw it instantaneously—you know, I know the guy really well—I saw instantaneously. He suddenly found a role for Nejma.

Then, when he got injured, instead of allowing the divorce and all the divorce discussion to go through, she's suddenly by his bedside in the hospital—after she'd refused to go to Africa. We had a plane ticket for her and everything to go to her husband, who was basically dying in Africa, and she had no interest in going. But now he's back at St. Vincent's Hospital and she's by his side, in control of who comes in and who doesn't come in. So I show up and I . . . You know I helped Nejma when she was running from her parents and so on and so forth. But I come in and I see Peter, and he's a bit cold to me. And Nejma says, "His relationship with you is going to be over." I said, "OK, fine." But she couldn't cancel me out then, because I was in charge of producing the Paris show, which was the single most important show of his life.

In the aftermath of the elephant incident, the business of Peter Beard was booming. His star had never been brighter, his name never better known. The famous elephant guy had flirted with danger one time too many and had finally been attacked by his beloved elephants. And survived! And thrived! The publicity and fanfare were immense.

In November, just two months after the attack, a show was arranged for Peter at the Center for Photography in Paris. Riva says he put up the $40,000 to mount the show, and set Peter up in Paris. During the opening, Peter inhabited the gallery space like a kind of wounded animal—one very aware that it is the main attraction, on crutches, playing to the crowd.

On the night of the opening, Peter brought in the 8" × 10" Polaroid camera he had then been using frequently in his work, to make photographs of the visitors, and of those photographs still more collages. It was a stroke of brilliance, to give him something to do, a performance with which the attendees could engage, or simply observe as Peter did his Peter thing. And he converted what is normally a stiff and staid event—a gallery opening, when people normally mill about sipping cheap white wine for a while before going off to dinner or plans elsewhere—into a raging party, a be-in, a happening, as only he was capable of doing.

In footage from the event, Peter is obviously limited physically by his injuries and by all the "jewelry," as he called it, inside of his joints. He leans a bit heavily on some of the models he is arranging for photos. He is distinctly handsy, as they might've said in old-time movies—decisive when directing them, not quite aggressive, but still it is enough to make for rather uncomfortable viewing. (I queried more than a dozen models with whom Peter worked during this period, either directly or through their representation, to talk about the climate and mood on his sets, but got not one reply.)

"The show was a great success," Peter Riva says. "[Peter's] got his mistress in a hotel that I'm paying for. Nejma doesn't show up, and then when she does, [she and Peter are] not together. It's kind of an odd thing. And I thought, *OK*, I guess the *gouvernante* thing is working out."

ALTHOUGH OUTWARDLY PETER SEEMED TO BE CARRYING ON with things, with life and the increasingly sensational shows, something, some light inside of him, went out around the time of the accident. He effectively retired from his life and work in Kenya. Even Zara, with whom he'd camped in Tsavo when she was young, never returned, never visited, or even met Peter's friends, his universe of people there. Maybe it was anticipating that, knowing that he was at the end of his game, that made Peter begin to set down a book of his picaresque tales in Old Africa for her, in a book that would be called *Zara's Tales*.

In the book, as he is working himself up to describe his experience at the business end of the elephant and his brush with death that followed, Peter quotes Blake. "You never know what is enough unless you know what is more than enough," he writes, and then proceeds to lay out his sort of manifesto, one he certainly seems to have obeyed. "So keep on jamming," he writes, "if for no other reason than to thicken up your one and only life, adding texture and bulk to the daily/yearly calendar, and possibly even coming up with something new. Yes, if you crave something new, something original, particularly when they keep saying, 'Less is more,' remember that I say: Too much is really just fine. Only by going too far can we break the boring mold and stumble into something a little different. Originality is a key goal for the old human nervous system. . . . The biggest and best homework assignment in life and art, and I'll give it to you right now, is to keep yourself excited, going forward, happy, *enthusiastic*. Look it up in a large etymological dictionary (even if you think you know what it means): 'eagerness, warmth, fervor, zeal, ardor, passion, devotion, having a god within.'"

When I asked Peter about this, I joked that he may well have had some sort of god within. And also a devil. And even after the accident, as he continued going forward, going way, way, way too far, breaking boring molds and stumbling into things somewhat differently, he remained astoundingly enthusiastic.

"Have you done a good job, do you think, of doing more than

enough, in filling your life and nervous system with originality?" I asked him.

"No," he said, without equivocation, without guilt or doubt or second-guessing.

"It doesn't give you a great sense of accomplishment to look back at all?"

After a moment he said, "I am liking it right now," and then veered into a consideration of a page in his diary. "I really like the way this came out, by the way. It's not great, but it's kind of perfect. It appeals to my . . . thing."

Not great, but kind of perfect.

AT THE END OF THAT YEAR, AFTER THE ELE INCIDENT AND THE show in Paris, in 1996, facing increasing threats of eviction due to unpaid taxes, Peter sold the forty-plus acres of Hog Ranch to the African Fund for Endangered Wildlife, the organization that owns the neighboring property, a bed-and-breakfast called Giraffe Manor, for $500,000—with the understanding that he could remain there as long as he was alive. The Manor, a former hunting lodge built in the style of a Scottish country house, has since the mid-1970s functioned as a sanctuary for Rothschild giraffes, complete with a breeding program and system to reintroduce them back into the wild. In more recent years, the photogenic and happily habituated giraffes have made the manor sort of internet famous, starring in myriad Instagrammers' posts, popping their heads into second-story windows for a snack, for example. And it is a bit funny to think that these influencers and celebrities are taking the very same sort of pictures Peter did, presumably with many of the selfsame giraffes.

CHAPTER 11

Pettiness and Futility

Most writers I know are, like me, envious of artists in other media. Musicians seem to be having a terrific time, doing something so tangibly satisfying, playing an instrument, and getting that immediate feedback from a live show. Painters and sculptors, too, at least according to Hollywood, are forever hosting cocktail parties in their sun-drenched ateliers, with beautiful models, socialites, and money people flitting all about. I remember the sculptor Robert Graham telling me once that he only ever sculpted nude women from live models, because *Why wouldn't you?* That kind of proves my point that writers exist in a kind of forever after-school detention, while all other artists are out playing with their friends, and every day is a Saturday.

Peter's long-term residency/be-in at The Time Is Always Now gallery in SoHo was probably the grand apotheosis of the artist as debauched party host. Throughout the early half of the 1990s, while a kind of rotating pop-up show remained on permanent display above him in the gallery's public area, Peter settled himself in the basement, on his knees, sprawled out amid his nest of prints and cuttings, inks and quills and bits of detritus, assembling his collages, while all around him a party raged. Models, musicians, scenesters, hucksters, hustlers, and what the gallery's owner, Peter Tunney, called riffraff all swarmed around him to be photographed with Peter's giant 8″ × 10″ Polaroid or just to drink, do drugs, hear Peter's stories, collect a Peter story for their own mythology, and, likely as not, walk off with an actual work of art to boot. "A lot of people took advantage of [Peter]," a friend of his told *New York* magazine, on condition of anonymity. "At his studio at night, [they'd say], 'Peter, I like that!' 'Oh all right, you can have it.'"

In the same way that he had become the ideal avatar for our adventurous impulses, shirtless on a perpetual safari, throwing himself at mayhem and adventure with sociopathic zeal, consequences and safety and all good sense be damned, Peter was, too, the perfect manifestation of the rock-star artist at the end of the twentieth century. Wildly debauched. The life of the party. Adored by women and men alike. Always up for an adventure. Always ready to make you a memory. Most days, he was installed at The Time Is Always Now until evening, when he and his retinue would stomp around the corner, to Cipriani on West Broadway, and make merry, Peter on his beloved bullshots, until the party moved again, maybe back to the gallery, to a bottle-service nightclub that was then the rage in Manhattan, where Peter would establish himself as a kind of installation piece, around whom models and scenesters would gather, a magical Tinker Bell basking in the attention of those hoping for a little hit of old-timey celebrity, for a story, a drink, a puff of a joint with the legend. And then Peter and his Lost Boys & Girls would carry on their celebrations at an after-party, at someone's apartment. . . .

Waking up with a hangover one morning during this time (he was nearly 60), Peter said, "New York is only good at night. [The problem is that] sometimes you have to wake up there in the morning."

The hottest hot spot of the day was Spy Bar, on Greene Street in SoHo. It had a kind of modern Studio 54 door policy, admitting only those deemed cool enough, and a models-and-bottle

VIP room in the back. One night in the winter of 1995, Peter went to Spy Bar to meet his then girlfriend, the Danish producer Rikke Mortensen, but was turned away at the door. In an act of wild Peter impetuousness, he attempted to leap the velvet rope and dash past the tight-shirted Cerberuses at the door.

Tunney said later, "He makes a run for it, they grab him and beat the shit out of him. They punched him, they kicked him, and they snapped his biceps tendon, which required surgery." When Peter was being wheeled into the operating room, a drip of anesthetic in his arm, he apparently asked the doctor if he could "get some of this stuff to go."

If you are going to make art, Peter said, "You need to learn how, as Bacon would say, to trigger the valves of sensation. You have to learn how to play your nervous system so that you get results that you didn't count on." Which has a bit of Rimbaud and the derangement of the sensations to it. And indeed Peter played his nervous system for all it was worth, to the very end.

"Peter would think nothing of taking a bunch of acid or ecstasy and going out into a snowy field," Tunney said, "just to experience it."

Peter's wife, Nejma, was a little less enamored of the chemicals and the people with whom Peter was consuming them, never mind what he'd get up to when under their influence. "There are two Peters," she said. "One is a completely loving, vulnerable human being, and the other is a complete publicity-hound monster who wants to be a celebrity, and to be around celebrities. That's his downfall. He's absolutely petrified of getting old; Peter wants to be young, and drugs are his escape. When we had an intervention for him, he said, 'I like my drugs, and I don't think I have a problem.' It's a complete avoidance of reality."

"I've met so many wonderful people on coke," Peter said, when asked about this. "I have nothing bad to say about it. I really enjoy coke. . . . Got any?"

The publisher and filmmaker James Crump made Peter's acquaintance at this time, when he sought him out to put together a book of Peter's pictures for his imprint, Arena Editions. Crump marvels that, despite the volume of cocaine, alcohol, and marijuana, Peter never seemed out of it, let alone out of control. It was almost as if the drugs and alcohol were straightening him out. When he was the center of attention, Peter had enormous stores of patience and consideration for others, Crump says. At a signing of the book, Peter made special, personalized signatures—really hand- or footprints in ink, with long detailed inscriptions—for each of the many dozens of fans who had gathered for the occasion. As long as people remained in line, waiting for his signature, Peter went right on signing and stepping on books, for six hours after the signing had been scheduled to conclude, according to Crump.

The same meticulous care went into the work, as ever, but cataloging and archiving the work from this period was something else entirely. Tunney admitted to *New York* magazine that there is not a terrifically accurate record of the work Peter made during this time. "He didn't want to do editions or stuff like that. He wanted each piece to be a living, breathing work of art."

When Nejma began to intervene in this process, "breaking up the party," as Tunney called it, she called into question the authenticity of some of the pieces that'd been sold through Tunney's gallery. The comedian David Spade, recipient of one of the pieces whose authenticity came into question, sued Peter, Nejma, and Tunney. The case, like almost all others having to do with Peter and/or his work, was settled out of court and sealed, and neither Spade nor any of the other living parties mentioned will discuss the terms of the settlement. But then, Peter had always been quite cavalier with his pieces after he'd completed them. As his friend the photographer Sante D'Orazio noticed when he visited him during this time, "The mailman comes to pick up the mail, and he gives him a print! I'm like, 'Holy shit.' That's how he was with everybody."

The Los Angeles gallerist David Fahey, who had been working with Peter at the time and helped arrange for the Arena Editions book with James Crump, said that Peter had always claimed that a little wear and tear did his work good, that he would often leave pieces stacked up or scattered about in his garage in Montauk, exposed to the elements, as if the wind and water and weather were the final, finishing component of his work—which, if he'd taken anything away from his experience with the diaries at Lake Turkana that his colleague Wildman had saved, perhaps they were.

But once things started to go this direction, Nejma brought an end to the time of The Time Is Always Now—at least the action is always attributed to her in the retelling of events by those involved, and even Tunney himself says it was in all of their best interests. "If Nejma didn't come and break up the party, I'm pretty sure I'd be dead," he told *New York* magazine. "I think it's fair to say that Nejma probably thought we were having too much fun, not doing things professionally enough, not knowing where the money was going," Tunney said. "I was basically just plowing all the money back into the whole operation. It was an enormously expensive thing. But just when it was becoming a substantial thing, Nejma came in with the lawyers and said, 'The party's over, I'm in charge.' And Peter said, 'There's nothing I can do.'"

Nejma and the lawyers then went after pieces she deemed outstanding, not properly paid for, given or possessed under false or expired circumstances. According to friends of Peter's, she sort of declared war on the crowd that had gathered around him, accusing them of theft, of having pieces they didn't pay for, of taking advantage of Peter. When she and her lawyers could not physically repossess pieces, she would file them with the Art Loss Register, which alerted insurance agencies and law enforcement to their disputed status and made them all but impossible to resell.

"I wonder how many paintings she got back from cocaine dealers," Peter Riva says as a joke, kind of. According to *New York* magazine, in 2011, "Amaranth, Nello, and Cipriani, to name just a few [New York] places, have walls jammed with Beards. 'Half the bars in Montauk have Beard photos on the walls,' says one old friend of Peter's. 'Not to mention in the south of France. He'd use a photo to pay off a $20,000 bar bill.'"

"I think Peter expected her to clean up stuff for him." Peter's friend and Montauk neighbor, the painter and filmmaker Julian Schnabel, said. "I think she was trying to protect him from himself. If someone is being very self-destructive and you love them, where do you draw the line?"

"She's trying to control the purse strings and keep him on a short leash," a friend of Peter's told *New York* magazine. "She's eager to establish him before he dies as an important artist. That's going to be her nest egg."

At the time, Nejma, who controlled the family finances as well as the income and spending of the studio (before Peter's brother Anson apparently took it over closer to Peter's death), put Peter on an allowance. Friends of his claimed to *Vanity Fair* that this arrangement forced him to negotiate side deals, selling off pieces of his work under the table to pay for health care or send money to lovers. "Other people asserted that Beard had friends manage money for him without Nejma's knowledge," *Vanity Fair* reported. "One friend, Elizabeth Fekkai, said she arranged for a sale of Beard's work so he could pay a $26,700 dental bill. He also allegedly sold work without Nejma's knowledge, including to pay a $10,000 bill for a girlfriend." (Nejma declined to comment on the allegations for *Vanity Fair*.)

Still, all this doesn't seem to have covered his costs. "If Peter needed money, I gave him some money," Peter Tunney told *New York* magazine. "We literally spent every day together."

Other times, Peter would rebel more directly, telling a friend, for instance, that he was going "on strike with Nejma . . . she took away the keys to the car and we aren't speaking and she won't send me any money."

One night in the early aughts, according to a *New York Post* article citing court documents, Peter came home with two young women who Nejma took to be Russian hookers. Nejma reportedly called the police, claiming that Peter was threatening suicide— and actually had him committed. Though he was eventually released, and would continue to mount mini-rebellions for much of the rest of his life, even though they were met each time with the same force, and with his health and spirit diminishing, he would cave.

DEPENDING ON WITH WHOM YOU ARE SPEAKING—AND, IN- deed, the version of the story they are then telling—Peter either fled to Cassis, to escape Nejma's ever-tightening grip on his life, his finances, and his fun, or Nejma sent him away to get him out of the glare of the New York media, away from the temptations of New York nightlife, its women and its drugs. "He needed inspiration and to get away from the parasites and harpies," Nejma told the *Wall Street Journal.* The irony, friends in Cassis say, is that those things and everything else were in great abundance in the south of France. Peter had no trouble finding a girlfriend, bringing in opportunistic visitors from the demimonde of Europe, and he soon had a ready supply of cocaine in this place where many of the big bosses from the time of the French Connection, when drugs were being exported to Manhattan from Marseilles, built their beach homes.

"You're gonna send a guy twenty minutes from Marseilles and think there are no drugs around?" Peter's cousin Christopher Schroll asks. "That's crazy."

Peter had been making periodic visits to Cassis since his cousin

Jerome Hill had set up camp there in the late 1950s, purchasing property on a low limestone cliff across from the port. At the time, the only building standing on the property was an old arsenal, La Batterie, which had been fortified by Napoléon's army, as well as the former Panorama Hotel, where in 1920 Winston Churchill painted *Daybreak at Cassis,* and from which he made his visits to the nearby coves (the Calanques, as they are known). The area had always been a favorite destination for English artists, including Bloomsbury groupers Duncan Grant, Virginia Woolf, and Vanessa Bell, all of whom came to enjoy the light and heat so radically different from that of London. Jerome Hill, too, came to Cassis to paint, and made friends with the grandees of the time who didn't mind a little sun and fun. Peter took a photo of Jerome and Brigitte Bardot at La Batterie in 1959 and continued to make embellished prints of it for the rest of his life.

In 1961, Peter brought his then fiancée, Astrid Heeren, a German actress who, a few years later, would play a love interest of Steve McQueen's Thomas Crown in *The Thomas Crown Affair.* In 1967, after their disappointing (to Minnie) honeymoon to Mozambique, where her parents had rented them a cottage, Peter and his new bride, Minnie Cushing, and her parents, visited Jerome and stayed at the newly built house on the property, Pierrefroide, with their pet bush baby sleeping with them in the bed. And over the course of forty years, Peter came back—in 1984 when he was arranging for his exhibition as part of the Rencontres photo fair in Arles, and then again in 1997 when putting together a show of his work at the Nord-Pinus, also in Arles.

Throughout this time, Peter's partner in crime was his second cousin, Jerome Hill's nephew, Christopher Schroll. Schroll had first visited Cassis with his family for the summer of 1952, and he and his mother and father too kept coming back periodically, to visit his uncle. "I hooked up with Peter in '65," Schroll says, of the summer when the two lads shared a room in Pierrefroide.

We were like a couple of kids, you know, always daring one another to jump off higher and higher cliffs, throwing rocks at the lighthouse across the way there, seeing who could hit highest on the lighthouse. We were a lot alike. We would sit up there with a pair of binoculars [looking down on the pebbly beach adjacent to Jerome's property], until we'd see this young pulchritude down there with her mom. And Peter would be off. I'd say, "You're gonna go down there?" And he'd say, "You bet your ass I'm going down there." And he'd take his camera down as if he were just casually passing, totally unsuspecting, and I was following all this through the binoculars, and would have to report it all to Peter later. Sure enough, when the cocktail hour would come, the girl would be there, Peter having made his case to her mother. . . . I mean he was like that. Unmitigated gall. He once nearly talked a couple into bringing him along with them on their honeymoon. And he could get away with [things like that]. He was so charming.

There were stretches of time when Peter and Schroll wouldn't see each other, but then pick right back up where they left off when they did. In 2005, a good portion of the Hill extended family, along with Jerome's nearest and dearest, got together at the Algonquin Hotel, Jerome's home away from home, to celebrate what would have been his one-hundredth birthday (he had passed in 1972).

A year later, Schroll says, Nejma called him and asked, "Can you take Peter?"

He laughs as he tells me he replied, "Um, in what sense? Like, footing the bill or . . ."

Nejma explained that she was hoping Schroll could set Peter up in Cassis. "Clean him out, maybe," get him away from . . .

everything. And so Schroll met Peter in Nice and "after a few days of carousing," bopping around the Côte d'Azur, even heading up to Geneva, running around, going out on Schroll's boat, which was then in Nice, they made their way to Cassis, "to work," Schroll says, sort of facetiously, having a bit of fun with the idea that Peter's project was to clean himself out.

They set Peter up in the top floor of the former Panorama Hotel, where Winston Churchill had stayed before him, and he immediately set about papering his nest with prints and all manner of ephemera, spending his days kneeling on the floor in a whirlwind of paint and glue and ink and blood to make his doodles, his collages, his diaries. As he did everywhere, he obsessively collected rocks from the seaside, "and we set about hauling them up to the third floor," Schroll says. Peter stayed in his room at the Panorama for a season, and then moved into an apartment above one of the restaurants on the port, working all the while, producing diary pages and his larger-scale collages. Though it should be said that, even if his practices were much the same, the work from this period suffers a bit from the technology of the time. Many of the prints Peter clipped and inserted into his collages made in the 2000s are of very poor quality, digital, and look a bit like not very good bootlegs of Peter Beards.

In 2008 Peter was invited by Pirelli, the tire company, to make one of its famous calendars, which had been considered a very big deal for a photographer. The calendars have historically been famous for the nudity of their subjects, the overt sexuality, and they are always a bit of a sensation, offering a photographer a huge canvas on which to explore an idea, a vision—like shooting twelve magazine cover stories at once. Peter took the production to Botswana, to shoot several of the best-known models of the time—Daria Werbowy, Lara Stone, Malgosia Bela, Emanuela de Paula, Mariacarla Boscono—in typical Peter Beard scenarios. And though some of the actual photographs themselves are extraordinary—one of Bela, topless, walking in a parade of elephants, is incredible by any standard—the collages Peter made of the photos are not. In fact, the Peter Beardness, the cutting up and writing on the images, makes the final images a bit of a mess. Images gone too digital and pixelated look absurdly out of sync with their backdrops. Nudes of Charlotte Kemp Muhl, cut from the calendar, look more like something for a nineties issue of *Hustler* than anything else. The overall effect is a bit hokey, as if Peter Beard were making a rather unflattering pastiche of Peter Beard.

IN 2008 NINA ZINAI WAS THIRTY-FOUR AND WORKING IN A restaurant in Cassis, where she had moved from her native Marseilles, thinking that, if and when she had children, she would prefer to raise them somewhere a bit quieter than the big, hectic city where she'd grown up. Her childhood home and life had been spartan, she says. Her parents, Algerians, had little in the way of money, and so she learned to do with less. Her tiny apartment in Cassis was all that she needed. When she encountered an older man, seventy at the time, wandering the port in a length of fabric cinched around his waist, she took him to be a bit unwell mentally. The man was barefoot, and his hands were covered in filth and ink, she says, and she would have thought nothing more of it if he hadn't started talking to her a mile a minute, making grand romantic overtures, inviting her to his apartment above a restaurant on the port, and telling her over and over how she was the one and simply *had* to be with him.

Having managed to extract herself then, Nina soon saw the *kikoi*-wearing madman again when she walked into a restaurant where he was having lunch in the company of a forest of "top models," as she says, all of whom he immediately disregarded to make a beeline to her. Again, he made quite an impression. A few days later, when the madman's secretary, Gustavo, called Nina, she learned that he was, in fact, an artist, and hoped to show her his work, again inviting her to the apartment above the restaurant. Almost immediately, Nina says, she was entirely under Peter's spell. After visiting him at his apartment, they went to the nearby Roches Blanches hotel, up on a bluff just west of the port, the hotel where Jerome Hill had had his salon-style lunches every day. There Peter took photographs of Nina.

Very quickly, they were madly in love, but Nina noticed something was a bit off with Peter, she says. She noticed a pattern of big fancy people, as she calls them, coming to visit Peter, always bringing him some cocaine, and leaving with bits and pieces of his work as informal payment. And while she worried for him, she says, as long as Peter had drugs, he was happy.

Nina says that she is just "a simple person" and didn't know these big fancy people who were coming to meet Peter, but she knew it had to stop, and so, slowly at first, and then rather dramatically, she took on the role of Peter's mother, caretaker, boss, and protector that so many others had occupied before. Nina, who, as people in Cassis repeatedly brought to my attention, looks astonishingly similar to a younger Nejma, became the bad cop in Peter's life that Nejma had been up to that point. The definitive moment took place when a big delivery came Peter's way, from someone in Switzerland, she says. The delivery, Nina discovered, was a massive amount of coke, which she, in very short order, dumped down the toilet. Amazingly, Peter agreed that she was in the right and threw himself into her care.

"For a very long time," Nina says, "he was my child." And every day she would bathe him, dry him with a hair dryer because the towel hurt him too much, applying creams and swaddling him like a baby in her care and affection. For three years she kept Peter entirely away from coke—quite an accomplishment, she says proudly, considering the mountains he had been consuming up until that point.

"Clear of coke from 2009 to 2011?" Chris Schroll asks in disbelief when I relate the story. "Well, *she's nice*," he says, implying he knows different. He starts to say, "Well, we all . . ." and then says, as if he is happy to shoulder some blame, if blame indeed it is, "I certainly put his nose in it, if you will."

When Nina and Peter would take little trips, like to St. Tropez down the coast, Nina acted like "a bodyguard," she says, keeping the sleazy and degenerate away from Peter—or, more precisely, keeping him away from them. "Peter thought everyone was nice and good," she says. Like a child. And he regularly called her his angel, for protecting him, for mothering him the way she did. But Peter's other bodyguard, Nejma, still had control of all of the money the studio brought in (apparently as much as $2 million a year around this time). Still, Nina and Peter very happily made do, Nina says. She cooked for them. They lived very simply. As long as Peter had paper and ink and they had each other, they were happy.

A friend of Jerome Hill and Chris Schroll tells me that, shortly before Jerome died, he asked Schroll to take care of Peter. They both knew how Peter was with money—and life—and Jerome was sort of passing down guardianship within the family to his nephew. "Something like that," Schroll says, agreeing with this characterization. And Nina says that when Chris Schroll noticed the financial pinch Nina and Peter were feeling, Schroll assured her that, if they needed money, she only had to ask. Nina demurred.

Peter and Schroll, sometimes with Nina, started taking little trips—"to Rome, around France, to London . . . and then for months, to California and Hawaii, things that were a bit spendier," Schroll says. Anyway, the trips were more expensive than Peter could afford on the credit card Nejma had given him with its €300 (or Schroll thinks €200) per month limit. And so Schroll agreed with Peter to buy 10–15 of his big Taschen monographs, which had recently come out, embellished in all of Peter's ways, for $10,000 apiece, cash, which went straight to Peter, so that he had some walking-around money. (Through her attorney, Nejma denied putting Peter on an allowance in Cassis.)

Right around this time, in late 2008, Sophie Soulayrol, a local neurologist, who was then working with City Hall, learned of Peter's presence in town through an associate of Jerome Hill's and thought it'd be great for the town to celebrate him. She and Peter met and cooked up the idea for an exhibition in Cassis, but back in New York, Nejma didn't want anyone to know that Peter had fled the city (or was in a kind of exile), and she put the brakes on any of Peter's art getting to France, Sophie says, all but ending their plans. Until Sophie had an inspiration. Why didn't they project images of Peter's against the massive cliff face just behind the beach in Cassis and invite the whole town out for a sandy celebration. Peter, of course, loved the idea of his work being enlarged up to a thousand times actual size on a rock face where it could be seen for miles, and so as they began prepping the party, Sophie, along with the mayor of Cassis, arranged for Peter (and Nina) to move into a stately whitewashed two-story home, the former customs house of the port, right on the edge of the beach, just below the cliff face where the images would be projected. He was putting on the exhibition gratis, but Nejma had made one stipulation, Sophie says: they could have no press or publicity of the event. No one was to know that Peter lived in Cassis, and, presumably, lived with another woman. Nejma's attorney denied Sophie's account of the show in Cassis.

When, in 2011, Peter had to get hip surgery, Nina says, Nejma booked him a one-way ticket to Manhattan and an appointment with the doctor who'd attended to him in the wake of his elephant accident. As the trip and surgery loomed, Nina says, Peter would have moments in which he dwelt very heavily on his death. He insisted to her that she make sure that he was cremated and that his ashes be scattered at Hog Ranch. Those were among the wishes he expressed to her. But as Nina suspected, and as his friends agreed, if Peter took that plane to New York, he'd never come back. And indeed, he never did.

"Peter is a coward," Sophie says, implying that if he didn't want to go, he didn't have to. He was only hiding behind Nejma, the bad cop, so that he could be all lovey-dovey and just never formally break up with Nina, never be the bad guy, never be responsible. Which fairly well checks out, frankly. "He certainly benefited from [the arrangement with Nejma]," wherein he could play the victim and avoid responsibility, Schroll says. "But it hemmed him in, too. He was like an animal in a cage."

Upon Peter's return to New York, this comparison to a caged animal became even more apt. He was shut away in Montauk and all but cut off from the world, friends say. "It was really sad," Schroll says. Lee Radziwill, who had come to visit Peter in Cassis and remained on very warm and tender terms with him, came to visit him after his return and "was left on the doorstep," Schroll says. Friends who called the house were told Peter was unavailable. Anyone daring enough to drop by was simply chucked out.

"In the fall of 2011," Schroll says, "around Thanksgiving time," just after Peter had come back from Cassis and was readying himself for the battery of tests and doctor's appointments, Schroll went to visit him. "We drank and ate and talked, with football on the TV. Then one day we went to Nobu, and Peter says, 'Do you have other things you are doing in town or did you just come to visit me?' I said, 'I'm here to see you.' And then he said, 'I think this is the last time we'll see each other.'"

Schroll says that he wasn't explicit on the matter, but he suspects Peter saw tough times ahead and was trying to cut him off to spare Schroll's feelings. For years afterward, Schroll would call and be told that Peter was unavailable. They never spoke again.

IN 2012, WHEN HE FINALLY DID HAVE HIS HIP-REPLACEMENT surgery, Peter suffered "a series of strokes" that from then on impaired his speech and, it is suggested, affected his brain function. Peter's friend in Cassis, with whom he arranged an exhibition of his pictures on the cliffs of Cap Canaille, Sophie Soulayrol, happens to be a neurologist; when she heard of Peter's diagnosis of dementia, she was a bit surprised. In all of her time spent with Peter, she says, his mind remained laser sharp.

Schroll, too, says that as long as he knew Peter his mind was sharp. He says that Peter was more than capable of playing a little spacy, "faking," as Schroll calls it, "if he wanted to avoid dealing with something." Peter was a great one for pretending he didn't know what you were talking about if he wanted to avoid the subject. But friends who saw him in later years, after 2016, do say they noticed lapses in lucidity, forgetfulness.

In 2013, Peter had surgery related to prostate cancer. At the time he went missing, he was taking pills for a heart condition and was advised not to go twenty-four hours without taking them. When he walked out on March 31, 2020, the pills were left at his bedside.

CHAPTER 12

Camp Hero

I keep thinking about Peter's hands, hammered into flat, angular shapes at the knuckles, caked with dense, semi-opaque calluses, as if they'd been fired a matte bisque, like some sort of Pleistocene tools. Which of course they were. The hands are our tools, as animals, digging, sifting, lifting, moving. They are what make us us, what give us the upper hand, as it were. And I wonder if that's why I keep seeing them in my mind, if his hands were the best testaments to Peter's effort to uncivilize himself, to make himself back into a man of the Pleistocene, to free himself from the life and society he was born into, and return himself to the earth, the soil.

Of course Peter really did return himself to the earth. As best we can tell, on the afternoon of March 31, 2020, Peter got up and out of the house, all on his own volition, and wandered into the woodland bordering his property to the east, into a protected area called Camp Hero. It is impossible to know now whether he knew upon leaving the house that he would not return, did not wish to return, or whether he became disoriented and got lost in the fast-falling darkness, if he was scared, if he suffered, or if he settled down to sleep.

After nineteen days of searches for him, it was a hunter, wandering through the thick woods east of Peter's house, who saw some bright-colored clothing and alerted the police. Later that day, the family confirmed that the body the police had recovered, only a few hundred yards from their front door, was indeed Peter's. In the statement they released, expressing their heartbreak at the discovery, they wrote, "Peter defined what it means to be open: open to new ideas, new encounters, new people, new ways of living and being. Always insatiably curious, he pursued his passions without restraints and perceived reality through a unique lens."

At the risk of sounding insensitive, I cannot help but think that this exit left is signature Peter, that it bears the imprimatur of the same dramaturge responsible for all his most outlandish behavior, his grand gestures, his theatrical flourishes, and his very clearly stated intent to return himself to the wilderness. "Wild-deer-ness," as Peter liked to call it, was to him less a geographical place on a map than a state of being, the original way of being, to which he hoped his whole life to wander into and, I imagine, return to completely someday.

Of course, the very idea of a wilderness, a here-there-be-dragons terra incognita off any known maps, beyond our fenced-in "civilized" farms and cities, is a white European idea. This othering of untouched nature and wildlife, separating humans from the land and from all the beasts in creation, was the original sin, to Peter's mind. Thinking we were somehow apart, distinct, above the rest of nature, he believed, was a delusion we had fallen into and then relied on as we destroyed the world for our convenience. Perhaps his whole life, his life's work and legacy, will be his Cassandra cry to reintegrate with nature, just as he did himself.

Or maybe I'm projecting, although he did create the kind of canvas, with his life and works, that lends itself to such interpretation. He asked for it. Or am I giving him too much credit?

In perfectly Peter fashion, he seems to have posed the question, made the provocative move, and then left us to contemplate the meaning: of his end, of his entire curriculum vitae, of his life and his work. Peter Tunney, Peter's gallerist and facilitator in the nineties and early aughts, is now an artist himself, living in Miami. When I managed to get ahold of him, I wondered aloud whether Peter and his work might be due a reevaluation. Did Tunney think, for example, that Peter would get a major museum retrospective? This seemed to offend Tunney, who said he had already done that, with The Time Is Always Now, that the work was done. He hung up on me, and never again responded to my queries and calls.

I wonder if that's true, if we've heard the last word from paradise, as it were. Still, I think Peter Beard's legacy is largely undecided, a work in progress. Will it be his images that remain in our collective consciousness, for example, or his image? Will it be important, or necessary, for posterity to separate the artwork from the man who made it, especially when his life is both subject and meta-text of so much of the art? Will that even be possible?

Will Peter be remembered for his worst behavior, or his best? Will it be for his influence on lifestyle, fashion, art, and conservation that he will be remembered? Or will he always be associated with allegations made against him, with actions and a persona that were projected onto him?

Will he be inflated into a kind of idea, a symbol, used either to celebrate or demonize that with which he becomes associated? A mythic bogeyman if bad or a paragon if good? It seems notable that, after spending years thinking about him, years before his death and the years since, I believe any and all of these potentials are possible.

Peter played with very powerful ideas and themes. He created some of the most potent images of the twentieth century. His life, both person-to-person and in the image he projected onto popular culture, connected with people in a way that very few do.

For better or worse, there will certainly never be another person like him, in part because he was the right sort of person for the right sort of time. He was born rich and beautiful in a time and place that celebrated him as a symbol of wealth and beauty. Given license to express himself as he did, to behave as he did, he made a picture of himself that chimed with appetites and interests of his day.

"I think Peter will be seen as an important figure," Bob Colacello told me, "both aesthetically, in the history of photography, but also because of his social awareness, his very early warning signs about what was going on in Africa."

This despite Peter not always being the easiest person to deal with, as Colacello says. "I think people were quick to turn off to him, and they were sort of bored by being lectured. And now that everybody is recognizing the cataclysmic threats, they're wishing that we'd listened to him better."

You are only free to love someone when the person is dead, Camus believed. So I wonder, will Peter's work suffer without his jester/impresario performance around its exhibition, coloring it with stories of run-ins with lions and elephants? Or will we begin to see it anew, more clearly perhaps? Will it start to speak for itself?

IN HIS BOOK *ZARA'S TALES*, PETER WROTE THAT THE POINT OF life was to "keep yourself excited, going forward, happy, enthusiastic." And he was nothing if not enthused. When I visited him for the weekend in 2016, at his home in Montauk, I asked him if he had done a good job filling up his one life and nervous system with originality.

"No," he said.

"No?! Do you feel like there is something you've missed?"

He dissembled, muttered about being an escapist, not to be

taken too seriously. And then, of his work, said, "This is a lazy man's thing."

"Do you have a particular moment that you like to look back on?" I asked. "Were there great golden days?"

"Absolutely," he said, "there's wonders. I'd like it all to feel that way."

Index

Index

Index

Index

Index

Index

Index